SEXUAL REVOLUTIONS

GENDER AND ARCHAEOLOGY SERIES

SERIES EDITOR:
Sarah Milledge Nelson
University of Denver

This series focuses on ways to understand gender in the past through archaeology. This is a topic poised for significant advances in both method and theory, which in turn can improve all archaeology. The possibilities of new methodological rigor as well as new insights into past cultures are what make gendered archaeology a vigorous and thriving subfield.

The series welcomes single-authored books on themes in this topic area, particularly ones with comparative focus. Edited collections with a strong theoretical or methodological orientation will also be considered. Audiences are practicing archaeologists and advanced students in the field.

EDITORIAL BOARD
Philip Duke, Fort Lewis College
Alice Kehoe, Marquette University
Janet Levy, University of North Carolina, Charlotte
Margaret Nelson, Arizona State University
Thomas Patterson, University of California, Riverside
K. Anne Pyburn, Indiana University
Ruth Whitehouse, University College, London

BOOKS IN THE SERIES
Volume 1, *In Pursuit of Gender: Worldwide Archaeological Approaches*, Sarah Milledge Nelson and Myriam Rosen-Ayalon, Editors
Volume 2, *Gender and the Archaeology of Death*, Bettina Arnold and Nancy L. Wicker, Editors
Volume 3, *Ancient Maya Women*, Traci Ardren, Editor
Volume 4, *Sexual Revolutions: Gender and Labor at the Dawn of Agriculture*, Jane Peterson
Volume 5, *Ancient Queens: Archaeological Explorations*, Sarah Milledge Nelson, Editor

SUBMISSION GUIDELINES
Prospective authors of single or coathored books and editors of anthologies should submit a letter of introduction, the manuscript or a four-to-ten-page proposal, a book outline, and a curriculum vitae. Please send your book manuscript/proposal packet to:

Gender and Archaeology Series
AltaMira Press
1630 North Main Street #367
Walnut Creek, CA 94596
(925) 938-7243
www.altamirapress.com

SEXUAL REVOLUTIONS

Gender and Labor at the Dawn of Agriculture

JANE PETERSON

ALTAMIRA PRESS
A Division of Rowman & Littlefield Publishers, Inc.
Walnut Creek • Lanham • New York • Oxford

ALTAMIRA PRESS
A Division of Rowman & Littlefield Publishers, Inc.
1630 North Main Street, #367
Walnut Creek, CA 94596
www.altamirapress.com

Rowman & Littlefield Publishers, Inc.
A Member of the Rowman & Littlefield Publishing Group
4720 Boston Way
Lanham, MD 20706

PO Box 317
Oxford
OX2 9RU, UK

Village drawings courtesy of Julie Longhill.

British Library Cataloguing in Publication Information Available

Library of Congress Cataloging-in-Publication Data

Peterson, Jane, 1960-
  Sexual revolutions : gender and labor at the dawn of agriculture / Jane Peterson.
    p. cm. – (Gender and archaeology series ; v. 4)
  Includes bibliographical references and index.
  ISBN 0-7591-0256-2 – ISBN 0-7591-0257-0 (pbk.)
  Social archaeology. 2. Feminist archaeology. 3. Sexual division of labor—
  History. 4. Agriculture—Social aspects—History. 5. Middle East—Antiquities.
  6. Excavations (Archaeology)—Middle East. I. Title. II. Series.

CC72.4 .P48 2002
306.3'615—dc21

                                                                    2002003219

Printed in the United States of America

♾™ The paper used in this publication meets the minimum requirements of American National Standard for Information Sciences—Permanence of Paper for Printed Library Materials, ANSI/NISO Z39.48–1992.

This book is dedicated to my parents—
Beverly and Roland Peterson,
Who shared with me their love of nature and the written word

Contents

List of Figures and Tables

Figures

Tables

Foreword

SARAH MILLEDGE NELSON

IT IS A PLEASURE to present Jane Peterson's *Sexual Revolutions: Gender and Labor at the Dawn of Agriculture* as the fourth volume in the Gender and Archaeology series. Gender in archaeology has distinctly come of age with this volume on gender in the transition to agriculture and beyond. Peterson presents the reader with a well-reasoned whole, consisting of theories, methods, and descriptive material. This book is firmly based in theory and responsive to other work that has been accomplished on gendered activities of early farming, but it is also grounded in data of specific times and places. Her area is the southern Levant, where she shows the power of gender analysis when applied to prior excavations. Her data, which make up the core of the book, are the human bones from the Natufian to the Early Bronze Age. In her analysis, Peterson demonstrates how these bones can shed important light on the changes in gendered labor patterns with the shift to farming and animal husbandry.

The body has been the subject of much attention from feminist (and other) scholarship, but bodies in the past have received less attention. Here the author uses bodies from mortuary contexts to contrast populations before and after the "Neolithic revolution." She considers the question of the extent to which the origin of agriculture was a work revolution for women and men. By examining bodies from the same region both before and after agriculture was established, one can look at a slice of time and correlate changes in the bones with artifactual and spatial data. Human skeletal remains thus reveal a great deal in this book. The social organization of labor stands revealed in the shadows of musculature left on the bones of men and women.

While Peterson does critique previous models of gender in early agriculture, she goes beyond mere critique by providing a rationale for how and why her particular data set sheds new light on the problem. Gender in the context of the origins of agriculture has been structured as a problem of which sex does what work. The central question of the organization of labor and how jobs are organized and who does them has been elusive for the Neolithic everywhere. The problem of gendered labor in the Neolithic has been difficult to crack, especially in cases where there are no graphic illustrations on walls or pots or sculptural representations of men and/or women performing daily activities. Furthermore, the Neolithic is a time when, almost by definition, there is no written record and myths are difficult to extrapolate so far back in time, especially when labor practices are being sought.

Yet assumptions have been continually made about women's work—in food production and food preparation and as artisans and caretakers—that lead to generalizations about gender roles. Feminist archaeology tries to go beyond such stereotypes to find data that allow these (and other) activities to be demonstrated to be gendered rather than merely assumed. Peterson's work does just that. There have been many critiques of the androcentric versions of the past, especially the origins of agriculture, but fewer attempts to find new ways to solve the problems. Peterson blends the results of her study of human bones in the southern Levant, from Natufian times to the Early Bronze Age, with thoughtful discussion of the meanings of her findings.

This approach shows that gender studies can be both scientific and thoroughly grounded in feminist theory. It is a breakthrough in the interplay of method and theory. Peterson is fully aware of the possible pitfalls of her data on musculoskeletal stress markers, and she argues her interpretations carefully. A gendered archaeology is truly better archaeology.

Acknowledgments

THIS BOOK REPRESENTS a distillation and extension of my dissertation work completed at Arizona State University in 1994. I owe a deep debt of gratitude to my chair, Geoffrey Clark, for his support and interest in my research. I also thank the other members of my committee, Stephen Falconer, Charles Redman, and Katherine Spielmann, for their patience, logic, and critiques. Special appreciation goes out to Diane Hawkey, who provided an introduction and invaluable guidance in the identification and scoring of musculoskeletal stress markers (MSM).

Those who granted permission and access to skeletal collections also deserve recognition: B. Arensberg, L. Beck, B. Frolich, I. Hershkovitz, Z. Kafafi, D. Ortner, G. Rollefson, and P. Smith. Costs associated with travel and research were defrayed by awards from the National Science Foundation, the United States Information Agency, and Arizona State University.

There are many others who helped me stay focused on this project, provided intellectual and editorial input, and clarified priorities. These include Cheryl Claassen, Jim Holstein, Alice Kehoe, Gale Miller, Sarah Nelson, Nancy Peterson, Norman Sullivan, Bill Thomas, members of the 1997 MSM symposium presented at the annual meeting of the American Association of Physical Anthropologists, and the scholars who attended the Fourth Gender and Archaeology conference held in 1996.

For ensuring that this manuscript finally saw the light of day, I have Mitch Allen and Sarah Nelson to thank. They offered encouragement at some particularly difficult moments and answered my numerous questions with patience and humor.

Finally, most ardently, I thank Michael Gregory and my sons, Malcolm and Jackson. Without them, I would lack many of the insights about gender and work that inform this book.

An Investigation of Labor Patterns   I

T
HIS STUDY EXAMINES the roles of women and men directly before and after the adoption of settled, village farming as a way of life. It focuses on the regions of modern Israel, Palestine, and Jordan where archaeologists have early evidence for plant domestication, dating back some 10,000 years. Dramatic social changes most likely accompanied economic changes as human groups made the transition from hunting and gathering to farming and animal husbandry. Populations came together in larger, more permanent settlements. New daily and seasonal schedules were required to tend and process plant crops and care for herds of domestic animals. Researchers agree, in theory, that how the "first farmers" organized their work and their relationships with family and community members was crucial to the success of early agricultural villages. Yet little serious attention has been paid to understanding the social organization of labor. And so a stalemate exists: Archaeologists recognize the potential significance of labor organization and sexual work patterns but have not directly investigated the subjects.

These groups left behind no written accounts or graphic imagery that depicts their daily activities. Their graves contain relatively few mortuary offerings. Among the scant offerings, no patterns indicative of occupational roles have been discerned. And assumptions that link certain tools with either male or female tasks prove unwarranted ethnographically. Instead, the activities of these ancient people are explored using the only direct evidence prehistorians have for examining labor issues: human skeletal remains. As activity patterns are revealed, it is possible to ask a series of questions. How do male and female work patterns vary through time? Did a sexual division of labor exist throughout the era, or did the work of agriculture, as many historians have argued, cause a sexual division of labor?

Work Patterns and Sexual Divisions: Historical Background

Scholars from diverse backgrounds, ranging from biological anthropologists to feminist historians, have contemplated the origins and development of sexual labor patterns. Over the years, many researchers have argued that the foundation of sexual labor patterns is ultimately determined by biological differences and thus dates back to the earliest eras of hunting and gathering. In this view, the greater physical strength of males combined with females' burdens of pregnancy, nursing, and child care jointly predict who will carry out which tasks (Lerner 1986; Murdock 1949; Ortner 1974; Rosaldo and Lamphere 1974). Others reject a strict biological imperative but still view institutionalized sexual labor divisions as a fundamental part of what it means to be human (Brown 1970; Leibowitz 1986). Leibowitz argues that the divide between hunting (male domain) and hearth-based activities (female domain) was in place more than 100,000 years ago at the time of *Homo erectus* (Leibowitz 1986:64).

Another group of scholars single out the emergence of agriculture as the triggering event for institutionalized sexual labor patterns (Divale and Harris 1976; Lerner 1986; Meillassoux 1981). In many of these scenarios, farming leads to sharply defined sexual labor roles and even sows the seeds of widespread social inequality between the sexes (Aaby 1977; Chevillard and LeConte 1986; Divale and Harris 1976; Ehrenberg 1989; Meillassoux 1981). And certainly, ethnographers have noted a rise in sex-typed adult work and a decrease in female status among several specific groups who have undergone the transition from hunter-gatherers to farmers in modern contexts (cf. Draper 1975).

Near Eastern archaeologists have made a number of assumptions regarding sexual divisions of labor as well. For some, Paleolithic hunter-gatherer work patterns are structured principally by strict sexual divisions of labor defined by biological differences (Henry 1989). There are those who see the rise of agriculture as a time of significant social reorganization, a time when large nuclear or extended family units emerge to provide the labor for rigorous farming lifestyles (Flannery 1972). Still others suspect that new activities and schedules imposed by farming promoted increased differentiation between men's and women's activities (Bar-Yosef 1995). One of the most consistent descriptions of both hunter-gatherer and farming groups is that their social and economic activities centered on nuclear families (Byrd 2000; Henry 1989; Johnson and Earle 1987; Moore 1986; Olszewski 1991; Watson 1978). It is important to recognize that strictly defined sexual labor divisions are a corollary assumption often linked conceptually to the "nuclear family." To many archaeologists, nuclear families make sense because biological differences or culturally defined roles demarcate two distinct labor spheres for males and females. Thus, the dyad of one male and one female provides a complementary productive and reproductive unit (Evans-Pritchard 1961; Johnson and Earle 1987; Murdock 1949). So, reconstructions of the past that posit nuclear families as a primary socioeconomic unit implicitly suggest that sexual divisions of labor were already in place.

These diverse efforts to describe and model the social dynamics of prehistoric labor systems share several shortcomings. Their authors presume to know how prehistoric labor was organized. In fact, they do not. They cite no independent evidence from grave offerings, graphic portrayals in art, or texts that suggest distinct occupational spheres for women and men. Neither has human skeletal material been systematically studied for activity patterns.

Furthermore, authors often suggest that there was a uniform, developmental trajectory for sexual labor divisions as groups switched from foraging to farming. In fact, this seems highly unlikely. To the contrary, current scholarship emphasizes that sexual labor patterns are transformed and re-created in the context of specific sets of historic, economic, and social conditions (Moore 1988). Among the Beti of Cameroon, for example, traditional yam and millet crop production is described as a shared activity system, with men and women working side by side in the fields carrying out sex-specific, complementary tasks. Colonial policies aimed at encouraging maize and cassava production caused cultivation work to become more sexually segregated than had previously been the case (Guyer 1991).

Even though the sexual division of labor is often described as one of the most basic organizing principles of human social behavior (Leibowitz 1986), our understanding of the prehistoric past is not served by assuming that a particular work pattern existed for hunter-gatherers or early farmers. Instead, skeletal data are used to investigate whether activities and work were divided up among community members and, if so, whether any of those divisions suggest a sexual division of labor. By minimizing our assumptions about labor patterns and treating this as a baseline investigation, we avoid the politically charged and ill-supported ideology that sees fundamental differences between the sexes in labor and status as a natural and static component of human social relationships.

Social Models in Archaeology: Past and Future

Current Dissatisfaction

Most archaeologists agree that how work and family groups were organized is a key variable to understanding the development of farming economies (Bender 1978, 1985; Byrd 2000; Flannery 1973; Harris 1996; Hayden 1990; Kuijt 2000; Redman 1978; Smith 1976; Stark 1986). Yet our models continue to fail in their efforts to identify and address these factors adequately. Why the intellectual stalemate?

The dilemma is clarified by briefly discussing the nature of archaeological data as well as the influence that general systems theory has had on American archaeology for several decades. The record of human activity that prehistorians have to work with is frustratingly incomplete. Our window on the past gets smaller and smaller the farther back in time we go—the joint effects of organic decay and human disruption take their toll on the material culture record of the past. As the number and types of material objects decrease, archaeologists focus on data sets that preserve and can be measured: stone tools, pottery, long-term climate/ environmental changes, and the number and size of sites in an area, to name a few. Practically speaking, our explanations get reduced to what we can observe and measure. Admittedly, it is often difficult to tease out the social element from these data. But there is a tangible price to be paid when archaeologists stop trying to find creative avenues to identify and study human agency. Ultimately, we run the risk of deluding ourselves that the social realm is less influential in culture process simply because it is hard to measure.

From the theoretical perspective, systems theory has been influential in how archaeologists model the large number of social, technological, environmental, and demographic variables that simultaneously define culture and influence culture change. Open a book about the rise of agriculture or the rise of civilization, and you are apt to see elaborate flow charts with variables (technology, environment, and population growth) confined to boxes linked by arrows that designate negative and positive feedback loops. One of the implicit messages a reader gets from these systems diagrams is that cultures function in complex yet predictable ways. What these diagrams do not communicate effectively is that humans have a role in shaping culture process rather than being passive recipients of culture. Humans are not "pushed" and "pulled" around the landscape by changes in the physical environment and technology but are active participants directing culture change. Cowgill (1975) stated this same point in a more scholarly way when he said that systems-centered views of culture process perceive the dynamic change in the behavioral realm as the result of the deterministic, systemic context rather than any active participation by human agents. More recently, other archaeologists have argued that systems approaches are incompatible with the goal of examining the dynamics of social change (Brumfiel 1992; Wylie 1991a, 1991b).

From a Levantine perspective, adhering to systemic models of human behavior has constrained the extent to which social processes have been addressed by archaeologists who study the rise of agriculture. Researchers continue to look toward large-scale environmental change, technological innovation, population pressure, or some combination of these factors to explain the dynamics behind the transition to agriculture (Blumler 1996; Blumler and Byrne 1990; Edwards 1989; Harris 1986; Henry 1989; Hillman 1996; Layton, Foley, and Williams 1991; MacNeish 1992; McCorriston 1992; Redding 1989; Rindos 1980). Near Eastern climate change—with the emergence of a longer, drier summer growing season—is the dominant model used to explain why human groups were "pushed" to develop agriculture (McCorriston and Hole 1991).

With fragmentary data sets and limited theoretical insights, it is really not surprising to find archaeologists borrowing prepackaged, generalized concepts about sexual labor divisions from sociologists, historians, and cultural anthropologists without seeking any empirical validation from the archaeological record (Crabtree 1991; Peterson 1994).

The Potential of Engendered Analyses

One specific avenue for exploring the social context of culture change is to focus on the roles and relationships between men and women. An "engendered" perspective departs from a systems approach because it focuses explicitly on the participants and recognizes that "human goals are achieved via the manipulation of two interrelated systems [social and natural]" (Brumfiel 1992:559).

In order to investigate potential sexual divisions of labor, it is necessary to establish empirically whether certain tasks or patterns of activity can be assigned to one sex, the other, or both. This essential first step has been described as "task differentiation" (Conkey and Spector 1984; Spector 1982). Researchers agree that establishing how a specific group divides up tasks depends on evidence specific to each case, not on expansive, untested notions about what constitutes "women's work" and "men's work." Guidelines for establishing task differentiation exist, but these often rely on direct historic or ethnographic connections that link a living group with their archaeological ancestors (Conkey and Spector 1984; Spector 1982). Among the successful studies of gender in archaeology, many rely on textual evidence or oral tradition to divide tasks by sex (Becker 2000; Brumfiel 1991; Hastorf 1991; Holliman 2000; Jackson 1991; Wright 1996).

Searching for a starting point, perhaps a model focusing on Near Eastern ethnographic data would provide a reasonable analogy for sexual divisions of labor in prehistoric contexts. There is a wealth of ethnographic literature that documents traditional agricultural practices, sexual divisions of labor, as well as village and household organization (Horne 1994; Jacobs 1979; Kamp 1987, 1993; Kramer 1979, 1982a, 1982b; Watson 1978, 1979a, 1979b).

However, there are substantial problems with using modern ethnographic data from the Near East as a starting point for establishing task differentiation. Historical circumstances, particularly with respect to gender organization, make the connection between prehistoric past and ethnographic present—from "first farmer" to "modern farmer"—questionable. The strength of Islam as an ideolog-ical system defining social and economic roles for men and women in the Near East cannot be underestimated. In many part of the Muslim world, a subordinate position for women, one of economic dependency and not active participation, is the current ideal (Whyte 1978). In general, physical segregation by sex, both at home and in school, begins between age six and puberty. In this context, the as-sociation between females and the private, domestic sphere becomes entrenched. In most Muslim countries, the rate of female participation in economic activities outside the household setting is very low compared with other countries at simi-lar levels of economic development (Whyte 1978).

In subsistence agricultural settings, the degree to which the Islamic model of ideal behavior is carried out varies. And herein lies the second problem with using the ethnographic record as a basis for task differentiation. Several examples show that there is no single pattern of sexual labor that we can realistically choose as a starting point. In light of the heavy labor demands of small-scale farming economies, the sphere deemed appropriate for women is often enlarged to include agricultural tasks. In Turkey, Cosar (1978) argues that women perform the bulk of agricultural production. For these women, work in the fields is compulsory and completely integrated with home and family life. Men often plow the fields, but planting, tending, harvesting, and processing are frequently accomplished exclu-sively by women. In a study of rural, western Iran, Watson describes a fairly strict division of labor between the sexes (Watson 1979a). Men typically take on a ma-jority of agricultural tasks, including plowing, sowing, harvesting, and threshing. Women winnow the grain from chaff, care for animals, produce secondary animal products (wool, yogurt, and cheese), collect fuel and water, prepare meals, and en-gage in craft activities. Among Shiite Muslim villagers in southern Lebanon, Pe-ters (1978) emphasizes the "interchangeability" of tasks. Through their teenage years, boys and girls work jointly in family fields, sharing all tasks. Once they be-come adults, plowing, terrace repairs, and irrigation are tasks allocated to males, but most other tasks are typically accomplished by mixed-sex groups. Men and boys sometimes help with cleaning and food preparation chores. These three brief ethnographic snapshots indicate the range of organizational options that are prac-ticed. This variation, in combination with the influence of Islamic ideologies, mandates looking beyond ethnographic accounts for a starting point in our ex-ploration of labor patterns.

In this context, human skeletal material becomes an especially significant data set. Estimations of biological sex are often reported in bioarchaeological studies. Sex is often a central axis of data presentation and analysis. In some few cases, an explicitly engendered perspective is a central theme: where sexual patterning is used to address issues of role, status, and activity variability between males and females (Bridges 1985; Bumsted et al. 1990; Gray 1996; Holliman 2000; Larsen 1982; Molleson 1989, 1994; Robb 1994, 1998). To examine changes in prehistoric labor patterns, the suite of data collectively known as markers of occupational stress (MOS) is of particular interest. Studies of trauma, dental wear, arthritis, bone structure, and muscle development have all been used to discuss workload and activity patterns (Kennedy 1989). When analyzed and interpreted within and between sex categories, MOS can provide information germane to labor divisions within a population.

Sex and Gender Terminology

A note concerning terminology is appropriate at this point. I will employ the distinction between "sex" as a biologically determined variable and "gender" as a cultural construct that has been repeatedly voiced (Conkey and Spector 1984; O'Kelley and Carney 1986). Sex generally refers to one of two categories defined on the basis of external genitalia. From the osteological perspective, it refers to an estimation of these two categories based on standard skeletal criteria (Bass 1971). While there is often close correspondence between sex and gender categories, some cultures define additional gender role options. The Native American "two spirit" corresponds to a third gender category, combining male and female activity and identity within a single individual (Holliman 1997; Roscoe 1991).

The standard, dichotomous osteological estimation of sex provides the analytical basis of this research, hence the consistent use of "female" and "male" in the remainder of the text. The occasional use of the terms "gender" or "engendered" acknowledges the possibility that sexual identity is a more complex, less dichotomous, and culturally specific construct. The sexual labor system can be viewed as part of this larger, more inclusive gender system. However, the exploration and identification of gender identities in the prehistoric southern Levant outside those defined along biological lines await study.

Study Area and Chronology

The causes and consequences of the rise of domestication economies are particularly salient issues in the southern Levant of western Asia, where the world's first settled agricultural villages were established (Figure 1.1). A long tradition of prehistoric research in this region provides a wealth of archaeological data from a number of well-excavated and well-reported sites. Excellent preservation of architecture, plant and animal food remains, and human osteological material provide essential empirical foundations.

The primary data discussed in this book span the periods before, during, and after the development of agricultural economies—roughly 12,500 to 5,000 years

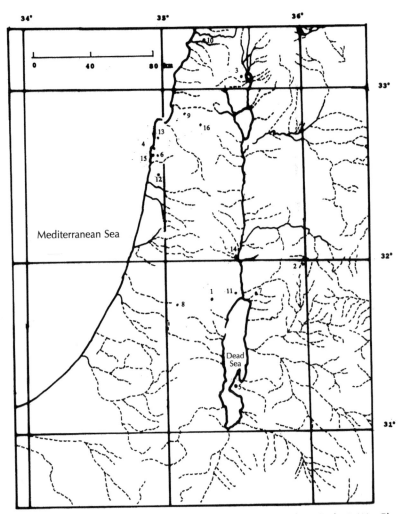

Figure 1.1   Locations of primary sites mentioned in the text. 1–Abou Gosh. 2–'Ain Ghazal. 3–'Ain Mallaha. 4–Atlit Yam. 5–Bab edh-Dhra. 6–El Wad. 7–Ghassul. 8–Hatoula. 9–Hayonim Cave and Terrace. 10–Horvat Galil. 11–Jericho. 12–Kebara. 13–Nahal Oren. 14–Netiv Hagdud. 15–Newe Yam. 16–Yiftahel.

ago. (Table I.I). I examined a total of 158 skeletons from fourteen sites for this study (Table I.2). The Natufians were semi-sedentary hunter-gatherers who used wild plants intensively and hunted game, primarily gazelle. During the Pre-Pottery Neolithic periods, groups employed domestic plants and animals in sedentary village contexts for the first time. However, there is growing evidence that communities in different regions relied on different mixes of wild and domestic species. During the succeeding Pottery Neolithic and Chalcolithic periods, domestic ani-

Table 1.1 Archaeological Chronology for the Southern Levant

Period	Analytical Units	Approximate Dates (B.P.)[1]
Terminal Epipaleolithic	Early Natufian	12,500–11,500
	Late Natufian	11,500–10,000
Pre-Pottery Neolithic	Pre-Pottery Neolithic A	10,500–9,300
	Pre-Pottery Neolithic B	9,300–8,000
	Pre-Pottery Neolithic C	8,000–7,700
Pottery Neolithic	Yarkmukian	7,700–6,200
	Munhata	(combined phases)
Chalcolithic	Ghassulian	6,200–5,500
	Wadi Rabah	
Early Bronze I[2]	Early Bronze IA and IB	5,500–5,000

[1]B.P. = Before Present. Date ranges are synthesized from the following sources: Gilead (1988); Richard
(1987); Rollefson, Simmons, and Kafafi (1992); and Valla (1987a).
[2]Bronze Age period in Palestine often referred to as Canaanite periods.

Table 1.2 Inventory of Skeletal Sample

Period/Site	F	M	Total	Primary Osteological References
Natufian				
'Ain Mallaha	9	12	21	Perrot and Ladiray (1988), Soliveres-Massei (1988)
El Wad	6	10	16	Peabody Museum Inventory
Hayonim Cave	5	12	17	Belfer-Cohen (1988)
Kebara	1	5	6	Peabody Museum Inventory
Nahal Oren	6	6	12	Crognier and Dupouy-Madre (1974); Tel Aviv University Inventory
Subtotal	27	45	72	
Neolithic				
Abou Gosh	1	2	3	Lechevallier (1978), Arensburg, Smith, and Yakar (1978)
'Ain Ghazal	3	5	8	Field notes, Yarmouk University Inventory
Atlit Yam	3	3	6	Hershkovitz and Galili (1990), Tel Aviv University Inventory
Horvat Galil	2	1	3	Hershkovitz and Gopher (1988), Tel Aviv University Inventory
Hatoula	2	4	6	LeMort (1989), CNRS Jerusalem Inventory
Netiv Hagdud	1	1	2	Belfer-Cohen, et al. (1990), Tel Aviv University Inventory
Newe Yam	1	1	2	Tel Aviv University Inventory
Yiftahel	2	2	4	Hershkovitz, Garfinkel, and Arensberg (1986), Tel Aviv University Inventory
Subtotal	15	19	34	
Early Bronze I				
Bab edh-Dhra	23	29	52	Inventory provided by Frolich and Ortner
Total	65	93	158	

mals became increasingly important. A range of settlement types reflects a variety of cultural solutions to this new economic base. Some groups lived in sedentary, mixed agricultural settlements, while others seem to have been more mobile, with a greater reliance on domesticated animals and their products. There is a paucity of human osteological data from the Pottery Neolithic and Chalcolithic periods. Fortunately, broadly similar, regionally diverse economic patterns extend into the initial Early Bronze I time period, for which there are data available. During the Early Bronze I, an agropastoral lifestyle, one that relied on domestic plants, herded animals, and animal by-products, emerged. The human skeletal data used in this study come primarily from Natufian, Pre-Pottery Neolithic, and Early Bronze I sites.

Organization

This book is organized into six chapters, including this introduction. Chapter 2 lays out the regional culture history in the southern Levant. A synopsis of current Natufian, Pre-Pottery Neolithic, Pottery Neolithic, Chalcolithic, and Early Bronze I research is provided. Several major socioeconomic transformations occur in this time range that are typically assumed to have influenced the sexual division of labor, including increased sedentism, the rise of agriculture, the first domestication of sheep/goat, and finally the use of animals for milk, wool, and burden bearing (secondary products sensu Sherratt 1983).

Chapter 3 is an overview of the trends within bioarchaeology related to constructing prehistoric patterns of habitual activity and occupation. Long-bone robusticity, joint modification, trauma, tooth wear, and musculoskeletal stress markers (MSM) are considered in detail. Whenever possible, I have drawn examples from case studies that specifically address the development of farming economies. Recent methodological advances as well as limitations in using MSM are discussed. It is important to temper our optimism about the potentials of bioarchaeological data with the reality of osteological material sometimes more than 10,000 years old. Similarly, activity is only one variable that contributes to the development of many occupational markers. Just as with traditional material culture studies, integrating multiple lines of bioarchaeological evidence produces the strongest explanations.

Chapter 4 narrows the bioarchaeological focus to an examination of Near Eastern studies that pertain to reconstructing activity patterns. These studies provide an important backdrop against which the detailed MSM research can be interpreted and integrated. The MSM data derived from my own research are analyzed in Chapter 5. The analysis validates the existence of some sexual labor divisions for at least two of the three periods: the Natufian and the Early Bronze I.

Distinctions between male and female activities and activity load change in both character and intensity through time. One clear pattern of sexually divided labor occurs during the Natufian, when male participation in hunting appears to be significant. However, I characterize the overall sexual division of labor as weak during the Natufian because, beyond the muscle signatures associated with hunting, males and females often have broadly similar MSM profiles. Even fewer differences in activity and workload were discerned between Neolithic males and females. Neolithic labor patterns are marked by a convergence in MSM profiles, leaving open the question of sexually divided labor. Subsequently, during the Early Bronze I, activity patterns shift again. Female activity levels increase substantially relative to their male counterparts, and MSM profiles suggest that more pronounced divisions of sexual labor developed during the Early Bronze I period relative to either the Natufian or the Neolithic.

In Chapter 6, I explore how the MSM results fit into a broader context consisting of bioarchaeological, archaeological, ethnographic, and feminist arguments about sexual labor divisions and the rise of agriculture. A preliminary model outlining the nature and pace of changes in the sexual labor system is offered in conclusion.

This study represents an attempt to integrate social variables more fully into models of the development of domestication economies. I take the position that the dynamics of social change are highly relevant to the nature and pace of agropastoral developments. Work patterns and sexual labor divisions, derived from bioarchaeological data, provide a unique opportunity to ask more compelling questions about a wider range of human behaviors in the past.

Archaeological Evidence from the Southern Levant

2

⊞

IN ORDER TO recognize critical junctures in task reorganization, we begin by exploring the archaeological evidence for subsistence and settlement change in the southern Levant. A general chronology for each time period is presented. Particular attention is paid to material culture indicative of shifts in daily activities. Each chronological section also contains a general assessment describing current interpretations about social structure, family organization, and work. Not surprisingly, researchers are not always in consensus. Each section ends with a summary of the expected changes in habitual activity based on the currently available archaeological data. This survey emphasizes the regions that produced the skeletal populations used in this study: the Mediterranean coastal and forest zones, the Jordan Valley, and the fertile areas of the western Jordanian plateau (see Figure 1.1). Cultural variations in the arid and semiarid zones of the Sinai, Negev, and eastern Jordanian plateau are not treated comprehensively here.

The skeletal samples I examined came from Natufian, Pre-Pottery Neolithic, Pottery Neolithic, and Early Bronze I (EBI) contexts (see Table 1.2). A number of archaeological, postdepositional, curatorial, logistic, and personal considerations influenced the osteological collections chosen for analysis. For example, permission from the Syrian director-general of antiquities to examine the Tell Ramad came six months after I had finished my collections research. The researchers currently analyzing the material from Basta and Tell Aswad did not reply to my inquiries. In several cases, the physical anthropologists most familiar with material provided details that discouraged me from using their collections. In some cases, I was informed that the collection was composed almost exclusively of children or neonates (Ghassul) or that poor cortical preservation would have made the identification and scoring of musculoskeletal stress markers (MSM) impossible. Much of the large Pre-Pottery Neolithic collection from Jericho is still undergoing conservation, but the analyst explained that what little postcranial material was preserved was too fragmentary to be of use (Rohrer-Ertl, personal communication).

So, although the sample represents a wide range of social and economic stages in the cultural trajectory of the southern Levant, there are also significant gaps. Appropriate skeletal material from Chalcolithic contexts was not available and material from the Pottery Neolithic very scarce. Regardless of the presence or absence of skeletal material, each time period is described here to provide a continuous time line of cultural adaptations in the study area.

Several other sampling issues require mention at the outset. The Natufian and Pre-Pottery Neolithic samples are composed of material from multiple sites. Furthermore, these samples come from different chronological phases within these periods. Typically, variation between Natufian sites and phases was not statistically significant, so the period is treated as a single analytical entity (Peterson 1994). Unfortunately, this same assumption could not be validated for the Pre-Pottery Neolithic sample. Treating the Neolithic period as a single temporal unit of analysis undoubtedly masks intersite diachronic and regional variability. Until sample sizes within regions and phases increase, however, there is no satisfying alternative. The EBI sample comes from a single site: Bab edh-Dhra. The assumption that the activity spectrum at this one EBI site represents regional patterns should also be the subject of more rigorous analysis as additional samples become available.

Natufian Period

Archaeological Context

Seventy-two Natufian skeletons were included in this study (Table 1.2). The sites represented are Kebara, El Wad, Nahal Oren, Hayonim Cave, and 'Ain Mallaha. The first four of these are located in the hilly piedmont just east of the narrow coastal plain of present-day Israel. 'Ain Mallaha is located in the northern Jordan Valley, in the now dry Houleh Basin.

The final Epipaleolithic archaeological manifestation in the Levant is called the Natufian. The term "Natufian" was coined originally by Dorothy Garrod during her excavations at Shukbah Cave in 1928 (Garrod 1932). Additional explorations in the Mount Carmel area (Garrod and Bate 1937) and the Judean Hills (Neuville 1951) further defined the terminal Epipaleolithic period in the Levant. Since then, Natufian sites have been discovered throughout the temperate Mediterranean zone, semiarid hilly zones, and even steppe/desert areas (Bar-Yosef and Goren 1973; Betts 1988; Byrd 1989a; Byrd and Colledge 1991; Cauvin 1991; Copeland 1991; Crabtree, Campana, and Belfer-Cohen 1989; Edwards 1991; Garrard et al. 1989; Goring-Morris 1987; Henry 1976; Moore 1991;

Muheisen et al. 1988; Perrot 1966; Ronen and Lechevallier 1991; Sellars 1998; Stekelis and Yizraely 1963).

This period is divided into Early and Late phases. The Early phase covers the period 12,500–11,500 B.P., while the Late spans the years 11,500–10,500 B.P. The division is defined primarily on the basis of retouch styles on the backing of microliths. The Early Natufian microliths are characterized by bifacial, Helwan retouch; the Late Natufian ones are typically backed using an abrupt, bipolar technique (Bar-Yosef and Valla 1979; Byrd 1989b).

Environmental conditions were apparently in a state of flux during the Natufian, although the nature of these changes is still a source of controversy. Researchers are divided as to whether the Early Natufian should be characterized as a relatively moist period but agree that the Late Natufian was a period of increased aridity (Bar-Yosef and Belfer-Cohen 1989; Henry 1986). As a result of drier conditions, the Mediterranean forest zones contracted northward and probably westward (Baruch and Bottema 1991). Settlement patterns were affected, as some large Early Natufian sites are abandoned. Other sites, closer to reliable water sources, exhibit continuous occupation through the Late Natufian period.

During this 2,000-year period, scholars generally agree on two cultural trends with significance in terms of labor organization and structure. First, the Natufian is characterized by increased sedentism. This phenomenon can be documented through architectural remains, settlement distribution, burial practices, and faunal studies (Bar-Yosef and Belfer-Cohen 1991; Davis 1983; Tchernov 1984). Second, Natufian diets consisted of relatively large quantities of cereals and other plant foods according to human osteological, dental, and ground stone findings (Smith 1991, 1995; Smith, Bar-Yosef, and Sillen 1984; Wright 1992, 1993). Some dietary variability between sites and between Early and Late phases of the Natufian has also recently been discussed (Sillen 1984; Sillen and Lee-Thorp 1991).

Cave, terrace, and open-air sites range in size from 15 to 100 square meters, on the small end of the scale, to more than 1,000 square meters (Bar-Yosef and Belfer-Cohen 1989). Henry (1989) notes that large sites tend to be concentrated on ecotones between grassland and forest mosaics and argues that such strategic placement of villages took advantage of several resource catchment zones. A variety of smaller, open-air sites occur throughout the area and can be characterized generally as campsites or as extractive loci (Henry 1989; Hovers 1993).

The first well-preserved, substantial architecture in the Levant occurs during the Natufian period. Structures have been uncovered from a number of large sites (Bar-Yosef and Goren 1973; Edwards 1991; Henry 1976; Henry and Leroi-Gourhan 1976; Marks and Larson 1977; Muheisen et al. 1988; Perrot 1966; Stekelis and Yizraely 1963). Typically, individual circular and semicircular structures are arranged in loose clusters or linear arrangements. Many of the structures have stone foundations. Others appear to have been excavated partially into the ground so that a solid earth wall provided the foundation (Figure 2.1). In either case, superstructures of timber, reeds, thatch, or wattle/daub have been postulated. Structures range in size from 2.5 to 10 meters in diameter, with an average of 3 to 5 meters in diameter (Olszewski 1991). An oval house, built of undressed local stones at Nahal Oren, is described as containing interior "silos" (Stekelis and Yizraely 1963).

At large sites without domestic dwellings, other architectural features, such as terrace walls, pavements, and curbs, have been excavated (Betts 1988; Garrod 1932; Garrod and Bate 1937; Neuville 1951; Turville-Petre 1932). Bar-Yosef (1991) describes an oval structure at Hayonim as a lime-processing kiln because of the presence of pounded lime and charred areas.

So, some Natufian groups excavated house foundations, produced plaster, transported heavy stones for building materials, and dug underground storage

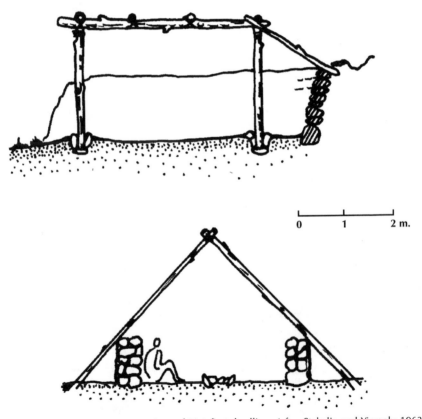

Figure 2.1   Artists' reconstructions of Natufian dwellings (after Stekelis and Yizraely 1963, top, and Valla 1991, bottom).

pits—all significant energy expenditures that suggest continuous seasonal or permanent residence. Permanence of settlement is indicated by the high densities of lithic debris, the presence of human commensals (house mouse, rat, and sparrow), and age and seasonality markers in gazelle remains (Bar-Yosef and Belfer-Cohen 1992). So, too, the establishment of well-defined cemetery areas is often associated with more sedentary occupation.

Burial areas tend to be in close proximity to habitation areas. Mortuary treatment sometimes included elaborate decoration of the body. A variety of shell, bone, and stone ornaments are often associated with graves. The types of grave goods represented provide few direct clues regarding occupation or activity. Both primary and secondary interments occur, as do individual and collective graves. Corpses have been found in flexed, semiflexed, extended, and seated positions (Belfer-Cohen 1991).

Burials also bring to mind a consideration of the symbolic realm. Animal bones are sometimes found in burials. Often the faunal remains do not reflect food offerings per se: a turtle carapace, gazelle horns, horse teeth, and so on. Only occasionally is there evidence for the use of red ocher (Valla 1995). Grave locations are sometimes marked with stone slabs, mortars, or cup-marked stones. These artifacts are often found in burial pits as well (Feidel 1979). The stones might have served to mark graves, symbolically immobilize the deceased, protect the remains from scavengers, indicate something about the status/activities of the deceased, or some combination of these purposes. During the Late Natufian, the practice of skull removal appears, but we do not know what became of the skulls. A tradition of figurative art that features animal forms can be seen in items from burial and domestic contexts.

Bar-Yosef and Belfer-Cohen (1989) make the case that Natufian material culture is typified by a fundamental unity at the basic technological and typological levels. An examination of artifacts can provide data pertinent to widespread economic activities. Natufian chipped stone industries are characterized by a formal tool technology based on the production of blades and bladelets that are retouched to form a variety of geometric forms. The "type fossil" of the Natufian is the lunate (Figure 2.2).

Sickle blades are also consistently present in chipped stone assemblages in relatively low frequencies, except in extreme southern areas (Bar-Yosef 1991). Use wear studies indicate that some sickle blades were used to harvest cereals (Anderson 1991, 1999; Unger-Hamilton 1991). There is also a macrolithic and a massive tool component associated with Natufian assemblages, including scrapers and elongated, bifacial picks (Bar-Yosef and Belfer-Cohen 1989) (Figure 2.2).

The proportion of Natufian sites containing ground stone tools increases sharply from earlier Epipaleolithic (Kebaran) contexts (Wright 1992, 1993). The

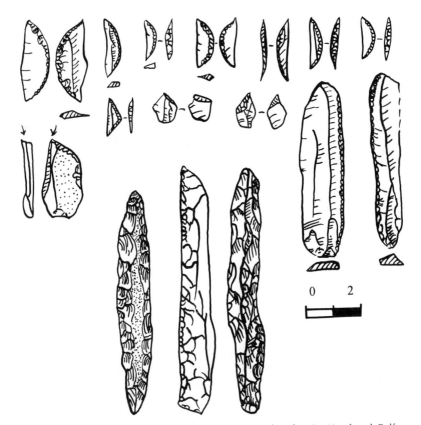

Figure 2.2   Examples of Natufian chipped stone tools (after Bar-Yosef and Belfer-Cohen 1989).

ground stone assemblages from Natufian sites are composed of a range of morphological types: pestles, mortars, bowls, slabs, querns, hand stones, and so on. Deep-hole conical mortars, both freestanding and bedrock forms, are apparently unique to the Natufian (Wright 1993) (Figure 2.3). While local limestone and basalt materials were often readily available, at Hayonim basalt was transported from at least 30 kilometers from the site (Bar-Yosef and Goren 1973).

A variety of bone tools also occurs for the first time during the Natufian period. Sickle hafts, pointed implements, spatulas, and barbed points have been found, suggesting cereal collection, sewing and skin working, and fishing, respectively (Bar-Yosef and Belfer-Cohen 1989) (Figure 2.4). Morphological and use-wear analyses suggest that the objects from Hayonim were probably used as fasteners for clothing, ornaments, skin preparation tools, sickles, and hunting and fishing tools (Campana 1989, 1991).

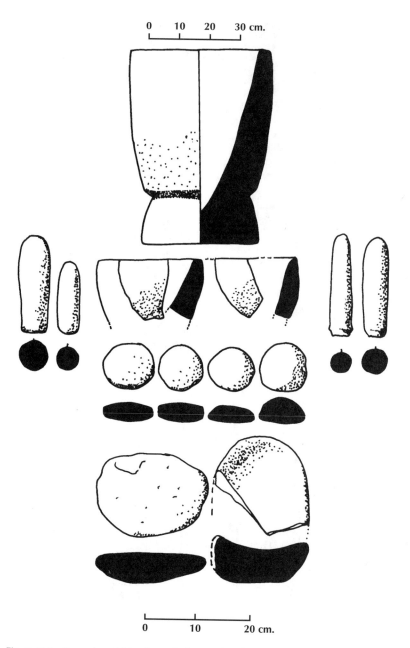

Figure 2.3   Examples of Natufian grinding tools (after Perrot 1966). Note different scale used for top mortar.

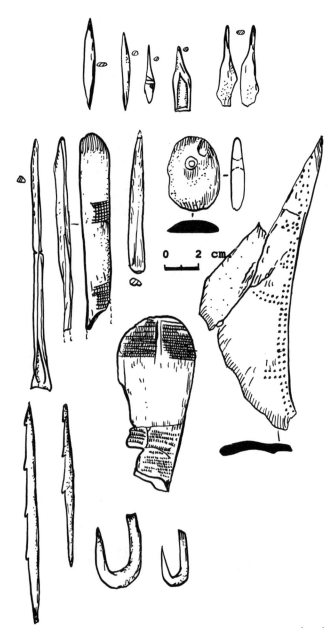

Figure 2.4 Examples of Natufian bone tools (after Bar-Yosef and Belfer-Cohen 1989 and Turville-Petre 1932).

Wild faunal remains recovered from Natufian sites include onager (*Equus hemionus*), cattle (*Bos primigenius*), gazelle (*Gazella* sp.), and goat (*Ovis* sp.); sheep (*Capra* sp.), ibex (*Capra ibex*), wild boar (*Sus scrofa*), and various genera of deer (*Dama mesopotamica, Capreolus capreolus,* and *Cervus elaphus*) are some of the larger forms present. Among these, gazelle bone typically dominates faunal assemblages in terms of the number of identified specimens (Henry 1989). More systematic retrieval techniques at recent excavations have provided evidence for a greater faunal diversity, including hare, various bird species, fish, reptiles, and lizards (Edwards 1991; Henry and Leroi-Gourhan 1976; Ronen and Lechevallier 1991).

Charred seeds and charcoal samples provide botanical evidence for plant food utilization. Wild einkorn wheat (*Triticum boeticum*), wild barley (*Hordeum spontaneum*), wild annual and perennial rye (*Secale cereale* and *S. montanum*), acorn (*Quercus* sp.), lentil (*Lens* sp.), chickpea (*Cicer* sp.), and field pea (*Pisum* sp.) have all been identified, along with a variety of weedy species with economic potential (Hillman, Colledge, and Harris 1989; Potts, Colledge, and Edwards 1985). Remains of pistachio and almond were recovered from 'Ain Mallaha (Perrot 1993a).

Dental studies support the notion that large quantities of ground cereals were being incorporated into the diets of Natufian populations (Smith 1972, 1991; Smith, Bar-Yosef, and Sillen 1984). Patterns of dental disease suggest that their diet was relatively high in abrasive, caries-producing matter. Strontium-to-calcium ratios also support the conclusion that Natufian diets were omnivorous, containing substantial amounts of vegetable foods relative to meat (Sillen and Lee-Thorp 1991).

The current view of Natufian lifeways consists of semi-sedentary hunter-gatherers who harvested a variety of wild plant and animal resources from their environments. At certain favorable environmental locations, dwellings were built and "residential camps" maintained. These same locations were often used as burial areas.

Natufian Social Structure

Historically, most researchers have focused on Natufian social organization at the level of the community. They have asked, "How socially complex were these groups? Were there status differences between group members? How were those differences defined?" Answers rely heavily on interpretations of mortuary remains. Far less attention has been paid to the organization of families and work.

An ongoing debate centers on the type and degree of status differentiation apparent at Natufian sites. From his analysis of the El Wad burials and grave goods, Wright (1978) concluded that ranking and subgroup affiliation were present. Belfer-Cohen (1995) challenged his interpretation, maintaining that there is no evidence for social stratification during the Natufian. Kuijt (1996) suggests that by the Late Natufian, mortuary ritual served to maintain balance and cohesion among individuals and groups that were increasingly socially differentiated. In a comprehensive and systematic review of the Natufian mortuary data, Grindell (1998:207, 235) argues against Kuijt's position, stating that there is remarkably little evidence for social differentiation of any kind. Her analysis of the burial evidence indicates that Natufian social organization was fundamentally egalitarian.

Both burials and architecture have been used to discuss family size and composition. An examination of the age and sex compositions of the multiple or group burials at Hayonim Cave indicates that they often do not represent nuclear families (Bar-Yosef 1988; Belfer-Cohen 1990; Peterson 1994). Two very different interpretations of domestic architecture have emerged. Small interior dimensions are, in fact, typical of Natufian structures. Later dwellings at Mallaha, for instance, average 12 square meters, with many falling in the 8-to-10-square-meter range (Valla 1991). All the structures at Hayonim Cave fall below 10 square meters (estimates based on map in Belfer-Cohen 1988). Excavators note that not all these structures are dwellings, yet a habitation component is considered to be present (Bar-Yosef and Goren 1973).

The inhabitants of small Natufian residences are considered by some to be nuclear families (Byrd 2000; Henry 1989; Olszewski 1991). Others, using ethnographic analogs, suggest that one person, or at most two people, lived in Natufian houses (Flannery 1972; Valla 1991). Ethnographically derived individual floorspace requirements suggest that 7 to 10 square meters is a reasonable estimate range for a single individual (see Kramer 1979; LeBlanc 1971; Naroll 1962; Watson 1978).

I have already voiced hesitance in assuming that nuclear families were the sole productive and residential units in the prehistoric past because of the highly segregated labor scenarios that they tend to imply. Given the current burial and architectural data sets, there are good reasons to keep an open mind about the size and composition of household units during the Natufian.

When it comes to describing the organization of work, three distinctive models can be found. Flannery (1972) published an influential model of prehistoric social organization for Near Eastern communities on either side of the agricultural transition. Sexual labor divisions are one organizational axis that he explores. At preagricultural Natufian sites, Flannery attributes most productive work to single-sex task groups, not families (Flannery 1972:25, 31). Groups of males are responsible for hunting and butchering animal game. Groups of females collect and process plant resources. The resources obtained by single-sex groups are later shared by the entire community—which he tentatively states might be composed of related adult males and their polygynous households. The basis for Flannery's sexual labor divisions is never made explicit. Both males and females are viewed as being fairly mobile, spending considerable time away from the camps.

Communal work patterns are also emphasized by Crabtree (1991), but she rejects a strict division of labor by sex or age as a necessary corollary. Crabtree focuses on the seasonal nature of stable plant resources used by Natufian groups: acorns and cereals. Based on faunal evidence from several sites, she suggests that gazelle hunting may have been conducted seasonally and involved game drives. Relying on Great Basin ethnographic accounts, she argues that large, coordinated work parties would have been the most sufficient way to exploit seasonal resources. All able-bodied group members, regardless of sex or age, would have participated. Crabtree cites grave goods that crosscut sex and age categories in further support of her claim.

A third model of Natufian sexual labor patterns comes from Henry (1989), who emphasizes a highly segregated labor system. He envisions a prehistoric scenario in which males and females are responsible for distinctive sets of tasks that are carried out in spatially distinctive settings. Henry begins by linking certain artifacts and certain sexes. Unfortunately, he cites no independent archaeological or ethnographic evidence in support of these sex-based assignments. Women are viewed as the manufacturers and users of stone bowls, ostrich egg bottles, and hide-working tools (Henry 1989:202). The inference is that these are domestic items used by women who operate largely in a domestic sphere. Flint tools are male objects (Henry 1989:208). Men are viewed as more mobile, engaging in long-distance hunting, trading, and warfare. This scenario clearly corresponds to a highly segregated female/passive/domestic versus male/active/public paradigm that has been the focus of continued criticism for over a decade (Brumbach and Jarvenpa 1997; Conkey and Spector 1984; Conkey and Williams 1991; Watson and Kennedy 1991).

Flannery, Crabtree, and Henry have very different visions of Natufian social structure and labor organization. All three scenarios have ethnographic parallels. Sexual labor patterns encompass a wide spectrum of options, ranging from tasks being equally shared to tasks being highly sex segregated. So how is one to choose which of the three scenarios is most plausible? With that question in mind, I turn first to the archaeological record for a discussion of documented Natufian activities. Ultimately, these data, alongside the bioarchaeological data, suggest the most likely model for labor patterns among these complex hunter-gatherers.

Natufian Activity Expectations

Habitual activities among Natufian groups certainly would have included hunting, perhaps communally. Leather working was undoubtedly a significant undertaking by Natufian craftspeople. One can imagine the importance of animal skins as a resource for carrying bags, tents, and many other uses (Grigson 1995). One group of bone tools described as scrapers or *lissoirs* shows microscopic wear consistent with leather working (Campana 1989, 1991). The intensive collection of plant foods is another expected activity realm, as are the tasks involved in processing them. The increase in grinding stones is a material correlate of the increase in the importance of cereals. Fiber technology would be equally important in providing basketry, netting, cordage, and the like. There are artifactual correlates to these activities (Campana 1989, 1991) as well as dental evidence suggestive of fiber processing (Molleson 1994). The material record also attests to the production of stone tools and items of personal adornment. Less frequent but important activities would have included the range of tasks involved in constructing dwellings and graves.

Pre-Pottery Neolithic Period

Archaeological Context

I included thirty-two Pre-Pottery Neolithic (PPN) skeletons in this study (Table 1.2). They came from seven sites. Netiv Hagdud is located in the lower Jordan Valley. Hatoula is in the Judean Hills of central Palestine. Atlit Yam is a submerged site located on a shallow coastal shelf off the northern Carmel coast. Yiftahel and Horvat Galil are in the Galilee. Abou Gosh is 15 kilometers southwest of Jerusalem, and 'Ain Ghazal is in the northern suburbs of Amman.

The transition from the Natufian to the PPN was first established stratigraphically by Kathleen Kenyon at Jericho (Kenyon 1957). The cultural elements of the PPN represent, in many ways, the continuation and expansion of trends established during the Natufian. In general, the PPN can be characterized as a period when domesticated plants and animals first appear, gradually increasing in economic importance through time. Large villages were established. Multiple occupation layers and architectural remodeling are used to infer continuous site use by a fairly sedentary population.

The PPN sites date from the end of the Late Natufian period: 10,500 B.P. to between 8,000 and 7,700 B.P. The era is broadly divided into three chronological segments. The Pre-Pottery Neolithic A (PPNA; ca. 10,300 B.P.–9,300 B.P.) and the Pre-Pottery Neolithic B (PPNB; ca. 9,300 B.P.–8,000 B.P.) were first identified by Kenyon during her excavations of Jericho (Kenyon 1957). The Pre-Pottery Neolithic C (PPNC), defined recently at the Jordanian site of 'Ain Ghazal, spans the time period from 8,000 B.P. to roughly 7,700 B.P. (Rollefson 1990).

Regional settlement patterns throughout the PPN reflect certain crucial resource parameters. Where water resources were dependable and perennial, sedentary lifeways were sustained. Wild resources were increasingly supplemented with cultivated cereals and legumes and finally domesticated caprovines. In more marginal settings, settlements were often smaller; reflecting the more limited productive capacities of the resources in the landscape (Henry 1985). All PPN habitation sites reflect semi- to fully sedentary adaptations.

For those of us working in the southern Levant, this is a very exciting time. Large portions of the settlement map that were previously archaeological terra incognita are beginning to fill in. Our models are just now beginning to consider the full range of regional and environmental settings. Systematic survey and excavation in the southern Sinai (Bar-Yosef 1981, 1984), southern Negev (Goring-Morris and Gopher 1983), and Jordan (Gebel and Bienert 1997; Kafafi, Caneva, and Palumbo 1999; Peterson 2000b; Rollefson 1998, 1999; Simmons and al-Najjar 1999) are providing the much-needed data.

Current research results suggest that PPNA lifeways represent in situ developments from Natufian precursors. This conclusion is supported by continuous occupational and stratigraphic sequences at archaeological sites as well as similarities in a variety of tool forms, architecture, and burial customs (Kenyon 1957; Kirkbride 1966; Noy, Legge, and Higgs 1973; Perrot and Ladiray 1988; Stekelis and Yizraely 1963).

Overall, sites increase in size and number from the PPNA to the PPNB. Open-air sites dominate, although terrace and cave sites also occur infrequently. Sites vary in size from 0.2 to 12 hectares (Stager 1992). Functional differences likely account for some of the range in site sizes, as both habitation sites and short-term, limited activity sites seem to be represented. Moving from the PPNA to PPNB, there is a trend from smaller to larger "villages." For example, PPNA Jericho and Netiv Hagdud cover areas of 1 to 3 hectares. Several PPNB sites, such as Basta, 'Ain Ghazal, and Wadi Shu'eib, are much larger, up to 12 hectares or even larger. Population estimates for these sites range from 375 to 450 for the largest PPNA villages to more than 1,000 for the PPNB villages (Bar-Yosef and Belfer-Cohen 1991). By the PPNC, however, the settlement pattern may be characterized by a much smaller core of year-round denizens and groups of dispersed, seasonal inhabitants (Rollefson and Kohler-Rollefson 1989). Environmental degradation at large villages is cited as the primary cause for socioeconomic changes (Rollefson 1996).

For the sites included in this analysis, there seems to be an evolutionary trend from round to rectangular domestic architecture as we move from the PPNA to the PPNB. At several PPNA sites, the typical house is a circular hut structure with a mud floor and a timber and wattle/daub superstructure (Bar-Yosef, Gopher, et al. 1992; Kenyon 1981; Kuijt, Mabry, and Palumbo 1991; Noy, Schuldenrein, and Tchernov 1980). Structure size varies, and the smallest may have been used for storage rather than habitation.

Rectangular structures are typical during the PPNB. Stone foundations are a common feature. Partitions in the form of piers or dividing walls sometimes divide interior spaces (Banning and Byrd 1987; Braun 1997; Byrd and Banning 1988; Lechevallier 1978) (Figure 2.5). Building materials vary depending on the raw materials available locally. Unbaked mud bricks were used at Jericho (e.g., Kenyon 1981). The use of lime plaster as floor, hearth, and wall coverings is very typical (e.g., Rollefson, Simmons, and Kafafi 1992).

A new PPNB architectural tradition is emerging from recent excavations in southern Jordan that departs from the freestanding individual structures just described. A number of sites in central and southern Jordan have domestic architecture consisting of interconnected building complexes. In some cases, the complexes seem to be defined by a large, central room surrounded by smaller rooms (Gebel and Beinert 1997; Mahasneh 1997; Peterson 2000c; Simmons and al-Najjar 1999; Waheeb and Fino 1997). Large multiroomed structures are more typical of the PPNC domestic structures at 'Ain Ghazal, similar to those found at

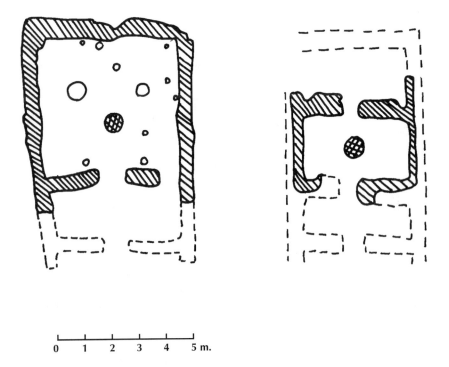

Figure 2.5   Pre-Pottery Neolithic B architecture from 'Ain Ghazal (after Banning and Byrd 1987).

Basta and Beidha. Some of these structures had two or more stories. Massive courtyard walls are also found in the PPNC levels at 'Ain Ghazal (Kafafi and Rollefson 1995; Rollefson and Kafafi 1994; Rollefson et al. 1992). Several structures that are functionally distinctive from their domestic counterparts have also been described. The tower and retaining walls at PPNA Jericho are a well-known example (Kenyon 1981). Locus 8 at PPNA Netiv Hagdud is an oval building with an interior partition. The structure is one of the larger at the site. More than seventy grinding stones and three adult skulls were found in Locus 8. The structure is described as functionally distinctive, but no further interpretations are offered (Bar-Yosef and Gopher 1997; Bar-Yosef, Gopher, et al. 1992). A circular/apsidal building, utilized and refurbished during four phases of 'Ain Ghazal's PPN occupation, contains a unique red painted plaster hearth. Rollefson describes it as a shrine. A PPNC "temple" at 'Ain Ghazal contains altars formed from large stone slabs and internal partitions that restrict access and visual pathways (Rollefson 1998).

Mortuary customs throughout the PPN are fairly consistent and represent an intensification of ritual compared with the Natufian (Grindell 1998). Human skeletons are typically found beneath the floors of domestic structures but also occasionally in middens. Both individual and group burials occur. Group burials are more frequent during the PPNC. Skulls are often detached from adult bodies, leaving only the mandible behind. Skulls, single and in groups, are often found in separate pits. The removed skulls are often embellished with painted decoration, plaster "refleshing," inlaid shell eyes, and bitumen coating (Butler 1989; Lechevallier 1978). Similar proportions of male and female skulls are treated in this manner (Grindell 1998). Ethnographic parallels link this practice to ancestor cults (Cauvin 1972; Feidel 1979). An increase in ritual activity involving ancestors suggests that the definition and maintenance of family or community generational connections was increasingly important. Secondary burial of multiple skulls in communal spaces may also provide opportunities for large celebrations that serve to reaffirm a village's egalitarian ethos and connections between and among households (Kuijt 2000).

In addition to the possible public/ritual structures, new developments in figurative art are rich in symbolic content. PPN traditions of figurative art expand to include plaster human statuary. Examples have been described from Jericho, Nahal Hemar Cave, and 'Ain Ghazal (Tubb and Grissom 1995). The most extensive collection (parts of approximately thirty-four statues) comes from two caches at 'Ain Ghazal. Their wide-open, highly decorated eyes are their most prominent feature. Morphologically, most are androgynous, although three have sexual characteristics to indicate that they are female (Tubb and Grissom 1995). The statues appear to have been ritually buried. Like the plastered skulls, the statues may also be related to ancestor worship. Smaller carved stone and baked clay figurines also occur. It has been noted that human forms, particularly females, occur more frequently in the PPNA compared to the preceding Natufian period (Bar-Yosef and Belfer-Cohen 1992).

Stone tool industries undergo a series of developments during the PPN. PPNA assemblages initially contain a microlithic component that phases out rather quickly. More common tools in the PPNA are burins, scrapers, and somewhat irregular blades. Some of these have lustrous edges associated with cutting silicaceous plants, such as grasses or reeds (Unger-Hamilton 1991). Projectile points, described as arrowheads, also appear during this period (Bar-Yosef 1981). Alternatively, an emphasis on blade production characterizes the chipped stone assemblages of PPNB. Both unmodified and retouched blades are used as sickles and reaping knives. Again, macro- and microscopic surface use wear indicates their role in harvesting plants (Anderson 1999). Some have argued that flourishing PPNB communities spawned lithic craftspeople skilled in using naviform core-and-blade technology to produce the standardized blades used for many tools (Quintero and Wilke 1995). Other chipped stone tools include borers, burins, and scrapers (Figure 2.6).

Several new types of large, heavy tools make their first appearance, in any significant number, during the PPN. Axes, adzes, chisels, and picks are shaped using unifacial and bifacial techniques on both volcanic and metamorphic materials. Ground and polished axes make their first appearance during the PPN and are considered a "type fossil" of the aceramic Neolithic in general (Wright 1992). Many are roughly oval to triangular in plan. Functional differentiation among these tools is based primarily on the length and shape of the working edge. The butt ends are often carefully trimmed and shaped for hafting in a handle. Axes and adzes are typically defined as implements for felling trees and working wood. Picks, with narrower, more pointed profiles, are associated with breaking up and turning soil. Ax and adze rejuvenation flakes attest to frequent resharpening and reuse of these tools, which must have been relatively "expensive" to produce (Figure 2.7).

When compared to the Natufian period, a larger proportion of the PPN sites contain ground stone tools (Wright 1992, 1993). Among the artifact types represented, grinding slabs and querns become more prevalent (Figure 2.7). An emphasis on grinding, rather than pounding using mortars and pestles, represents a more intensive use of cereal grain. Comparing Natufian and PPN dentition, an increase in dental pathology supports a model of increased reliance on carbohydrates (Smith 1989a, 1991; Smith, Bar-Yosef, and Sillen 1984).

The plant food economy of the PPN is a mixed one, composed of both wild and domestic species. During the PPNA, the first unequivocal domestic cereal

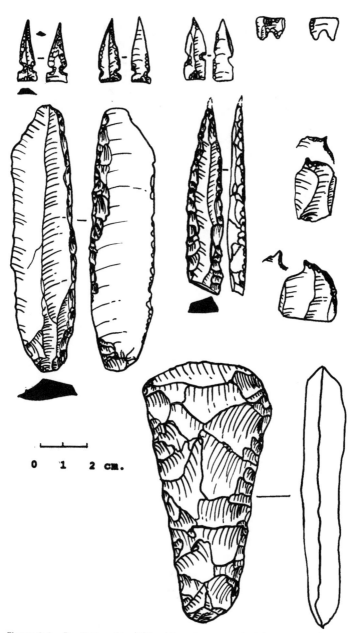

Figure 2.6   Pre-Pottery Neolithic chipped stone tools (after Bar-Yosef, Gopher, et al. 1992).

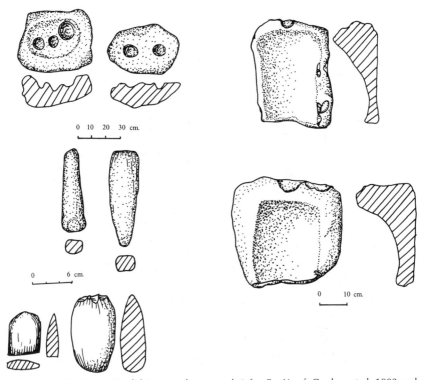

0 10 20 30 cm.

0   6 cm.

0   10 cm.

Figure 2.7   Pre-Pottery Neolithic ground stone tools (after Bar Yosef, Gopher, et al. 1992 and Wright 1992).

grains appear: emmer wheat (*Triticum dicoccum*) and two-row hulled barley (*Hordeum distichum*) (Hopf 1969; Noy 1977). In the PPNB, the first evidence for domestic einkorn wheat (*Triticum monococcum*) occurs (Hopf 1969). A variety of legumes are also present, including peas (*Pisum* sp.), lentils (*Lens* sp.), chickpeas (*Cicer* sp.), and horsebeans (*Vicia faba*). Wild grass and weed seeds are also typical. Olive (*Olea europeaea*), oak (*Quercus* sp.), pomegranate (*Punica granata*), pistachio (*Pistachia atlantica*), fig (*Ficus carica*), and carob (*Ceratonia siliqua*) have also been identified from PPN contexts (Bar-Yosef, Gopher, et al. 1992; Bar-Yosef and Kislev 1989; Garfinkel 1987b; Hopf 1969; Liphschitz 1989; Noy 1977).

Faunal resources during the PPNA seem to indicate the continued and exclusive use of wild species: sheep (*Ovis* sp.), goats (*Capra* sp.), wild boar (*Sus scrofa*), cattle (*Bos primigenius*), onager (*Equus hemionus*), and gazelle (*Gazella* sp.). Water and fine sieving at recent excavations has expanded the diversity of species represented to include a variety of avifauna and aquatic species (Bar-Yosef, Gopher, et al. 1992). The remains of more than 2,000 birds at Netiv Hagdud, some species of which are seasonal migrants, make the case for site occupation over at least a nine-month period (Tchernov 1994).

During the PPNB, domestic goat has been identified by both metrical analysis and culling patterns (Clutton-Brock 1979; Ducos 1978; Kohler-Rollefson 1989). Wild animals continue to be used as well. By the PPNC, however, domestic animals dominate the faunal spectrum, with pigs, dogs, and possibly cattle identified at 'Ain Ghazal (Kohler-Rollefson 1989).

The bone tool assemblages from PPN sites contain a variety of implements: awls, needles, battens, and spatulas. Combined with ground stone weights and spindle whorls, these assemblages indicate weaving activities (Wright 1992). This inference is dramatically supported by examples of both linen and bast textiles made from flax and palm fibers, respectively, that have been preserved in the Nahal Hemar Cave in the Dead Sea depression. Textile manufacturing techniques include hand weaving, knotting, and loom use (Bar-Yosef, Schick, and Alon 1993).

At Yiftahel, long-distance procurement of greenstone raw materials is documented. Finished beads, production debris, as well as pieces of unmodified raw material have been found. The precise provenance of the greenstone has yet to be determined, but it must be related to copper-bearing strata—the closest of which occur at the Wadi Feinan in Jordan (270 kilometers distant) and Timna in the southern Araba (350 kilometers distant) (Garfinkel 1987a).

PPN Social Structure

Several authors have speculated about the social complexity of PPN groups. Moore (1985) described PPN social systems as egalitarian on the basis of a lack of differentiation among the mortuary data. Grindell's more recent study also supports low levels of social differentiation. She argues that the mortuary patterns indicate that strong group boundaries may have developed (us vs. them) but little internal differentiation (elites vs. peasants) (Grindell 1998). The lack of internal differentiation is reflected in burial data where certain individuals do not stand out by virtue of large amounts of grave goods or specialized, costly interments. Rather, there appear to be a small number of burials in which individuals are buried haphazardly in unusual contexts. She makes the case that these may represent individuals with negative status within the group, mentioning witchcraft accusations specifically (Grindell 1998).

Looking at the regional PPN map has led others to hypothesize that there was some level of social complexity present during the PPNB. Large PPNB sites (sometimes referred to as "mega-sites") are viewed as wealthier and the focus of ritual and religious activities. Families or lineage groups are viewed as being arranged hierarchically (Bar-Yosef 1995; Bar-Yosef and Belfer-Cohen 1989).

Others have argued that despite gross differences in size, there is little evidence that even the largest sites were qualitatively different in ways that suggest that they were focal points of centralized political or economic functions (Hole 2000).

In terms of family composition and organization, the PPN may have witnessed an increased emphasis on the family as social unit. The reverence of ancestors, inferred from the specialized treatment of skulls and statuary, is an important line of evidence. Kramer (1982a) states that the proximity or close packing of houses may also indicate close family relationships. Compelling evidence is offered by the results of careful stratigraphic excavations that revealed multiple remodeling episodes within certain structures (Banning and Byrd 1987; Braun 1997; Lechevallier 1978; Moore, Hillman, and Legge 2000). Large rooms are sometimes subdivided by adding short interior partition walls, or piers. Rooms are also added and demolished. Banning and Byrd (1987) argue convincingly that remodeling was a response to the changing needs of the household unit as members were added and dispersed. These changes are equated with a family's developmental cycle. The willingness to remodel space reflects a cohesive sense to the household unit not previously documented.

A variety of family structures and marriage patterns have been suggested, and the lack of consensus indicates both a paucity of relevant data and the possibility for diachronic and regional variability in these social features across the PPN landscape. Flannery (1972) holds that family groups inhabit the new, rectangular PPN dwellings. He states that productive tasks once performed by single-sex task groups during the Natufian are now accomplished by large nuclear or extended families. Large families, with lots of children, are seen as providing labor for the great many unskilled tasks required by a farming life. Polygyny has also been suggested as a logical solution to PPN labor demands (Hershkovitz and Gopher 1990).

However, little architectural or demographic evidence can be cited in support of large families during the PPN of the southern Levant. While structures generally increase in terms of interior floor space in comparison with the Natufian, they are by no means expansive. Estimates of the co-residential unit size are typically between three and four individuals (Byrd 2000). Synthesizing ethnographic and skeletal data from the Levant, Hershkovitz and Gopher (1990) have estimated the number of live births per female at 5.6, of which a significant number would not reach maturity.

The interconnected, shared-wall architectural tradition emerging from sites in southern Jordan has also been explained as housing for extended or joint families (Gebel, Hermansen, and Niebuhr 1999). These conclusions need to be strengthened with room functional analyses and the identification of redundancy of certain features and/or artifact classes (Peterson 2000c). It seems premature to interpret the domestic architecture in the southern Levant as synonymous with large, agglutinated PPN structures in the northern Levant (e.g., Akkermans, Fokken, and Waterbolk 1981; Voigt 1990; Watson 1979a).

So how are these families coping with the new and complex suite of tasks that are part of a farming and herding lifestyle? While most authors seem to agree that agricultural lifestyles imply increased labor demands, few seem to deal with the question, Who is doing the agricultural work?

Commentary about domestic social organization and sexual divisions is scanty. Bar-Yosef (1995) suggests that gender-based activity differences would increase with the establishment of farming communities. Women, he maintains, would have had new agricultural tasks and additional child care duties added to their workload. Men, meanwhile, would be increasingly involved in long-distance forays, presumably to acquire nonlocal materials. Bar-Yosef's statements imply that women were actively engaged in agricultural activities. Bar-Yosef and Belfer-Cohen (1992) make a related point when they make the case that the appearance of female figurines during the PPN is a cultural expression for a growing dichotomy between males and females.

Flannery suggests that men and women may be working more closely as a cooperative economic unit, albeit not necessarily sharing significant tasks. Children may be put to work before they reached adulthood. He implies that women may be responsible for processing cereals because he associates grinding slabs (and also cooking pots and needles) with women's activities (1972:39). But of the men, we hear only that they are still involved in hunting. Men are associated with spear points, arrowheads, and microlithic projectiles (Flannery 1972:39). As previously stated, there are no independent archaeological bases for these artifact associations with one sex or the other.

PPN Activity Expectations

What does the archaeological record for the PPN suggest in terms of habitual activities? There is good reason to believe that the physically taxing tasks of felling trees and chopping wood increased during the PPN. The construction and remodeling of more substantial houses would have required wood resources. Large posthole features document the use of wooden beams for the wall supports. Additional wood resources may have also been used in ceiling and wall construction. Clearing agricultural land may have also required timbering activities. But the most constant and habitual timbering activity was probably related to plaster production. Plaster was applied to floors, walls, skulls, statues, and so on. Floors were typically replastered many times during the use of a dwelling (Banning and Byrd 1987; Peterson 2000b). The chunks of limestone have, first, to be heated, requiring a substantial amount of fuel. And the fuel requirements for plaster production "entailed a colossal drain on local stands of trees" (Rollefson et al. 1992:468).

Despite the equation of PPN with the first unequivocal use of domestic plant foods, some PPNB sites do not contain such evidence (e.g., Yiftahel). Furthermore, there is still debate about whether barley from PPNA contexts is being intentionally cultivated or collected from wild stands (Bar-Yosef and Belfer-Cohen 1991). Cultivation of wild cereals may not have required planting per se, as wild barley and wheat appear to germinate better using broadcast sowing techniques (Anderson 1991). However, large bifacial tools described as hoes and adzes suggest that soil was worked to some degree prior to planting. Harvesting was also, obviously, undertaken. Just how much and how intensive the other soil preparation tasks were (harrowing, weeding, and watering) remains unknown. It seems likely that the PPN, taken as a whole, represents a transitional period in terms of agricultural activities. The full suite of agricultural tasks we traditionally associate with extensive farming may not have been in place until the PPNB or even later.

By the PPNB, the first evidence of domestic caprovines occurs. The use of domestic animals diminished the need for hunting and fishing to acquire meat protein. However, wild species continue to be present in all faunal assemblages. Projectile points, suitable for hafting onto dart or arrow shafts, indicate that hunting continued. Tools and faunal evidence for fishing are also present. Again, it is sensible to view the PPN as transitional with respect to the use of domesticated animal resources. Hunting may have become progressively less important throughout the period. And the transition was likely uneven over time and space.

Processing both cereals and lime for plaster would have necessitated pounding and grinding. Ground stone tools become ubiquitous at PPN sites (Wright 1993). Grinding stones are typically found associated with every house and found in large numbers in some structures. The number of querns relative to mortars increases (Wright 1993). To many, this indicates the widespread use of more intensive processing of cereal grains—a process that now involves dehusking, crushing, and grinding. The labor output involved in producing ground cereal through this three-stage process increases, but so do several important qualities of the grain product. Cereal grain that is ground has increased nutritional value and can be stored for longer periods of time compared to grain that is simply dehusked and coarsely crushed (Bender 1966; Stahl 1989).

PPN textile evidence suggests that both flax and palm fibers were already being manufactured (Bar-Yosef et al. 1993). Either band looms or staked horizontal looms were probably used to produce woven linen and bast textiles (Barber 1991). Rugs, bags, mats, cloth, and blankets were all important household items. Twined and knotted plant fibers would have also had a variety of uses—basketry, cordage, matting, and so on. Individuals at Neolithic Abu Hureyra in Syria used their teeth to process fibers (Molleson 1994).

Burden bearing would have been a regular part of the activity sphere for PPN villagers. On a daily basis, firewood and water had to be carried home. Less often, but still regularly, the raw materials for chipped and ground stone tools would have to be obtained and brought back to the site. Wood, stone, limestone, and earth construction materials were required for house construction. While some of these same tasks structured Natufian days as well, the rigors of burden bearing would have increased during the PPN.

Pottery Neolithic Period

Archaeological Context

The Pottery Neolithic (PN) skeletal material I examined came from Newe Yam (Table I.2) Two adult specimens of ascertainable sex were included in this study. Newe Yam is located five kilometers due west of the Carmel caves. It is now submerged, but when occupied it stood 250 meters from the shore along the banks of the Mughara River (Wreschner 1983). Because of the small sample, the material was incorporated into the PPN sample.

The PN period (ca. 8,000–6,200 B.P.) is arguably the least well understood in the chronological sequence. Efforts to reconstruct social and economic features of the PN are hampered by regional culture historical sequences based on little information, older excavation techniques, and what may prove to be a real diversity in adaptive milieus.

Recent survey and excavation projects have effectively challenged the traditional reconstruction of widespread depopulation in the southern and central Levant during the PN. Several projects now show that PN strata overlay PPN levels, drawing the "hiatus" theory into question (Gilead 1990; Kafafi 1988a, 1998; MacDonald 1988, 1992; Marder et al. 1996; Muheisen et al. 1988; Rollefson et al. 1992; Simmons et al. 2001). Nevertheless, settlement systems did undergo significant adjustments, particularly in the central and southern Levant (Mahesneh 1989). Many large PPN sites located in woodland areas were abandoned, while the number of ephemeral sites, especially in the eastern Jordanian desert, increased (Betts 1988; Garrard et al. 1989). At those sites with continuous occupational strata from Pre-Pottery to PN periods, significant changes occur. Sites typically decrease in size, and domestic architectural styles are transformed (Rollefson et al. 1992).

Rectilinear and curvilinear structures co-occur at some sites (Gilead 1990; Kafafi 1988a; Rollefson et al. 1992; Wreschner 1983). The widespread practice of covering house floors with lime plaster is replaced by mud-plastering techniques. Houses are fewer in number and more dispersed relative to the dense, closely packed PPN houses (Kafafi and Rollefson 1995). During the initial phase of the PN in the southern Levant, domestic structures are often semi-subterranean pit structures, like those from Jericho and Ghassul (Kenyon 1981; Levy 1993). Larger, multichambered rectilinear houses may represent a later development in PN architecture (Kenyon 1981; Perrot 1993b).

A paucity of PN human burials and published analyses makes generalizations regarding mortuary practice difficult. Grave goods tend to be very sparse. Spatially, interments still occur within the site limits but in more diverse contexts. In-house, subfloor burials, similar to the PPN pattern, are found at Shaar Hagolan, Habashan Street, and Munhata (Gopher 1995). In contrast, bodies at Byblos are typically placed in outdoor graves between houses (Dunand 1973). Jar burials of infants occur at Tel Teo, Tel Dan, and Nahal Zehora II (Gopher 1995; Gopher and Orrelle 1995). In Jordan, single interments without grave goods occur (Kafafi 1998). There is no evidence of the continuation of postmortem removal, separate burial, and/or decoration of skulls (Kafafi 1998). Analysis of PN skeletons from Lod, Newe Yam, and Nahal Zehora are under way and may provide additional insights (Smith 1995).

The one common trait among most PN sites is, of course, the occurrence of ceramics (Figure 2.8). Pottery provides a new medium for a variety of decorations

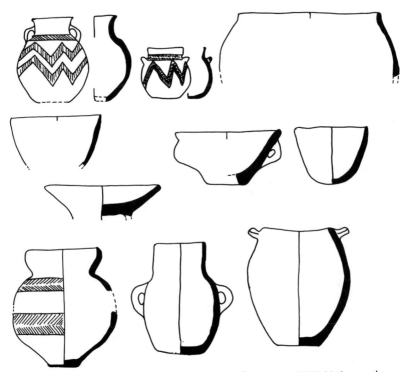

Figure 2.8   Pottery Neolithic ceramic vessel forms (after Amiran 1970). Various scales.

that undoubtedly were imbued with rich symbolic content. The decorative component of PN ceramics has, unfortunately, not been systematically investigated (Gopher 1995). Several PN sites have yielded large numbers of pottery and stone anthropomorphic figurines. These have typically been related to religious activities involving fertility rituals (Stekelis 1972)—a premature conclusion, according to others (Gopher 1995).

Common ceramic forms include globular jars and bowls. Made by a coil-and-scrape technique, coarse wares were tempered with grit and straw. Based primarily on ceramic form and surface treatment, several geographic and temporal divisions within the PN have been proposed. Stager (1992) divides the PN into Yarmoukian, Munhata, and Wadi Rabah phases, while Gopher (1995) prefers Yarmukian, Lodian, and Wadi Rabah culture distinctions.

Continued production of blades used as composite elements in sickles (demonstrated by sheen) indicates that agricultural activity is ongoing (Crowfoot Payne 1983; Gopher 1995). Arrowhead frequencies decrease notably and would seem to correspond with faunal assemblages that are increasingly composed of domestic species (Gopher 1995). At 'Ain Ghazal, an increasingly expedient PN technology was reflected in larger amounts of flake debitage, fewer prepared platforms, and fewer tools (Rollefson et al. 1992). About the same proportion of PN and PPN sites investigated by Wright (1993) contained ground stone. However, a decline in the density and diversity of ground stone tools occurs from the PPN to the PN at 'Ain Ghazal (Wright 1993). A decline in ground stone axes at Jericho is interpreted as a decline in wood clearance activity during this period (Wright 1992).

By the PN, domestic cattle (*Bos taurus*) and pig (*Sus scrofa*) are identified with certainty (Kohler-Rollefson 1989). Both PN Jericho and the desert site of Azraq 31 have wheat and barley present (Hopf 1969; Wright 1992). Macrobotanical evidence for domestic cereals and legumes was found at 'Ain Rahub (Neff 1988). The floral and faunal evidence is invoked to argue that many PN sites represent sedentary, mixed farming communities (Gilead 1990; Grigson 1995). Raising swine is not compatible, historically or ethnographically, with nomadic adaptations (Flannery 1983). Alternatively, others have suggested that PN groups are becoming increasingly pastoral, in part because of environmental degradation (Rollefson 1996; Rollefson and Kohler-Rollefson 1989; Rollefson et al. 1992).

As the PN archaeological record accumulates, a number of large, fully agricultural villages have come to light. Other sites contain a PN component that is commonly interpreted as more mobile and less focused on agricultural pursuits. Whether these roughly contemporaneous transient sites and the agricultural villages are manifestations of a single group or represent separate groups with distinctive economic systems is not yet understood.

Pottery Neolithic Social Structure

Few efforts have been made to reconstruct or even speculate about PN social structure. Kafafi (1998) hypothesizes that extended families may explain the larger houses and expanded outdoor courtyard spaces during the PN, but the data are very limited. He states further that increased craft specialization, livestock husbandry, and agriculture necessitated a certain, unspecified level of labor division (Kafafi 1998:134).

Current burial, material culture, and architectural data do not suggest to Gopher (1995) any social hierarchy. He does speculate, however, that the social system of the PN would have emphasized kin-based partnerships and alliances aimed at controlling resources, such as land, water, and pasturage.

Pottery Neolithic Activity Expectations

The need for hunted animal resources would have diminished among both PN settled farmers and more mobile pastorally based groups. The farmers have added domestic cattle and pig to their dietary spectrum. And presumably, the more mobile groups are relying increasingly on domestic sheep and goat resources.

For farming groups, a reduction in timbering activities makes sense, as the use of plaster declines and many fields may already be cleared. The daily tasks of obtaining fuel and water would not have changed. The need for crushed and ground cereals meant that processing tasks with ground stone tools would also been regular activities. Working leather and fibers would still be essential tasks.

Ceramic container technology introduces a new set of tasks that include obtaining the clay, hauling it to the site, mixing and tempering the clay, building vessels, and firing vessels. Increases in burden bearing would result from procuring not only the clay but also the fuel needed to fire the vessels.

For the segment of the PN population that may be more pastorally oriented, burden bearing may constitute a larger segment of the activity spectrum. In addition to daily household tasks that involve bringing resources to site, households would occasionally be packed up and moved to new locations. With no evidence for ancillary transport, humans would provide the muscle power to accomplish this.

Chalcolithic Period

Archaeological Context

Unfortunately, this study does not include any Chalcolithic skeletal material. There are human remains dating to the Chalcolithic, but they tend to be poorly preserved and fragmentary. Many of the skeletons represent children or neonates. These conditions not only make assessments of age and sex difficult or impossible but also often preclude the identification of MSM on cortical bone. However, there are significant social, technological, and symbolic changes taking place during the Chalcolithic. Some of these changes have implications for the following Early Bronze I period, for which there is a sizable sample. So it is worthwhile to summarize the major characteristics and developments that define the Chalcolithic.

The term "Chalcolithic" was apparently first used by W. F. Albright early in the 1930s to describe the cultural remnants excavated at the site of Ghassul in the northern Jordan Valley and elsewhere throughout Palestine (Gilead 1988; Levy 1986). The Chalcolithic spans the period from approximately 6,200 to 5,500 B.P. The transition from the Pottery Neolithic to the Chalcolithic is marked by the beginnings of copper processing, extensive production of decorated ceramics, and the earliest known examples of gold artifacts (Gopher and Tsuk 1996; Stager 1992).

Most active scholars involved in Chalcolithic research agree that the period represents an indigenous cultural entity growing out of Pottery Neolithic precursors. Notably, the type site of Ghassul appears to have grown out of local Late Neolithic traditions (Bourke 1997; Gopher 1995). Use of the Nahal Qanah burial cave in Pottery Neolithic, Chalcolithic, and Early Bronze I times also supports developmental continuity.

The Chalcolithic witnesses a hitherto unparalleled settlement in semiarid areas (Levy 1995; Stager 1992). This expansion has led some researchers to conclude that climatic conditions must have ameliorated, allowing human groups to establish more extensive settlements in these xeric areas (Gilead 1988). Regional surveys and large excavation projects in the Negev and the distinctive archaeological finds they have produced reflect the cultural diversity manifest during the Chalcolithic.

Various sites—villages, sanctuaries, burial caves, and ephemeral camps—are distributed in the Golan Heights, the coastal plain of Israel, the southern Jordan Valley, and the northern Negev (Gilead 1988). Some of the large sites, such as Ghassul, have substantial architecture and thick midden deposits, arguably the remnants of sedentary, long-term occupation. These sites are characteristic of rural communities practicing a mixed economy based on agriculture and village-based pastoralism (Gilead 1988; Levy 1993). More ephemeral sites may be the remains of nomadic pastoralists (Horwitz and Tchernov 1989). A growing notion of community or regional identity may be manifest in the public sanctuary complexes, such as those found at Ein Gedi and Gilat (Alon and Levy 1989; Ussishkin 1980).

"Broadhouse" domestic structures are typical in many regions. Broadhouses consist of rectangular structures with the entrances located on a long axis (Hennessy 1982). Sometimes small interior rooms occur, perhaps for storage (Levy

1986). These dwellings are often constructed using unworked stone foundations topped by layers of mud brick. Examples can be found at Shiqmim, Ghassul, and Abu Hamid (Bourke et al. 1995; Dollfus and Kafafi 1986; Levy 1987, 1993). Other features associated with the houses are pits, installations, ovens, enclosures, mud-brick pits containing storage jars, and small mud-brick structures. The chain-like house clusters in the Golan (Epstein 1977) and the subterranean oval rooms and passages at Beersheva (Perrot 1984) indicate substantial variation in domestic architecture.

Innovations in the symbolic and ideological realms are apparent in new Chalcolithic mortuary practices. Cemeteries, spatially segregated from habitation areas, are established for the first time at sites such as Shiqmim and Ghassul (Levy 1987, 1993). Secondary burials utilizing ceramic jars and small ossuaries occur, particularly in cave sites along the coastal plain of Israel. Substantial amounts of grave goods are found with some burials (Gopher and Tsuk 1996).

Chalcolithic agriculture is based on PN precedents for the most part: einkorn wheat (*Triticum monococcum*), emmer wheat (*Triticum dicoccum*), barley (*Hordeum* sp.), lentil (*L. esculenta*), pea (*Pisum* sp.), vetch (*Vicia* sp.), chickpea (*Cicer* sp.), and grass pea (*Lathyrus sativus*) (Dollfus and Kafafi 1986; Liphschitz 1989). Fruit trees also become important. Remains of olive (*Olea europaea*) become fairly ubiquitous at Chalcolithic sites. Fig (*Ficus carica*) and date (*Phoenix dactylifera*) also occur (Liphschitz 1989).

The question of irrigation technology arises with respect to some of the plant remains. Both wheat and olive would have required irrigation if the climate across the arid and semiarid settlement zone was similar to today's (Liphschitz 1989). However, evidence for irrigation is very scanty (Gilead 1988). Current data do not readily support the idea of complex, labor-intensive water management systems during the Chalcolithic.

Domestic species provided an increasing amount of meat protein requirements (Horwitz and Tchernov 1989). The dominant species are sheep (*Ovis aries*), goat (*Capra hircus*), cattle (*Bos taurus*), and pig (*Sus scrofa palustris*) (Dollfus and Kafafi 1986; Gilead 1990; Grigson 1987, 1995). The occurrence of pigs in relatively high frequencies at a number of sites is invoked to argue that large Chalcolithic sites represent sedentary, farming villages (Gilead 1988). As discussed for the PN, swine herding is not compatible with nomadic adaptations (Flannery 1983). Sites without domestic pig remains represent a sedentary component of the Chalcolithic settlement picture (Horwitz and Tchernov 1989).

A number of lines of evidence converge to support the notion that milk and milk by-products were important in Chalcolithic economies. Age and sex profiles of sheep and goats at Bir es-Safadi indicate that males were being culled from herds at younger ages (Grigson 1987). This pattern is consistent with a secondary products model of animal exploitation (Sherratt 1981, 1983). In addition, Kaplan describes ceramic churns as a "typical" fourth-millennium vessel type (Kaplan 1954) (Figure 2.9). These churns would have been used to turn milk into yogurt or cheese products, effectively increasing their "shelf life."

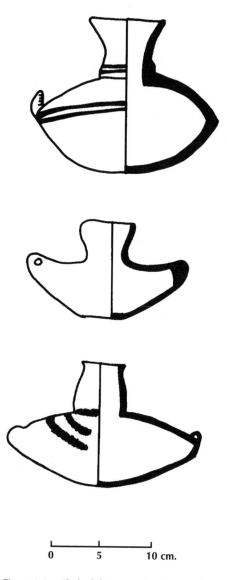

Figure 2.9   Chalcolithic ceramic churns (after Amiran 1970 and Gilead 1988).

Another development in the realm of animal husbandry worth discussing is the use of animals in transportation. Evidence from statuary indicates that donkeys and cattle were used as ancillary transport for the first time during the Chalcolithic (Epstein 1985). Pottery figurines of donkeys, laden with large jars or baskets, have been found in ossuary caves at Giv'atayim and Azor (Figure 2.10) (Kaplan 1969, 1976). An additional figurine fragment of the partial head of a bridled animal was found at a Jordan Valley site (Epstein 1977). The figurine from the sanctuary at Ein Gedi depicts a bull or cow carrying a churn (Ussishkin 1980). These figurines are important adjuncts to the archaeological record since domestic donkey remains (*Equid assinus*) occur only in later Early Bronze Age contexts (Finnegan 1981). Obviously, this development has implications for the activities of burden bearing from the Chalcolithic period onward. Transport of raw materials, agricultural produce, firewood, water, and all other heavy items could be facilitated by the domestication of this quintessential "beast of burden."

Various material culture items also provide insights into the daily activities of Chalcolithic people. Studies of chipped stone artifacts attest to a technology that is mainly flake based and includes an assortment of end scrapers, fan scrapers, piercers, borers, sickles, axes, adzes, and chisels (Dollfus and Kafafi 1986; Levy 1986). A decreasing number of arrowheads is consistent with a decrease in hunting (Levy 1986) but may also indicate use of morphologically similar copper points (Rosen 1986).

Wright (1992) offers a detailed appraisal of the ground stone assemblage from the Chalcolithic site of Abu Hamid. A range of cereal-processing tools used for dehusking/pounding (mortars, probably used with wooden pestles) and grinding (grinding slabs and hand stones) are present. The large size of the mortars and saddle querns suggests that grain processing was being carried out on a large scale. Basalt hoes and perforated stone discs are also present (Wright 1992). All these tools are consistent with a mixed-farming economy.

Sherds become the most common excavated artifacts, attesting to extensive pottery production during the Chalcolithic. Painted decorations, sometimes of elaborate design, become more common (Gilead 1988). Pottery containers appear in a range of forms, including bowls, pedestal bowls, cornets, basins, jars, churns, hole-mouth jars, and large storage jars (Commenge-Pellerin 1987). Petrographic studies of ceramics in the northern Negev indicate that pottery was produced and distributed within a restricted spatial range. Gilead (1988) asserts that the ceramic evidence supports the notion of ceramic production at a local scale, carried out by part-time specialists and households.

The hallmark of the Chalcolithic is the first heat-processed copper artifacts. Tools, containers, and decorative items are present in low quantities, primarily in

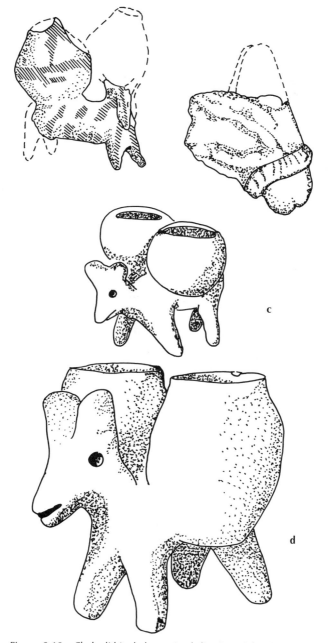

Figure 2.10 Chalcolithic laden animal figurines (after Epstein 1985). (a) From Ein Gedi. Height 18 cm. (b) From site near Yarmuk River. Fragment 7.5x4.5 cm. (c) From Giv'atayim. Height 7.4 cm. (d) From Azor. Height 7 cm.

the southernmost portions of the Levant (Gilead 1988). The potential sources of the raw copper ore coincide with this southern distribution, the known sources being located at Feinan in the Wadi 'Arabah (Hauptman and Weisgerber 1986) and in the Timna Valley, northwest of the Gulf of Aqaba (Rothenberg 1972).

Despite the large hoard of objects discovered at the cave of Nahal Mishmar, copper objects rarely occur in settlements. A detailed study of the forms and distribution of copper items was carried out at the site of Shiqmim (Shalev and Northover 1987). The assemblage is dominated by prosaic tools rather than decorative or ornamental prestige items. Furthermore, the copper artifacts are randomly distributed at the site (Shalev and Northover 1987). While involving some long-distance procurement of raw materials, the manufacture of these items does not appear to be the product of a centralized class of full-time specialists (Gilead 1988).

Chalcolithic Social Structure

When Chalcolithic scholars discuss social structure, they focus their attention on questions of social stratification and the identification of elites. Far less attention is paid to domestic social organization. In keeping with this emphasis, when the organization of work is considered, we read about the evidence for or against specialists and specialization in the realms of stone tool production, metallurgy, ritual knowledge, and long-distance trade. These aspects of activity and occupation are intimately related to the issues of social complexity. But there are, of course, other realms of activity and occupation to be considered. How did households manage and allocate their labor? How did farm families integrate new technologies and crops into their lives? If specialized production did occur, how did it affect their lives? Thinking about these fundamental questions is also important, as their answers reflect how the majority of Chalcolithic people lived.

The level of socioeconomic complexity in place during the Chalcolithic is the subject of some controversy. Based primarily on work in the Negev, Levy (1986, 1995) argues that a chiefdom-level political structure was in place during the Chalcolithic. He argues that a chiefly system, complete with hierarchical social ranking and a redistributive economy, arose out of the necessity of managing risk in a marginal environment. Mortuary treatments described as "chiefly" (at Nahal Qanah Cave) and settlement patterns described as "hierarchical" are cited as the archaeological correlates of this system. Conversely, Gilead (1988) argues that evidence for hierarchy and economic regulation are lacking. Instead, he offers a scenario of Chalcolithic societies as fundamentally egalitarian and practicing mixed farming like their PN precursors.

When the organization of work is discussed, it is typically in the context of evidence for or against craft specialization. Many (not all) consider craft specialization to be a hallmark of Chalcolithic society. The mining and production of copper artifacts provide the best case for craft specialization in the Chalcolithic. Questions about the scale (full or part time), location (household vs. workshop), consumption (few vs. many), and type (independent vs. attached) of specialization have yet to be fully addressed. Others have suggested that some ivory, stone, ceramic, and shell artifacts were made by a limited number of craftspeople as well (Kerner 1997; Levy 1995). As a rule, standardization of form is the primary criterion used to suggest specialization. Direct evidence from raw material source studies is absent. Beyond craft specialization, other divisions of labor are not discussed in any detail.

Family composition is another axis of social organization that tends to be ignored in discussions of Chalcolithic society. Architecturally, the broadroom houses of the Chalcolithic raise some interesting questions about family size and composition. But they are questions that have yet to be researched systematically.

Chalcolithic Activity Expectations

The use of donkeys and cattle as ancillary transport is potentially a significant factor influencing habitual activity patterns. Travelers to rural parts of the Mediterranean world are familiar with the range of tasks that donkeys accomplish. They provide transportation. They haul loads. It is easy to imagine that any number of burdensome tasks could be made less demanding by allowing donkeys to carry the load, from hauling the daily household requirements of water and fuel to transporting blocks of basalt from a distance to fashion grinding stones. Moving tools and agricultural products to and from fields is another obvious use for donkeys.

During the Chalcolithic, we have good reason to believe that people started making use of animal milk as an important dietary item. Animals require daily milking, sometimes twice a day, depending on the availability of water and fodder. This certainly constituted a habitual activity for some segment(s) of Chalcolithic society. The ceramic churns found at Chalcolithic sites suggest that some milk was also being processed into a semisolid form, which effectively lengthened its "shelf life." Ethnographic descriptions help us understand how these churns functioned. Milk is placed in the churn, which is suspended from a tripod by lug handles on the ends. A more standard jar can also be used, with a tight-fitting stopper. It would be placed on a sling mounted on a tripod. The motion of continuous rocking of the churn transforms the milk into yogurt or a buttery substance (Bronowski 1973; Cribb 1991). A ceramic statue of a seated woman with a churn from the site of Gilat (Alon 1977) provides a preliminary association between females and the production of secondary products from milk.

Tilling the soil by hand would have been an onerous task. Were domestic animals pulling plows? Plows are often inferred, but there is no direct evidence for their use during the Chalcolithic (Grigson 1995). Construction and maintenance of irrigation features (check dams, canals, and so on) are rigorous tasks. But again, their presence is still the subject of debate.

In the realm of craft production, stone tools, ceramic vessels, leather goods, basketry, and woven cloth appear to be the mainstays of household technology. There is a remnant of a horizontal ground loom from Nahal Mishmar Cave (Grigson 1995:257). This is the type of loom still used by Bedouin in the area to weave textiles.

The presence of a limited number of specialists producing household goods for consumers would have substantial implications for activity patterns. For example, are members of each household responsible for making the needed stone tools and ceramics, or are they acquired from specialists? This question is addressed more substantively in our discussion of the EBI in the next section.

Early Bronze I Period

Archaeological Context

The skeletal sample examined for the EBI period comes from the site of Bab edh-Dhra (Table 1.2). The site is located on the Lisan peninsula overlooking the Dead Sea in central Jordan. I included fifty-two skeletons.

Several commentators describe the EBI (ca. 5,500–5,000 B.P.) as a "pre-urban" period or a prelude to urbanism (Esse 1989; Stager 1992). Developments in settlement distribution, population density, economy, foreign relations, crafts, art, and religion foretell of the ensuing complexity of the Early Bronze II (EBII) (Ben-Tor 1992). G. E. Wright's ceramic analyses laid the foundation for the definitions and subdivision of the Early Bronze Age into the four periods (EBI–EBIV) that are widely accepted and remain in use to this day (Ben-Tor 1992). The EBI is sometimes further divided into two phases. The EBIA ceramic traditions still have strong links with the Chalcolithic at Ghassul, and trade relations with Egypt are weak. During the subsequent EBIB, ties between the southern Levant and Egypt increase because of unification under Narmer (Ben-Tor 1992).

Around 5,500 B.P., some large Chalcolithic settlements were abandoned (e.g., Abu Hamid and Teleilat Ghassul), other large sites were established (Bab edh-Dhra), and still others have both Chalcolithic and EBI remains (Tel Halif and Tel Teo). In general, settlement distribution in the EBI indicates population shifts into the moister Mediterranean climate zones and away from the semiarid and steppe zones in the south. One significant segment of the settlement picture focuses on the well-drained, agriculturally viable land, often along wadi systems where runoff irrigation could be practiced (Esse 1989) or annual rainfall in excess of 300 millimeters allowed for dry farming (Ben-Tor 1992). This suggests that at least part of the EBI population was making a living practicing agriculture year-round. A range of site sizes occurs. At the large end of the spectrum are sites that cover 20 hectares or more. Smaller villages also occur. In xeric environments, ephemeral settlements that seem to be more closely associated with a pastoral economic component continue (Esse 1989; Schaub and Rast 1984).

There is some regional variability in domestic architecture, but in general EBI villages share the basic elements of the Chalcolithic period: broadrooms, courtyards, benches, pits, and enclosure walls (Hanbury-Tenison 1986). Their walls enclose relatively large interior spaces, averaging 50 square meters (Ben-Tor 1992). The well-preserved architecture from Yiftahel shows examples of large curvilinear houses (Braun 1997). They are described as "sausage" shaped by the author and can be envisioned as broadroom houses with rounded ends.

From the EBIA levels at Bab edh-Dhra, only "stumps" of stone and brick walls were uncovered (Rast 1999:170). However, some 200 meters to the southwest of the site proper, survey results indicate the potential for more substantial EBIA settlement remains (Rast 1999:170). During the EBIB, a substantial settlement was established on the site. The remains of numerous mud-brick walls and extensive midden deposits have been excavated (Schaub and Rast 1984). Mudbrick houses, some with stone foundations, tend to consist of single square or rectangular rooms. Walls are plastered with mud inside and out. Roofs consist of wooden poles covered with reed matting and plaster (Schaub and Rast 1984). No dimensions are provided, and the excavators do not make any family size or organizational reconstructions based on the residential architecture.

Several other architectural forms occur during the EBI as well. Apsidal structures thought to be derived from precedents to the north occur at Megiddo, Yiftahel, and elsewhere (Ben-Tor 1992; Braun 1997). A number of functions have been suggested, including dwellings, elite residences, and temples (Ben-Tor 1992; Braun 1997). A cult or ceremonial function is more readily inferred from some other structures that are described as temples from Jericho, Ai, and Megiddo. Typically, a paved area defined by an enclosing wall houses a rectangular structure entered from one of the short walls (in contrast to a broadroom). Features described as platforms or altars are set against the wall opposite the doorway. Again, parallels with Chalcolithic antecedents are obvious (e.g., the sanctuary at Ein Gedi) (Ben-Tor 1992).

A number of large cemeteries dating to the EBI have been discovered. The mortuary patterns of EBI in the southern Levant are variable. Burials are found in natural caves, chamber tombs, shaft tombs, and charnel houses (Ortner 1981;

Richard 1987). Both primary and secondary burials occur. Remains are sometimes cremated, sometimes not. The number of individuals present ranges from a few to nearly 200 (Ben-Tor 1992). These bodies were not placed in tombs in a single episode of mass burial but represent reuse of burial areas over a long period of time. Most burial goods consist of pottery and, presumably, their contents (Schaub 1981). The lack of uniformity in burial programs between sites suggests cultural heterogeneity during the EBIB.

During the EBIA at Bab edh-Dhra, shaft tombs were carved out of the soft marl deposits. The EBIA graves tend to consist of multiple chambers off a single shaft, suggesting to the excavators that certain clans or families are adding new chambers to accommodate newly deceased members of their lineage over a period of time (Schaub 1981). Most of the EBIA tombs contain bone piles neatly stacked along with equally tidy arrangements of grave goods. The excavators believe that this represents the interment of a number of bodies in a single episode. The skeletal remains are typically disarticulated and incomplete. Bones appear to have been interred after the flesh had been removed (decarnation). Many of those affiliated with the excavations suppose that this mortuary pattern represents groups of seasonal visitors who returned regularly to the site with the remains of those who had died during their absence and entombed them simultaneously (Frolich and Ortner 1982; Rast 1999). However, among ethnographically documented societies that practice secondary burial, the majority live in sedentary villages, even if they have a strong pastoral component to their economy (Hershkovitz and Gopher 1990).

During the EBIB, both shaft tombs and charnel houses are reported (Rast 1981, 1999; Schaub 1981). Primary burials are the norm. Decomposed human remains were often pushed to the back and sides of EBIB tombs and charnel houses to accommodate a new interment (Rast 1999). In addition to the ubiquitous ceramic vessels, graves contained small amounts of jewelry, weaponry, and other household items.

Smith (1989b) argues that health and nutritional status decrease during the EBI relative to Epipaleolithic and Neolithic populations. Reductions in stature, given the evidence of population stability, most likely reflects poor health in early years rather than genetic change. This view is supported by high frequencies of enamel hypoplasia, caused by poor nutrition or disease during the formation and growth of teeth. Hypoplastic defects occur through the entire period of permanent tooth development (0–12 years), indicating chronic rather than periodic health problems (Smith 1989b). Her osteological analyses also indicate that there is no evidence from craniofacial morphology to suggest large-scale population movements into the Levant between Chalcolithic and EBI times (Smith 1989b). This argues decisively against those who would invoke populations moving into the southern Levant from other regions to explain the rise of the EBI.

Insufficient attention has been paid to primary economic data. Generally, the domestic animal species mix for Chalcolithic and Early Bronze contexts are very similar. Using meat-weight calculations, Grigson (1995) argues that cattle provided the bulk of meat for both periods. Faunal evidence indicating a significant loss of cortical bone in ewes reinforces the notion of intensive milking during the Early Bronze Age (Smith and Horwitz 1984). Examples of laden donkey figurines have been described (Epstein 1985). Evidence regarding plows is still equivocal. There are indications that donkeys were used for plowing in Mesopotamia by the third millennium B.C.E. (Postgate 1986). But it is premature to infer their use 1,000 years earlier in the Levant.

Domestic sheep/goat, pig, cow, and donkey are all represented at Bab edh-Dhra (Finnegan 1981). Unfortunately, Finnegan's results do not differentiate between EBIA and EBIB deposits. Since pigs are not compatible with a mobile lifestyle, their presence would provide direct empirical evidence useful in establishing the level of sedentism during the EBIA. An increased role for cattle is suggested not only by Grigson's meat-weight calculations but also by Ortner's (1982) paleopathological analyses. He cites several possible cases of tuberculosis in the EBI Bab edh-Dhra population that may be the result of increased human exposure to bovines (Ortner 1982). In contrast to the opinion of Rast and others, Grigson concludes that settled village farming prevailed as a way of life during the EBI. In her work, she sees no evidence for either full-scale nomadic pastoralism or even seminomadic pastoralism.

The hills, plains, and valleys of the relatively well watered Mediterranean zone offered groups the possibility of making a living practicing agriculture year-round. By the EBI, all the mainstays of the "Mediterranean" economy are now established. Data on plant foods and products reflect Chalcolithic precedents for the most part. Wheat, barley, flax, olive, pulses, fig, pistachio, and almond (*Prunus dulcus*) occur (Hanbury-Tenison 1986; McCreery 1981). The high frequency of caries and increases in dental attrition document the increased levels of cereal consumption among Early Bronze populations (Smith 1989b). At Bab edh-Dhra, grape (*Vitis vinifera*) pits were identified for the first time in EBI contexts (McCreery 1981). Unfortunately, the botanical information from Bab edh-Dhra does not differentiate between EBIA and EBIB deposits, either. However, McCreery also questions the interpretation of EBIA as a highly mobile, primarily pastoral group (McCreery, personal communication).

EBI material culture is thought to be derived from Chalcolithic technologies, but with some additions. From late EBI contexts at the large site of Megiddo stone tournettes provide unequivocal evidence for the use of slow-wheel pottery production (Stager 1992). This technological development increases the efficiency and potential for standardization of pottery production. Ceramic assemblages also become more varied in both style and form, with some evidence for at least four regionally specific ware types (Stager 1992) (Figure 2.11). This regionally based standardization is cited as evidence for a limited degree of craft specialization (Esse 1989). Ben-Tor (1992:90) also suggests that widely distributed but uniform small pottery vessels found as burial gifts may have been produced by a limited number of itinerant potters who went from site to site producing burial/gift ware for the inhabitants.

Chipped stone assemblages include many of the same tool forms that have been described previously: sickle blades, fan scrapers, axes, adzes, picks, and so on (Figure 2.12). Some research indicates the presence of a specialized Canaanean

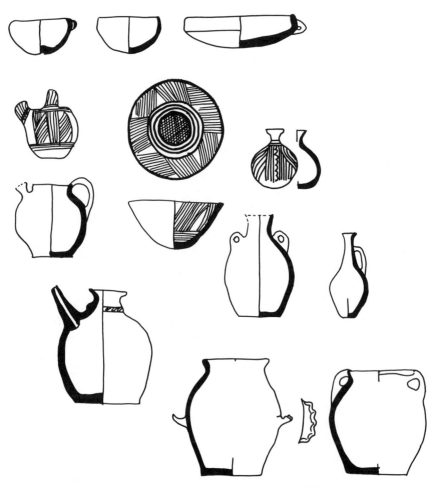

Figure 2.11   Early Bronze I ceramic vessel forms (after Amiran 1970). Various scales.

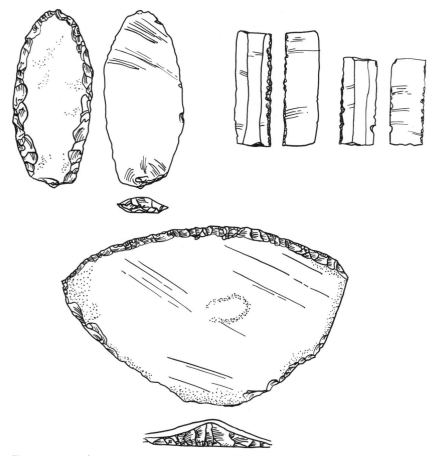

Figure 2.12   Early Bronze I chipped stone tools (after Crowfoot Payne 1983); scale 4:5.

blade industry. A limited number of workshops are envisioned that produced large, standardized flint blades that are subsequently distributed over a large area (Rosen 1983, 1997). At the same time, tools continue to be made from local stone, representing a nonspecialized aspect to lithic assemblages (Esse 1989).

Ground stone objects are common artifacts from EBI sites. They are fashioned primarily from locally available materials. The ground stone assemblage is also relatively unchanged, consisting of the familiar querns, mortars, pestles, and hand stones (Hanbury-Tenison 1986). Bowls, hand stones, and mortars are illustrated from the excavations at Yiftahel (Braun 1997). Grinding and plant processing appear to have been integral parts of EBI daily life.

Most metal items from the EBI are utilitarian objects. Most were made from copper, with alloyed bronze showing up only at the end of the period and in very small amounts. Ax heads, adzes, awls, and spearheads are reported (Stager 1992). A small number of gold and silver objects have also been found, representing contacts with Africa and Asia Minor, respectively (Ben-Tor 1992).

Examples of loom-woven textiles and basketry were preserved at Bab edh-Dhra. All cloth specimens were flax (Adovasio and Andrews 1981). The continued use of ground-staked, horizontal looms is presumed given the Chalcolithic precedents and Barber's (1991) technological and historical analysis. Clay and mud basket impressions indicate a number of twining, coiling, and plaiting techniques carried out with split reeds (Adovasio and Andrews 1981).

Trade with Egypt is documented during the EBI (Esse 1989). Coastal sites in the northern Sinai trace the overland trade route along which donkey caravans presumably traveled. Trading posts and mercantile enclaves occur along this route (Stager 1992). The goods moving into Egypt are thought to be copper ore, bitumen, wine, olive oil, wood resins, and artifacts. Egyptian pottery and distinctive chipped stone artifacts found in Palestine are evidence of goods moving northward from the Nile Valley (Stager 1992).

There are competing claims about how to best characterize the EBI. For some researchers, the EBI archaeological record demonstrates pronounced continuity with the Chalcolithic (Finnegan 1981; Grigson 1995; McCreery 1981; Smith 1989b). Others have concluded that there were extensive discontinuities between Chalcolithic and EBI lifeways. The abandonment of several large Chalcolithic sites (Ghassul, Abu Hamid) is equated with system collapse (Gophna 1995; Levy 1995). A more dispersed settlement pattern, with fewer large sites, is cited as evidence that at least some of the EBI population is increasingly nomadic, more dependent on animal products (Gophna 1995). For those, such as Levy, who see complex chiefdoms during the Chalcolithic and focus on the Beersheva region, fewer large sites and more rural settlements equals substantial discontinuity.

Contrasting characterizations of the lifeways of the EBI inhabitants at Bab edh-Dhra represents this same issue in microcosm. Some researchers claim that the EBIA-to-EBIB transitions represent a significant increase in sedentism and, presumably, agricultural activity, while others maintain that the two phases are broadly similar in terms of economics and mobility.

EBI Social Structure

What was daily life like during the EBI? This is a question that has received meager attention. Some economic specialization in lithic and ceramic production presents the possibility that socioeconomic relationships were becoming more interdependent and interdigitated. Some groups within the society are participating in trade networks in which goods from Egypt and Asia Minor are circulating. The tombs at Bab edh-Dhra represent a significant energy expenditure. But there is no one currently making the suggestion that these represent the emergence of incipient social inequality at the site. There is no evidence of fortification of the site until the EBII levels.

Size and organization of the domestic unit are also fairly hard to gauge given the currently available data sets. Larger houses may equate with larger household groups. Excavators at Yiftahel exposed an extensive horizontal exposure of EBI architecture. Some houses are large and multiroomed, others are small with no partitions. Functional distinctions do not appear to explain this diversity. Several hypotheses are entertained to account for this variability, including variation in family size and wealth (Braun 1997). Even with his firsthand familiarity, Braun is not comfortable supporting any one particular hypothesis at the moment.

Many suppose that the reuse of shaft tombs over time symbolically represents the reunification of kin or lineage members in death. Ethnographically, we know that maintaining a corporate cemetery is a logical way to lay claim to the ownership and inheritance of territorial resources (Charles and Buikstra 1983). Cemeteries are the places where ownership and inheritance are ritualized. Kin or lineage groups express their rights to control resources by establishing permanent burial areas—which in effect say that this land was used not only by me but also by my ancestors. It becomes the ritual home of their ancestors. So the delineation of family and lineage groups may be increasingly important to EBI villagers. Whether this resulted in a competition for resources is unclear. There is some evidence for hostility and interpersonal aggression from the human remains at Bab edh-Dhra (see discussion of traumatic injuries in Chapter 4).

The inhabitants at Bab edh-Dhra were making their living by some mix of farming and animal husbandry. Kin-based groups seem to be increasingly important in terms of claim to resources. We can suppose that much of the daily and seasonal work is still accomplished by family or other communal groups. A limited amount of productive work may have moved outside the household into the hands of specialists.

EBI Activity Expectations

On the basis of limited domestic architecture and burial evidence, excavators posit that a permanent, year-round village may not yet have been established at EBIA Bab edh-Dhra (Rast and Schaub 1981). In this scenario, agriculture may have been practiced in a more opportunistic, limited fashion by a group of seasonal site occupants who relied primarily on their flocks and their products. This is not an opinion shared by all those with firsthand knowledge of the site and its excavations (McCreery, personal communication). However, by EBIB, everyone seems to

agree that an agricultural village occupied year-round by at least some of its occupants has been established. These distinctions are not merely semantic since
roughly 71 percent of the Bab edh-Dhra skeletal sample used in this study comes
from contexts that are tentatively assigned to the EBIA occupation (Frolich and
Ortner 1982; Ortner 1981; Rast 1981).

Whichever interpretation holds true, the work of Burton and White (1984)
provides some interesting insights into expected activity loads. In a cross-cultural
examination of sexual labor divisions, Burton and White (1984) tried to identify
certain variables that have predictive value in discerning patterns of male and female agricultural participation. Among the best predictors were the number of
dry months and the importance of domesticated animals to subsistence. A long
dry season precipitates seasonal time pressures, requiring labor spurts. Under these
conditions, males tend to increase their participation in agriculture in order to
meet scheduling constraints. Marked dependence on domestic animals tends to
draw women out of the agricultural labor pool as they spend more of their time
caring for animals and processing animal products (Burton and White 1984).

Another significant factor influencing the EBI task spectrum includes the potential expansion of craft specialization into the ceramic realm. Some people may
be actively involved in a limited spectrum of activities, such as pottery production
and long-distance trade. It is worth noting that donkey and cattle are still being
used as beasts of burden, as laden donkey figurines attest (Ben-Tor 1992; Epstein
1977). Secondary milk products continue to be significant in the diet. Processing
grapes and olives into storable products such as wine and oil might require regular and rigorous muscle activity. Egyptian demand for a variety of raw materials
and food products may also be encouraging surplus production and processing of
certain items.

Conclusion

This discussion of archaeological data and diachronic trends in the southern Levant provides a broad outline of social, economic, and technological changes in the
region. Examinations of the social context of these changes are fairly limited and
often focus on identifying status differentiation and social complexity. Efforts to
investigate the organization of work and family are scarce and highly speculative.
Fortunately, bioarchaeological data have the potential to address questions of social context in substantive ways. The following chapter explores a number of case
studies where markers of occupational stress have provided socially relevant information about agricultural transitions in prehistory.

Markers of Occupational Stress   3

⊞

THE BIOARCHAEOLOGICAL CHALLENGE to investigating prehistoric labor organization lies in linking data sets relevant to activity with archaeological patterns. A skeptic could rightly note that many such social organizational research issues have yet to be addressed. As a result, much of the current theorizing about sexual labor patterning involves speculative, general theorizing. Yet even within the specific niche of Near Eastern prehistoric research, several authors have taken on the daunting task of describing a range of social behaviors (Banning and Byrd 1987, 1989; Flannery 1972; Hershkovitz and Galili 1990; Kuijt 2000; Molleson 1989, 1994; Rathbun 1984; Smith, Bloom, and Berkowitz 1984). Efforts to identify new empirical referents of sex and gender, integrate independent data sets, and improve innovative methodologies are primary concerns in achieving a more socially informed, empirically based research paradigm.

In honesty, there are significant methodological hurdles to face. Fundamentally, where does one start? How does one identify labor patterns dating back 10,000 years? For the time periods in question, there are no textual sources to provide clues about the organization of work. Neither are graphic illustrations preserved on ceramics, textiles, or any other media to serve as guides. In terms of ethnographic parallels, much has been written about the continuity from prehistoric to historic periods in the Levant (Hillman 1984, 1985; Horne 1994; Jacobs 1979; Kamp 1987; Kramer 1979, 1982b; Watson 1978, 1979a, 1979b). And those continuities are visually striking, especially in the areas of vernacular architecture and traditional farming techniques.

However, extending this analog back into the realm of prehistoric labor systems is problematic from several angles. First, as any student of Near Eastern cultures can attest, there is no one, monolithic pattern of sexual labor to be discerned. And neither have those divisions been static through time (Beck 1978;

Cosar 1978; Peters 1978; Tapper 1978; Tavakalian 1984; Watson 1979a). Furthermore, the strength of Islam as an ideological system, a system defining traditional roles for men and women, cannot be overlooked (see Chapter 1). I conclude that applying any one Near Eastern ethnographic analog as a model for prehistoric contexts is both culturally and historically inappropriate. These cautionary notes do not imply that the future of investigating labor patterns is stuck intractably in the realm of speculation.

Historical Overview

Searching for a way to establish task differentiation led me to consider a class of skeletal data described as markers of occupational stress (MOS), or activity-induced stress markers (Kennedy 1989). There are many categories of MOS, including trauma, joint modification, degenerative skeletal pathologies, dental attrition, cortical thickness, and diaphyseal strength. Efforts to measure and interpret MOS have a long and colorful history and have recently attracted increased attention from the bioarchaeological community. Those of us interested in reconstructing prehistoric labor patterns benefit. Provided here is a discussion of MOS analyses as they pertain to investigating sexual labor patterns. An important part of this synthesis involves outlining some of the prerequisites, pitfalls, and controversies surrounding MOS studies.

The early historical background of activity-induced skeletal changes was synthesized by Kennedy (1989). A few highlights from his summary are in order here. By the late nineteenth century, a number of anatomists and surgeons became aware of an array of morphological and size irregularities in the human skeleton that could be related to life habits (Kennedy 1989). Practitioners of industrial medicine had patients from the working classes whose bodies had been shaped by years of heavy physical labor (Kennedy 1989:130). These doctors described a number of specific, trade-related skeletal modifications, and the value of these clinical descriptions was quickly recognized by physical anthropologists (Kennedy 1989:131). More recently, the fields of industrial, sports, and forensic medicine have provided additional clinical diagnoses that refine the connections between activities and their skeletal manifestations (Hawkey and Merbs 1995).

MOS are the source of considerable debate in anthropological circles. Recent book-length treatments represent two contrasting sides of the debate (Jurmain 1999; Larsen 1997). Jurmain (1999) argues that it is too early in our study of most skeletal markers to make many meaningful links between observable MOS patterning and prehistoric behavior. He is concerned that researchers do not yet have a complete understanding of the various factors contributing to the development of many types of MOS (e.g., activity, hormones, metabolism, nutrition, genes, and disease). Jurmain feels that the limited number of clinical trials providing links between particular conditions and the activities that produced them detract from the utility of MOS. He tends to interpret variability among case study results as a reflection of our incomplete understanding of MOS.

Larsen's (1997, 2000) position is more optimistic. While acknowledging the multifactorial nature of many MOS, he assumes that bioarchaeological patterns reflect social dynamics within populations (1997). Larsen recognizes that additional research will strengthen our understanding of the complex connections between MOS and behavior, but he does not view current studies as "hamstrung" until such a time that we have delineated these connections fully. Instead, Larsen suggests that different patterns can be productively equated to different behaviors. A comprehensive analytical program that integrates various MOS and complementary archaeological data can inform about activity pattern in the past (Larsen 1997). Variable results between case studies examining, say, activity change across the forager-to-farmer transition may not reflect a lack of methodological rigor. Instead, varying patterns are accepted as reflecting real differences in the way different groups behaved under different, local circumstances (Larsen 1997, 2000).

Larsen's more optimistic perspective is shared by many who are currently involved in MOS analyses. And I tend to favor Larsen's position regarding the utility and potential of MOS patterning in reconstructing activity as well. Much work has still to be done. Current behavioral reconstructions will likely be amended or replaced as research proceeds—in my opinion, an altogether healthy and expected part of the analytical process.

Within the realm of an explicitly "engendered" research paradigm, the utility of bioarchaeological data has been recognized for some time. Studies have examined a variety of skeletal indicators of activity, differential nutrition, and mortuary programs in order to discuss gender role, status, and ideology (Bumsted et al. 1990; Claassen 1996; Cohen and Bennett 1993; Gray 1996; Holliman 1991, 2000; Wilson 1994, 1997). Yet in the Levant, despite its wealth of skeletal data and long-term research traditions, bioarchaeology and gender have been slow to converge in explicit and meaningful ways.

The following sections describe recent MOS research grounded in an anthropological paradigm. Specifically, I highlight those studies that investigate sexual divisions and the transition to agriculture. Broader, more general syntheses of osteological indications of occupation, nutrition, and community health can be found elsewhere (Iscan and Kennedy 1989; Jurmain 1999; Larsen 1987, 1997, 2000; Ortner and Putschar 1985). These sources should be consulted for in-depth considerations of etiology, morphology, and graphic illustrations.

Structural Changes

Julius Wolff succinctly summarized the position that bone not only is active but also responds to external forces. Wolff's law states that bone tissue places itself in the direction of functional demand (Larsen 1997; Wolff 1892). Stated another way, physical activity can influence the size, shape, and robusticity of bones. Bone remodeling occurs in response to various mechanical forces applied to the skeleton throughout life (Ruff and Larsen 1990). Within a particular population, patterns related to bone structure have potential implications for labor organization. Besides physical activity, factors affecting bone structure include genetics, hormones, nutrition, and disease (Bridges 1989). Thus, studies of changes in bone structure between and within populations must take other variables into consideration.

Relative robusticity and strength represent the biomechanical demands placed on bone as skeletal tissue is remodeled in response to mechanically demanding lifeways (Larsen 1984:394). Diaphyseal structure is assessed by cross-sectioning bones, using either nondestructive imaging technologies (e.g., radiographs and CAT scans) or physically cutting through the bone. Both the amount of cortical bone present and its distribution in cross section are of interest. Looking first at the amount of cortical bone, we can state that the thicker the bone, the more strength it possesses under compressive forces (Bridges 1995:112). An earlier study of Levantine populations from Natufian, Neolithic, and later agricultural populations compared cortical thickness in humeri to suggest differences in functional demand across time and between the sexes (Smith, Bloom, and Berkowitz 1984). These results are discussed in detail in Chapter 4.

But amount of cortical bone is only one factor in resisting force. How that bone is distributed in cross section is also of interest in assessing musculoskeletal stress. Using engineering formulae designed to estimate the strength of hollow beams (bones for us), it is possible to examine the cross-sectional geometry of an arm or a leg bone at various points along the diaphyses (Bridges 1995; Larsen 1987; Sumner et al. 1985). By looking at shape change in cross section, it is possible to document differences in the relative directions and types of forces placed on bones at various points along their shafts.

Biomechanical research of this kind has been applied particularly in the field of early hominid research (Churchill 1994; Lovejoy and Trikhaus 1980; Ruff et al. 1993; Trinkaus, Churchill, and Ruff 1994). But of more interest here are studies that focus on agricultural transitions. Unfortunately, there are few examples of studies examining the rise of agriculture in the Old World. One exception is the work of Jacobs (1993), who documented increased robusticity in both male and female Ukrainian skeletal samples moving from the Mesolithic to the Neolithic period.

The best-studied cases involving changes in physical activities with the emergence of agricultural subsistence regimes come from New World settings: coastal Georgia and northwestern Alabama. The two studies come to different conclusions about changes in activity, workload, and sexual labor. Different populations appear to have found different labor solutions in different, local circumstances.

In coastal Georgia, an overall decline in bone strength in upper and lower limbs suggests that workload decreased with the adoption of domestic plant foods. Comparisons of femur cross sections between precontact hunter-gatherer and agricultural samples document that femora become relatively weaker and flatter through time. This suggests a reduction in bone strength and mechanical stress. When differential nutritional quality between the sexes is taken into account, the authors suggest that changes in general activity levels declined equally for both sexes (Larsen 1987). Decreased mobility is seen as the primary cause for the changes in the lower limbs. The most significant pattern from the upper body (humeri) is the decrease in sexual dimorphism in the cross-sectional shape through time (Ruff and Larsen 1990). The convergence specifically involves a greater decrease in bilateral asymmetry among females relative to males, suggesting that the activity regimes of females were more profoundly affected by the transition to a subsistence regime based partially on maize agriculture (Fresia, Ruff, and Larsen 1990). The convergence in male and female humeral shape is equated with increased male participation in agricultural activities (Ruff and Larsen 1990).

Markedly different results emerged from analyses of Archaic and Mississippian populations from northwestern Alabama. Increases in measures of both upper- and lower-limb strength suggest that agricultural lifestyles were more physically demanding for both sexes, but particularly for females (Bridges 1985, 1989, 1995). Mississippian males had stronger femora than earlier hunter-gatherers, while their female counterparts were stronger in both upper and lower limbs (Bridges 1995). An increase in bilateral symmetry among females is one particularly pronounced pattern. It is associated, specifically, with increased strength in the middle to distal portions of left humeri. Maize processing using a two-handed pestle may be responsible for this pattern (Bridges 1989).

The point I am hoping to make with this brief synopsis is that the structural properties of bone are relevant to testing hypotheses regarding differential labor inputs and changing sexual labor patterns through time. Second, finer-grained inferences concerning activity type can be attempted by looking at patterns of lateralization and the specific location(s) of cross-sectional changes that occur. Finally, the patterns of activity level and activity type across the transition to agriculture vary regionally, suggesting that the search for a universally generalizable "origins" model for sexual labor change is unrealistic.

As a final methodological point, it bears noting that some skeletal collections are housed in locations that do not have access to imaging equipment. In these settings, bone robusticity is more typically measured by external shaft dimensions. Ideally, external dimensions should be supplemental to cross-sectional studies, although the two types of measurements have been shown to be correlated (Bridges 1995).

Joint Modification

Habitual postures and repetitive activities are reflected in a range of pathological and nonpathological skeletal modifications influenced by high mechanical demands. Nonpathological modifications on the hard tissue of the skeleton can occur as facets, bony extensions, grooves formed by ligaments, and so on. Repetitive body movements or heavy labor can also accelerate joint degeneration, creating pathological changes commonly referred to as osteoarthritis or degenerative joint disease (DJD).

Turning first to the nonpathological modifications, a great deal of attention has been paid to correlating faceting on the tibia and talus with a habitual squatting posture (Kennedy 1989). Studies of fossil hominids have frequently examined the presence of this particular anatomical variable (e.g., McCown and Keith 1939; Trinkaus 1975). Pronounced changes in the bones of the foot and toes (proximal phalanx and metatarsals) led Ubelaker (1979) to suggest that Ecuadorian populations along the southern coast spent longer periods of time kneeling, either at rest or at work. He suggests that grinding corn using ground stone tools is one activity that would have produced this bony signature.

Trinkaus (1975) expresses a cautionary note regarding the interpretations of squatting facets that applies, by extension, to the more general class of nonpathological articular modifications. The signatures for squatting, per se, may be influenced by a variety of other mechanically stressful activities. The conclusion that squatting, or any activity, alone is responsible for a particular bony characteristic unduly minimizes the cultural complexity and potential activity variability of prehistoric populations (Larsen 1987). This realization impresses on us the importance of interpreting these morphological features (as well as other MOS) using the most robust and integrative methods possible. It also highlights the role of our own mental templates in delimiting the range of possible activities.

The primary contributing factor to osteoarthritis is mechanical stress and physical activity, according to Larsen (1997:163). Joint degeneration appears to be accelerated under certain conditions of heavy labor (Steinbock 1976; Ortner and Putschar 1985). The skeletal manifestations of the disease are "lipping" (buildup of bone along the joint margins), "porosity" (breakdown of hard tissue on joint surfaces), and "polishing/eburnation" (development of smooth areas where the destruction of cartilage has exposed underlying bone) (Bridges 1992; Larsen 1987; Ortner and Putschar 1985; Steinbock 1976). Viewing mechanical stress as a cause of degeneration implies that its frequency, location, and severity are significant in reconstructing the activity patterns of past populations (Larsen 1987). Recent research issues range from examinations of early hominid posture and locomotion (e.g., Cook et al. 1983; Trinkaus 1975) to the relationship between status and workload (Tainter 1980).

The relative demands of hunting-gathering versus agricultural lifestyles have also been a concern for researchers of activity-related degenerative joint change. Even Jurmain (1999:88) notes that farmers seem to demonstrate the most consistent occupational association with osteoarthritis. And again, as with biomechanical studies of bone structure, the results are not consistent with a single, universal model of activity change. Bridges (1992) provides a detailed synthesis and critical discussion of a number of these. Results from various studies agree neither about the relative workload imposed by the two subsistence regimes (Bridges 1991a, 1992; Jurmain 1980, 1990; Sullivan 1977) nor about the relative labor contributions made by females and males (Bridges 1991a; Goodman et al. 1984; Larsen 1982; Pickering 1984, Williamson 2000).

One need not draw comparisons from far-flung regions to document this variability. Among studies within the eastern woodlands, the full spectrum of patterning is present. For example, Larsen's (1982) analysis of coastal Georgia populations documented a decrease in the frequency of DJD with the inception of agricultural economies. Sexually dimorphic patterning, however, increases—with males showing more DJD than females in the back, elbow, and knee. The pattern indicates that while agriculture generally meant easier workloads for the group as a whole, males may have been differentially participating in the more strenuous aspects of farming. In the lower Illinois River Valley, DJD increases most notably among females during the foraging-to-farming transition (Pickering 1984). And finally, at Dickson Mounds, no significant patterns of change in DJD occur for either males or females across the agricultural transition (Goodman et al. 1984). These cases imply that the amount of joint stress on populations moving from hunting and gathering to agricultural subsistence systems need not always be equivalent. Relevant variables that help account for these differences include agricultural techniques used, degree of reliance on domestic plant species, processing technology, local environments, and so on. So, too, different groups generated different labor solutions to handle the addition of agricultural chores.

Localization of arthritis in a particular joint or joints has often led to specific inferences about particular activities or occupations above and beyond general activity or workload level. Merbs's (1983) seminal study of osteoarthritic change among the Sadlermiut Eskimo provides a comprehensive picture of its relationship with specific activities and sexual divisions of labor. Merbs is fortunate to have ethnographic documentation to support and supplement his interpretations. Joint disease patterns in the jaws and postcrania of females appear to correspond with softening, processing, and sewing animal skins. Patterns among males reflect exertion of the upper body during harpoon use and kayak paddling. Shared patterns between the sexes in vertebral degeneration may be the result of sledding or tobogganing (Merbs 1983).

Joint modifications among the individuals from Mesolithic and Neolithic levels of the early agricultural settlement at Tell Abu Hureyra, Syria, have been comprehensively studied (Molleson 1989, 1994). Her findings document a variety of pathological and nonpathological changes germane to sexual labor roles during the transition to domestication economies. Molleson suggests that cereal processing in a kneeling posture with toes tucked under the foot is likely responsible for patterns. These results are discussed in detail in Chapter 4.

The studies that seem to me most successful in supporting activity and occupational inferences are those that integrate joint modifications with other lines of physical, archaeological, and ethnographic data. In the absence of multiple lines of convergent data, DJD patterns speak more directly to overall workload and general activity levels between and among populations (hunters vs. farmers and females vs. males). This opinion is hardly original. A number of researchers have cautioned that these DJD patterns alone are generally not sufficient to specify a particular activity that caused the degeneration (Bridges 1992; Jurmain 1991). The array of habitual activities that mechanically stress, say, the elbow may preclude linking any one activity with a pattern of DJD.

Behavioral reconstructions will certainly benefit from further methodological improvements and an improved understanding of etiology. Studies need to take into account age differences within populations because the development of arthritis is related to age (Bridges 1992). Discrepancies in scoring methods and presentation of data also adversely impact our ability to compare results from one study to another. These discrepancies have proven less problematic when evaluating sexually dimorphic patterning within a single population (Bridges 1992).

This brief discussion documents that, based on the role that activities play in the etiology of osteoarthritis, variable patterns of the disease have been used to support a range of hypotheses concerning level and type of physical labor.

Trauma

Traumatic injury can result from a variety of causes, including accidental injury, interpersonal conflict, self-mutilation, suicide, and surgical procedures (Merbs

1989). When trauma is manifest on the body's hard tissues, it provides insight into a group's exposure to risky activities, ranging from everyday tasks to violent confrontation. Classes of traumatic injury have been variously identified and grouped. Typically, they include fractures, crushing injuries, bone wounds made with sharp objects, and dislocations (Merbs 1989; Ortner and Putschar 1985; Steinbock 1976). Most discussion of trauma in archaeological contexts is directed at describing individual specimens. Population studies are less frequent. But it is the population-based studies that are particularly valuable from an occupational perspective. Here the distribution of traumas can identify differential activity patterns or at-risk groups (Burrell, Maas, and Van Gerven 1986; Jurmain 1991, 1999; Larsen 1997; Lovejoy and Heiple 1981; Merbs 1989). Meaningful patterns are likely to emerge in cases with large skeletal series that contain substantial numbers of traumatic injuries—conditions not often met.

Identification and interpretation of traumatic injuries require methodological rigor at a number of levels. The location and nature of a fracture are significant data. Fatigue fractures are typically caused by unusual bone stress or repeated microtrauma (Merbs 1989:162). Postmortem cultural and natural transformation processes must also be considered. And there is also a possibility of confusing trauma with other pathological conditions that are not the result of mechanical forces. The "cupping" of the central vertebral body that results from sickle cell anemia and tuberculosis, for example, can be confused with the modifications of the vertebral body associated with disk herniations of a traumatic nature (Merbs 1989).

In living populations, a variety of occupationally related traumas have been documented (Kennedy 1989). African grain porters who habitually carry loads in excess of 90 kilograms on their heads often suffer from what is described as "porter's neck." The weight and compressive force of these loads causes both fractures and dislocations in portions of cervical vertebra (Levy 1968). Stress fractures of the radius resulted from running with a heavy gun carried across the forearm (Farquharson-Roberts and Fulford 1980). Disk herniations, referred to as Schmorl's nodes, are frequently found in conjunction with vertebral compression fractures, suggesting that they are both produced by the same traumatic stresses (Merbs 1989:168). While this level of causal specificity is unlikely in prehistoric contexts, archaeological analyses that include information about trauma distribution/frequency by age, sex, and the areas of the body affected can clarify the social contexts and potential labor divisions underlying the injuries.

With the exception of timbering to clear fields, farming with handheld tools would not appear to introduce substantial new risks in terms of accidental injury. Trauma from violent encounters does appear to increase in some early agricultural settings. In Germany, for example, the spread of agriculture almost certainly entailed the colonization of lands already occupied by indigenous, Mesolithic hunter-gatherers by land-hungry farmers. This scenario seems to have spawned violent interpersonal confrontations in the case of Talheim, where a mass grave contained the bodies of thirty-five men, women, and children who had been killed by blows to the head with adzes (Keeley 1992).

Territorial conflicts can also emerge between neighboring groups as they become increasingly sedentary, a process that often goes hand in hand with agriculture (Powell 1992; Walker 1981). And even within a particular village, sedentism can pose social challenges that could result in increased traumatic injury. Options for defusing domestic conflicts may have become more limited as fissioning from one's social group became less feasible (Draper 1975; Gray 1996).

In one case study, patterns of trauma, spatial data from cemeteries, and pathological indicators of malnutrition and joint stress allowed researchers to discern patterns of warfare and community health among Oneota groups. The results have implications for occupation and sexual divisions of labor as well. A suite of characteristics were defined as evidence of violent death, including bones broken by arrows and other weapons; cut marks from scalping, decapitation, dismemberment; and cut marks made presumably by scavenging carnivores (Milner, Smith, and Anderson 1991:247). The relatively even ratio of male-to-female violent death, as well as single-sex group interments, led the authors to conclude that women working in agricultural fields may have been one target of raid-style warfare. The authors conclude that the mortality pattern in this group from the central Illinois River Valley suggests that women had a substantial role in subsistence practices (e.g., agricultural fieldwork) that took them away from the main settlement and placed them at risk (Milner et al. 1991:256).

A diachronic study of the human remains from Dickson Mounds, also in the Illinois River Valley, provides a second case study that used evidence of traumatic injuries to discuss activity and cultural milieu (Goodman et al. 1984). Data suggest that the frequency of postcranial trauma in adults increased notably for both sexes moving from hunting-gathering/mixed hunting-gathering and agriculture periods to the time of village-based agriculture. The pattern was particularly pronounced among males. The authors ascribe these results to the joint effects of increased physical work stress and/or interpersonal strife (Goodman et al. 1984:300).

Moving to the Near East, the literature regarding trauma is relatively scant. No systematic population-based or diachronic studies have been conducted. Rathbun's (1984) survey of twelve archaeological sites in Iran and Iraq indicates that trauma is not widely reported. In general, few cases of trauma have been reported from any Natufian or Neolithic sites in the southern Levant (Smith, Bar-Yosef, and Sillen 1984). This led Anna Belfer-Cohen to rebut the notion that agricultural origins in the Levant had their source in territorial circumscription (personal communication, 1994). Several individuals spread between a number of sites do exhibit traumatic injuries. The cases of traumatic injury reported are discussed in some detail in Chapter 4. Our first inklings of patterned traumatic injury from interpersonal violence come from Bab edh-Dhra, where at least three individuals suffered ax blows to the head (Ortner 1981, 1982).

This discussion and the related case studies demonstrate that patterns of trauma within populations can be used to discuss patterns of community health, activity, and conflict that enhance behavioral reconstructions.

Tooth Wear, Dental Trauma, and Caries

Wallace (1974) defines tooth wear as "the loss of the calcified tissues of a tooth by erosion, abrasion, attrition, or any combination of these" (385). Clearly, much of this wear patterning is attributable to diet. But in terms of inferring sexual labor divisions per se, we will leave aside the large body of evidence pertinent to diet and nutrition and focus on how wear can inform about occupation (Milner and Larsen 1991).

When humans use their teeth as tools or ancillary hands, a great degree of mechanical stress results (Larsen 1987). Humans who regularly hold or process nonfood objects with their teeth exhibit occupational wear. The range of activities under consideration includes processing animal hide and sinew, pressure flaking stone tools, and preparing fiber and cordage for weaving. Grooving on the occlusal (chewing) surfaces of anterior (front) teeth is a typical and widespread form of dental modification (Milner and Larsen 1991). There is general agreement that these grooves resulted from processing plant materials to make baskets, cordage, woven bags, nets, and the like. The wear presumably results from drawing plant materials through clamped teeth to remove outer layers or bark and expose pliable fibers within. Using teeth as clamps in the production of woven or plaited objects could also create occlusal grooving. Occlusal grooving has been reported among groups from Metal Age Italy (Robb 1994), the Great Basin (Larsen 1985), and the southeastern United States (Blakey and Beck 1984). Interproximal (between teeth) grooves have also occasionally been interpreted as resulting from plant fiber preparation (Schulz 1977). Narrow grooves on the anterior teeth from a prehistoric skeletal series from California correspond with patterns found on a historic series that were known to have processed plant fibers for cordage using their teeth (Schulz 1977).

Other forms of occupational dental wear include chipping, abrasion patterns, surface wear, and attrition (Milner and Larsen 1991). Extreme occlusal wear and attrition among Sadlermiut women is attributed to chewing on animal skins to soften them and stretching them while sewing (Merbs 1983:156–157). Eskimo men experience dental wear from using their teeth to hold fish lines, tow seals be-hind kayaks while paddling, crush the heads of birds, and crack seal bones (Merbs 1983; Turner and Cadien 1969). Aboriginal groups in the Northern Territory of Australia use teeth for a variety of tasks, ranging from stripping bark from tree branches, sharpening wooden tools, and pressure flaking stone tools (Barrett 1977). Pronounced abrasion of upper incisors, attrition of canines and premo-lars, and chipping are the respective corollaries of these activities (Barrett 1977; Milner and Larsen 1991).

Molleson (1994) analyzed the teeth from Abu Hureyra and provides a well-documented case study of occupational dental modification from the southern Levant. Grooving on the chewing surfaces of front teeth is linked to production of baskets and sieves by some of Abu Hureyra's Neolithic female residents. Ex-treme wear and enlarged joint surfaces led Molleson to tentatively identify another group of craftswomen who, she argues, were chewing plant stems, or "quids," to extract fibrous material for the production of mats and cordage (Molleson 1994). More in-depth discussion of these results, especially as they pertain to groups of household-based craft specialists, is found in Chapter 4.

Changes in the frequency of caries in skeletal populations have often been used to assess diet changes. Increases in caries and tooth loss are correlated with increases in domestic foodstuffs, particularly sticky carbohydrates. Sex-based caries patterns have been used to assess sexual labor patterns among both agricultural and hunting-gathering groups. Archaeological populations throughout North America demon-strate a consistent pattern of greater caries prevalence in females compared to males—a pattern that is also manifest among groups in Scandinavia, Europe, India, and Africa (Larsen 1997). Larsen concludes that this commonality reflects a general pattern of subsistence behavior among many agriculturalists and foragers. He claims that males have fewer caries because they consume more meat relative to the plant-rich diets of females. Supporting evidence is drawn from the ethnographic record that suggests that men, for the most part, are responsible for hunting as their pri-mary subsistence task. Several examples make it clear that, despite rules of sharing, hunters often consume much of their game. In contrast, women involved in plant gathering and preparation would have a higher proportion of plant foods in their diets (Larsen 1997). While the explanation is not entirely appropriate for Old World archaeological populations who relied on domestic animals and their prod-ucts for protein requirements, sex-based patterning in caries prevalence is another significant variable to consider in assessing occupation.

Thus, dental wear, trauma, and caries prevalence are potentially productive tools in building occupational inferences. That teeth tend to preserve so well is certainly one asset. Our ability to correlate prehistoric patterns with observations in living populations is another (Larsen and Kelley 1991).

Musculoskeletal Stress Markers

Repetitive and stressful loading at muscle sites results in bony remodeling. One form of this remodeling refers to the morphological changes at the muscle and ligament attachment sites visible on cortical bone. The changes take the form of surface irregularities, rough patches, bone buildup, and bone projections (Kennedy 1989; Larsen 1997). The operating assumption in the analysis of these morphological changes is that increased robusticity at these sites correlates with intensity and duration of use, among other things. Unlike cross-sectional analyses, this assumption is difficult to test in living populations because current imaging techniques cannot identify and measure these changes. Thus, the assumption linking morphology and activity has yet to be adequately tested in controlled clinical studies (Bridges 1997; Jurmain 1999; Nagy 1997). Nonetheless, many researchers find it reasonable to expect that more strongly developed markings result from more habitual and intense muscle use (Kennedy 1989; Larsen 1997; Merbs 1983). Furthermore, a variety of studies document that these markings vary in nonrandom patterns by sex, size, age, and subsistence strategy and in conjunction with other monitors of activity level. These findings lend continuing support to the link between musculoskeletal stress markers and mechanical factors (Churchill and Morris 1998; Hawkey 1988, 1998; Hawkey and Merbs 1995; Nagy 1997; Peterson 1994, 1997; Robb 1998; Shaibani, Workman, and Rothschild 1993).

Briefly, periosteum is the fibrous membrane that covers bones, and it is well supplied with blood vessels (Weineck 1986). When regular minor stress occurs, such as the "pull" of a muscle being used habitually, the number of capillaries that supply the periosteum increases (Wirhed 1984). This increased blood flow stimulates osteon remodeling, or the buildup of bone (Hawkey and Merbs 1995; Little 1973). A result is enlargement, or hypertrophy, of the bone at the muscle attachment site (Kennedy 1989; Weineck 1986). Rough patches and surface irregularities are formed at the attachment sites.

The terms originally used to describe these markings were "enthesite" and "enthesopathy," referring specifically to a buildup of extra bony material at attachment sites (Angel et al. 1987; Dutour 1986; Hawkey 1988; Kelley and Angel 1987; Kennedy 1983; Kennedy, Plummer, and Chiment 1986; Lai and Lovell 1992). "Enthesite" and "enthesopathy" are still terms that are used by many researchers (Jurmain 1999; Larsen 1997; Shaibani et al. 1993). A range of changes at muscle attachment sites—including pitting, grooving, and rugosity—has led others to adopt the more general term "musculoskeletal stress markers" (Hawkey and Merbs 1995), which will be used here.

As can be expected with any methodology that is emergent, the techniques for identifying, measuring, and interpreting musculoskeletal stress markers (MSM) are being reexamined and refined continuously. This flux, which should be considered healthy, can be simultaneously exciting and exasperating. The excitement comes as re-finements reinforce our assumptions that MSM are directly related to the amount and duration of habitual stress placed on a specific muscle (Berget and Churchill 1994; Hawkey and Merbs 1995). The exasperation comes when one's results are rather quickly in need of reassessment based on methodological improvements.

Interpretations of MSM patterns ultimately require that close attention be paid to a number of analytical criteria (Hawkey and Merbs 1995; Merbs 1983; Peterson 1998; Robb 1994; Stirland 1991). First, a positive relationship between MSM expression and age is now well documented; for example, muscle markings become generally more robust and well pronounced throughout the adult life span (Robb 1994; Hawkey 1988; Shaibani et al. 1993). To the degree possible, this en-courages us to make the finest-grained possible distinctions in our adult skeletal samples rather than lumping all postadolescents into a generic "adult" category. Genetics also plays a role, making patterns from more isolated, less mixed popu-lations more straightforward to interpret. Large, well-preserved samples are obvi-ously an asset, particularly in the arena of valid statistical testing (Stirland 1991). Inasmuch as our goal is to examine everyday activities and workload, it is also im-portant to control for trauma and pathology. Indications of these conditions on the skeletal elements being examined would typically exclude an individual from a sample (Hawkey 1988; Peterson 1994; Robb 1994).

Several coding standards of gross morphological expressions of MSM have been outlined (Hawkey 1988; Robb 1994). Both systems involve dividing the continuous range of surface markings into discrete grades (Hawkey 0–3; Robb 0–5) on the basis of observable criteria. They provide consistency in scoring by establishing identifiable thresholds for MSM scores via written and visual de-scriptions. Hawkey's method was established using more than 1,500 individuals from nine different regions of the world and has been most widely used (Hawkey 1988). Inter- and intraobserver error have proven negligible ($p < 0.5$) across a spectrum of studies (Hawkey and Street 1992; Nagy and Hawkey 1993; Peter-son 1994; Steen and Lane 1998). Using materials from the necropoli at Pon-tecagnano, Italy, Robb was able to accurately observe and seriate the range of sur-face MSM markings for forty-two muscle attachment sites (Robb 1994). His analysis included upper and lower limbs, as well as bones of the innominate, and has been applied elsewhere as well (Churchill and Morris 1998).

Research on MSM has spawned a number of methodological and analytical questions that have provided impetus for further study, including a 1997 sympo-sium at the meeting of the American Association of Physical Anthropologists (Peterson and Hawkey 1998). Concerns about controlling for bone size as an in-fluence on areal extent and therefore grade score have been expressed. Churchill and Morris (1998) examined the correlations between standardized muscle attachment area sizes and rugosity scores to examine this question among prehistoric hunter-gatherers of the southern coast of South Africa. The lack of significant negative correlations indicates that rugosity varies more as a function of activity than insertion size (Churchill and Morris 1998). Wilczak (1998) used digital imaging techniques to quantify insertion areas and explore their relationship to body size. She concludes that allometric differences are not sufficient to explain the variation demonstrated (Wilczak 1998). Attempts to link MSM patterns with individuals of known occupation also hold promise (Heilman, Roberts, and Knuesel 1997). Overall, the evidence linking mechanical stress as a causal factor in MSM morphology is growing, and our ability to control for other influential variables is becoming more sophisticated.

As MSM have emerged from the realm of qualitative, anecdotal descriptions, the search for appropriate quantitative methods has intensified. The search for pattern has frequently involved univariate analyses of lateralization (comparing left and right sides of the body) and sex differences, rank ordering individual MSM scores, bivariate comparisons of within- and between-skeleton MSM variability, and multivariate cluster analysis. Ultimately, our ability to make statements about workload and activity must take into account that muscles operate not in isolation but as synergistic groups. Observations of "marked" development or high muscle scores for single muscle attachment sites are insufficient for building detailed activity or workload reconstructions.

There are certain activities for which the synergistic muscle signatures and the skeletal stress patterns that result are fairly well understood. Throwing motions are an example because of the emphasis on treating injuries in sports medicine contexts. Kinematic and electromyographic studies abound. As a result, MSM inferences about throwing from prehistoric contexts are often well supported (Dutour 1986; Kennedy 1983; Peterson 1994). We have not developed detailed understandings of the correlation between muscle groups and activity for many other rigorous prehistoric activities.

Analysts must also confront the reality that many activities utilize similar muscle groups. It is likely unrealistic to think that one will be able to distinguish MSM patterns resulting from repetitive downward blows made when tilling the soil versus those made felling trees. Equifinality is a familiar issue for archaeologists and one that applies to interpreting MSM patterning.

Some activities are idiosyncratic enough in terms of the muscle activity to have relatively distinctive signatures. Analysts have built some good arguments for reconstructing rowing and paddling activities (Hawkey and Merbs 1995; Lai and Lovell 1992) and labor-intensive athletic endeavors, such as lacrosse (Stuart-MacAdam and Glencross 1997). The success in inferring these activities derives from the immense muscle demands placed on a unique suite of synergistic muscles.

The utility of having a background of detailed ethnographic and ethnohistoric documentation of activities in these cases is clear and has been previously noted (Merbs 1983).

I suspect that, at present, there are many activities and activity regimes that probably do not result in MSM signatures that are sufficiently unique or idiosyncratic to allow specific activity reconstructions given our archaeological reality. And that realization has implications for how we approach investigating sexual labor in many prehistoric contexts. Finding innovative ways to characterize more general patterns of activity level, range, and variation between the sexes may, in the long run, prove more productive than trying to squeeze MSM patterns into specific activity reconstructions.

That point brings us full circle to several important theoretical concerns. The search for specific activity patterns among data that are not always amenable to such fine-grained interpretations can open the door to assumption-laden speculation. Typically, I rely on archaeological materials to help delimit the range of activities, focusing on technology for subsistence. But clearly, the range of archaeologically visible activities does not represent the complete activity spectrum for any group. Artifacts can be valuable guides in building activity inference, but think of the range of strenuous activities that do not yield readily identifiable material correlates. Strenuous recreational and ritual activities are several examples that come to mind. So there is a danger of interpreting MSM signatures too narrowly with reference to well-preserved, obvious material culture correlates.

I also think we have to be on guard against interpreting "fuzzy" archaeological patterns in support of specific activity inferences that reflect our own gender and labor expectations rather than those that may have existed prehistorically. Robb (1994) notes, for example, that MSM patterning among males is typically ascribed to weapon use, while female patterning is explained as due to plant processing. Note the connection here between activity inference and plentiful stone tool categories. Given not only the vast activity spectrum to choose from but also our increasing knowledge of variability in sexual task divisions, this seems like a somewhat dangerous and overly narrow reading of the bioarchaeological data. Our inferences from MSM data are no more objective or sophisticated than the mindsets we bring to them. And efforts to provide precise interpretations in the absence of the necessary data resolution are problematic.

So, then, in terms of the agricultural transition, how fine grained can we hope to be in our goal of investigating sexual labor patterns? In an ideal world, we would like to be able to answer a variety of very detailed questions. Were males doing the majority of hunting? Were females primarily responsible for plant cultivation? Was everyone doing the same range of tasks? Were there specialists? If so, were they composed of mixed-sex groupings? And yet, answers at this level of resolution may not be forthcoming. While specific activities have been inferred with confidence in some cases, the bulk of studies warrant more general statements concerning activity range or task generalization versus specialization. These cautionary notes hardly mitigate our interest in MSM as a potential window into the prehistory of sexual labor patterns.

Having explored the historical, methodological, and theoretical aspects of MSM research in some depth, one can describe several research projects in order to illustrate the potential utility and applicability of this particular monitor of occupational stress. The seminal work by Hawkey and Merbs is an appropriate starting point. Although not couched explicitly within an engendered paradigm, the authors use sexual differences as a major interpretative vector (Hawkey 1988; Hawkey and Merbs 1995). Among Early period Thule adults, a sexual dichotomy of labor is suggested by the MSM analysis. As one example, high scores for a group of muscles in females suggest rowing of the large, skin-lined umiaks, or "women's boats." While this is consistent with ethnographic accounts, Hawkey maintains that the severe degree of muscle stress indicates that rowing tasks may be somewhat underestimated in these accounts (Hawkey and Merbs 1995:334). Males have high MSM scores for attachment sites consistent with the distinct, alternative rotary movements performed when propelling a kayak with a double-bladed paddle (Hawkey and Merbs 1995:335).

Robb's work in Italian Metal Age contexts provides a second case study that analyzes MSM from the perspective of how their expression and distribution reflect basic labor divisions by class and sex within society (Robb 1994, 1998). Clustering summary statistics of the muscle data, several labor groups could be identified: (1) those who performed specialized, physically stressful tasks (primarily males, one female); (2) those who performed generalized tasks at moderate activity levels (half the adult males and most of the females); and (3) those involved in less strenuous activities or who had not yet built up an MSM profile (typically the younger adults) (Robb 1994). Novel information about the organization of work, degree of task specialization, homogeneity of task level, and sexual division was derived without reference to specific activity reconstructions.

My own MSM research with Levantine Natufian, Neolithic, and Bronze Age populations suggests that both the timing and the intensity of labor changes differed for males and females during the development of agropastoral lifestyles (Peterson 1994, 1997, 1998, 2000a).

Conclusion

The MOS literature is expanding and becoming more mainstream. This review makes the case that integrating multiple lines of data whenever possible (artifactual, textual, multiple MOS, and so on) enhances both the scope and the detail of our activity reconstructions. The strength of a synthetic approach has been outlined in some detail elsewhere (Stuart-MacAdam and Glencross 1997). Although single data sets were emphasized in my previous discussion of various studies for the sake of convenience, it should be noted that many integrate multiple activity-related traits (Goodman et al. 1984; Hawkey 1988; Merbs 1983; Molleson 1989, 1994; Nagy 1997; Nagy and Hawkey 1993; Rathbun 1984; Robb 1994). Their respective activity reconstructions gain credibility and empirical validation from these efforts.

Bioarchaeological data can help reconstruct work patterns. Where sexual patterns exist, the data can be used to establish task differentiation. In some cases, the level of resolution of these tasks may be appropriate to support inferences about specific activities, especially where a direct historic, ethnographic link has been maintained. When dealing with the transitional periods for agriculture in the Levant, it proves productive also to look for coarser-grained, but still informative, patterns that indicate activity level, musculoskeletal specialization versus generalization, and so on. This is still an exciting and productive enhancement of our understanding of labor patterning. In the next two chapters, I present the Levantine data relevant to labor and occupation with the goal of enriching our models for the transition to domestication economies from an explicitly social organizational perspective.

Previous Skeletal Studies from the Levant **4**

⊞

AGAINST THIS GLOBAL backdrop of research in occupation and sex-based task differentiation, I will now narrow the geographic focus to the Levant. Historically, Levantine archaeologists recognized the behavioral significance of prehistoric human skeletal remains. Many early osteological studies focused on cranial morphology in order to examine questions of genetic continuity, ethnic affiliation, and population movements. Increasing concern for the interaction between biology and culture has led researchers to more inclusive discussions of population structure, pathology, trauma, and life stress.

This chapter summarizes the results of Near Eastern osteological studies that pertain to occupational stress. Taken together, these studies provide a range of statements and emergent patterns about activity and workload changes. Formulated as hypotheses, these statements provide the testable propositions used to examine and interpret the data on musculoskeletal stress markers (MSM). Some of the studies explicitly discuss sexually patterned activities or provide data that enabled me to do so. Others are significant because they provide background information about the factors, along with activity, that influence various indices of skeletal variability (disease, dietary stress, genetic continuity, and so on). Together, these studies provide the foundation and framework with which the MSM data of this project are integrated.

Briefly, osteological studies have characterized the Natufian as a time when certain traits exhibited pronounced sexual dimorphism, relatively healthy living conditions persisted, and patterns of pathology and trauma were consistent with other hunter-gatherers. The degree of sexual dimorphism present suggests substantial differences in some aspects of male and female activities. Both Natufian and Pre-Pottery Neolithic (PPN) groups appear to have consumed large amounts of cereals. Beyond diet, glimpses of changing PPN lifestyles and labor divisions in these first agricultural societies are garnered from several sites. Several researchers suggest that male and female work patterns converge during the PPN. The convergence is marked by more pronounced reorganization in male activities during the initial adoption of agriculture. The first pronounced declines in health, measured by a number of indices, occur during the Chalcolithic and continue into the Early Bronze I (EBI). Increasing dependence on cereals is typically cited as a primary cause of deteriorating health, but increased proximity to domestic animals and violent encounters with other humans may also have influenced community health. Hypotheses about labor organization are less well developed for the EBI. Whatever labor solutions EBI groups forged took place in the context of reliance on cereals and animal husbandry. I suggest that a fundamental reorganization of labor patterns between the sexes is part of that solution.

Extant Studies

Smith, Bloom, and Berkowitz (1984)

Change through time in humeral robusticity has been studied using radiographs and measuring cortical thickness (CCT). Smith, Bloom, and Berkowitz (1984) compared a sample of Natufian humeri from El Wad and 'Ain Mallaha to samples from Middle Bronze I, Roman/Byzantine, and Early Arab periods. Natufian males' CCT values were significantly higher than all other groups, of either sex. The Natufian population also displayed the most extreme sexual dimorphism (Smith, Bloom, and Berkowitz 1984:607). This supports the idea that Natufian males and females performed some different habitual activities.

The authors hypothesize that exceptionally high CCT values for Natufian men may be the result of male participation in activities requiring more arm muscle strength and mobility. Hunting with spear or atl atl is advanced as one activity that may be responsible for the pattern (Smith, Bloom, and Berkowitz 1984:608). Fortunately, the involvement of muscles in overhand throwing motions is fairly well documented. This tentative reconstruction is assessed with MSM data in Chapter 5.

One other finding is worthy of further exploration. The later time periods can all be described as economically agropastoral. Putting aside concerns about temporal change introducing variables that influence body robusticity, as we proceed from hunting and gathering to farming lifestyles, it appears that males undergo more significant changes in CCT values and consequently more significant changes in functional demands than females (Smith, Bloom, and Berkowitz 1984:608). Can we infer that female activity levels and tasks exhibit more stability and continuity through time for females compared to males? Comparing MSM profiles of populations with known health, nutrition, and genetic similarities helps answer that question.

Belfer-Cohen, Schepartz, and Arensburg (1991)

These authors provide an updated and impressive examination of Natufian skeletal material from Israel. All five sites sampled are likewise included in my MSM study: Hayonim Cave, Kebara, 'Ain Mallaha, Nahal Oren, and El Wad. In addition to the detailed analysis of Natufian material, some general comparisons with Neolithic groups from the Levant are advanced.

Levantine Neolithic agricultural adaptations are sometimes viewed as a response to resource stress (Henry 1989, cited in Belfer-Cohen et al. 1991:422). If true, this would make it more difficult to link patterns in skeletal morphology to activity since differences in health and nutrition introduce another axis of variability. However, their comprehensive review of the evidence suggests that underlying nutritional stress is not a feature of the Late Natufian (Belfer-Cohen et al. 1991:422). This position gains additional support from the in-depth dental and archaeological analyses in which the Natufian and PPN study populations exhibit pronounced continuity among a variety of dietary monitors (Bar-Yosef and Belfer-Cohen 1989:490; Smith 1989a; Smith, Bar-Yosef, and Sillen 1984:129).

Arthritis among Natufians is very rare, largely because of an underrepresentation of older adults in the skeletal population (Belfer-Cohen et al. 1991:421). Only five cases of arthritis are listed: four from El Wad and one from Hayonim Cave. The examples are consistent with what is described as the "normal 'wear and tear' of the hunting and gathering lifeway" (Belfer-Cohen et al. 1991:420). The osteological signatures used to identify arthritis consist of joint surface modification and osteophyte formation on vertebrae.

Rathbun (1984)

Stature reflects both long-term selective pressures and the "plastic" changes resulting from stress during an individual's lifetime, including activity (Frayer and Wolpoff 1985; Smith 1989b). Stature cannot accurately be portrayed as a measure of occupational stress, per se. But stature comparisons have often been used to advance hypotheses related to activity level and the sexual division of labor through time. In part, this is due to the fact that stature estimates have been a standard part of osteological analysis and reporting while many of the other occupational referents have not. Practical necessity dictates that archaeologists work with the data they have at hand.

Calculations made from intact femora provide the most accurate estimates of stature. But given the incomplete and fragmentary nature of many prehistoric collections, other indices can also be used (e.g., from both femoral fragments and other skeletal elements). Unfortunately, the variety of skeletal elements used to produce estimates, as well as the lack of explicit mention of which formulae are used in the calculations, hampers comparisons between sites and periods.

A diachronic study was conducted by Ted Rathbun, who compared stature estimates and pathology patterns from a number of sites in Iran and Iraq. His results suggest one potential pattern of sexual labor change for the southern Levant. Rathbun compared stature estimates between the sexes within and between a number of time periods: preagricultural (including Upper Paleolithic and Epipaleolithic), Neolithic, Chalcolithic, Bronze Age, and Iron Age. Within-period sex comparisons of stature indicate significant differences for all periods except the Neolithic (Rathbun 1984:146). Female stature tends to be more stable through time, while male stature shows diachronic fluctuations (Rathbun 1984:146–147). The possibility of greater activity change for males through time is worth examining, particularly in light of the CCT results that displayed a similar pattern. Furthermore, a hypothesis that activity levels were most similar between sexes during the Neolithic is worth exploring further.

Smith, Bar-Yosef, and Sillen (1984)

This study is a synthesis of a variety of data sets related to the rise and development of agriculture in the Levant. The authors, like Rathbun, examine data from several time periods. Their goal is to address issues of dietary change spanning the Middle Paleolithic (Mousterian), Natufian, Neolithic, Chalcolithic, Bronze Age, Hellenistic, and Arab time periods. Results from Natufian and Neolithic osteological collections are particularly pertinent here. The Bronze Age sample includes Middle Bronze material and is not directly comparable to the EBI sample used in my MSM analyses.

Several potential axes of variation appear to have held constant through time. The authors conclude that Natufian and Neolithic groups were generally healthy and that it is only in later periods (Middle Bronze and later) that health standards declined markedly (Smith, Bar-Yosef, and Sillen 1984:129). An overall assessment of cranial morphology and dentition also suggests population continuity.

The stature estimates provide some patterns that parallel Rathbun's findings and others that differ. The samples used by Smith and colleagues are larger than Rathbun's and come exclusively from southern Levantine sites. One interesting parallel is the relative stability of female stature through time compared to men's (Smith, Bar-Yosef, and Sillen 1984:112–113). On the other hand, fluctuations in male stature are pronounced looking at the Pre-Pottery Neolithic B (PPNB) sample. The largest population of PPNB males, from Jericho, increases significantly in stature (171 centimeters) compared to both Pre-Pottery Neolithic A (PPNA) males from Jericho (167 centimeters) and Natufian males (167 centimeters). The increase is not maintained in later populations. Could it be that males' workloads increased significantly during the PPNB, while females' activities and activity levels remained more stable through these periods? The authors state that skeletal pathology, including evidence for arthritis, has not been comprehensively reported for Neolithic populations (Smith, Bar-Yosef, and Sillen 1984:120)—a situation that has, unfortunately, not improved significantly since the publication of that article. Traumatic injuries are rare, suggesting that Neolithic groups were not particularly prone to injuries from aggression or accident (Smith, Bar-Yosef, and Sillen 1984).

The authors emphasize that neither during the transition from Early to Late Natufian nor during that from Natufian to Neolithic periods are there indications of environmental or nutritional stress. Not until the Bronze Ages do we see health status deteriorating as a result, perhaps, of increased density of human settlements (Smith, Bar-Yosef, and Sillen 1984:129–130). Being able to hold health status relatively constant for the Natufian and Neolithic periods makes comparisons of their MSM profiles subject to less variation. Natufian and Neolithic MSM patterns can be interpreted without fear of the biasing effects of substantial, population-wide health changes. This same assumption may not hold true for the Early Bronze Age sample, so temporal comparisons between this and earlier groups are more likely skewed by declining health as it affects activity and workload.

Molleson (1989, 1994, 2000)

Theya Molleson has done pathbreaking studies aimed at assessing habitual activity patterns from Near Eastern osteological collections. Her work is integrative in that she combines observations from dental wear patterns, joint modifications, and MSM to discuss prehistoric activities across the transition from hunting and gathering to an agricultural economy. Her skeletal material comes from the site of Abu Hureyra in the Euphrates River Valley in present-day northern Syria (Molleson 2000). The deposits in which the skeletons were found are contemporaneous with the Natufian and PPN in the southern Levant, although slightly different nomenclature is used in Syria (Moore 1986).

In her writings, Molleson suggests that certain villagers at Abu Hureyra knelt on the ground habitually with their toes curled back up under their feet. Impressions, and bony ridges around those impressions, on toe bones (metatarsals and phalanges) indicate that the foot was habitually held in a position that pushed the toes up (maximized dorsiflexion). In conjunction with other skeletal indications, Molleson concludes that grinding grain in a kneeling position was the activity most likely to cause these skeletal changes. In support, she notes pronounced attachment sites for the biceps and deltoid muscles that are expressed bilaterally (on both right and left arms), arthritic changes in the knee joint and lower dorsal spine, extreme tooth wear, and the presence of querns from the levels that produced the skeletal material.

Molleson also identifies several distinct groups of female craft specialists on the basis of dental wear and modification. Thin grooves on the chewing (occlusal) surfaces of anterior teeth were present in a few females. She argues that these individuals were manipulating plant fibers by using their teeth as third, or ancillary, hands—just as Larsen observed among the Great Basin Paiute (Molleson 1994:74). Several other individuals exhibit extreme, uneven tooth wear combined with pronounced enlargement of the mandibular joint surface. In this case, Molleson (1994:74) suggests that some females were chewing plant stems to extract fibrous materials to produce string cordage. The author views these specialized roles as natural outgrowths of the role division that seems to appear as a part of increased plant utilization (Molleson 1994:74).

Molleson addresses questions of sexual divisions of labor directly. The Abu Hureyra sample indicates a "rather loose division of roles . . . among these early Neolithic people," one in which females carried out most of the daily food preparation (Molleson 1994:73). In the final site volume, Molleson's view appears to have changed slightly. Here she suggests rather more substantial divisions in which males hunted and made a variety of tools, while females spun, wove, ground grain, and made baskets (Molleson 2000). Some of these activity patterns derive from her skeletal data as per the grinding and fiber production activities discussed previously. In contrast, other activity reconstructions—such as hunting and tool production—are more highly speculative.

Molleson's conclusions are often quite convincing, particularly when several independent lines of skeletal evidence are used to bolster her behavioral reconstructions. I treat the conclusions made without reference to skeletal patterns with a bit more skepticism.

Hershkovitz and Galili (1990)

A detailed osteological study of the human remains from the site of Atlit Yam sheds light on the activities and health of a PPNB population that lived along the northern coast of Israel. A total of twenty-four skeletons were retrieved beginning in 1983 (Hershkovitz, Galili, and Ring 1991). Fifteen individuals are presented in detail in the 1990 article, presumably representing the most complete, intact specimens. Among the adults, two were identified as male, five as female. Notable morphological similarities between the Atlit Yam residents and the Natufian residents of Nahal Oren, located 2 kilometers to the east, indicate genetic continuity (Hershkovitz and Galili 1990:353).

Because of coastline changes, the site is now located about 300 to 400 meters offshore in about 8 to 12 meters of water (Hershkovitz and Galili 1990:320). Various markers of occupational stress, in conjunction with archaeological finds, led the authors to conclude that the inhabitants were involved in a number of marine activities, including deep-sea fishing, diving, and fishnet production. Floral and faunal remains show that the residents at Atlit Yam hunted and farmed as well. What are the social strategies that lie behind such a diverse economic base?

Cord and fiber preparation for fishnets, baskets, containers, or mats is indicated in the extreme wear of the teeth on one individual whose sex is indeterminate (Hershkovitz and Galili 1990:351–352). The authors further suppose that divers collected marine foods available in the lagoon. On the temporal bone of one individual, the authors describe a buildup of bone forming a long ridge at the opening of the ear canal (auditory exostoses) (Hershkovitz and Galili 1990:344, 350–351). This feature has been linked elsewhere to diving for aquatic resources that habitually exposes the ear canal to cold water (Frayer 1988; Kennedy 1989:138). Again the sex of this individual is indeterminate. More generically, cases of "flattening" of long bones and overdevelopment of certain areas of muscle attachment are described as potentially indicative of a occupational stress. They do not discuss sex patterns among these features or attempt any activity-specific interpretations.

Focusing on the evidence for diving and fiber preparation, the authors speculate about sexual labor patterns, or at least what some males may have been doing. Males, they state, appear to have been responsible for fishing and other marine food exploitation. They make the broad assertion that among groups engaged in fishing, "males are predominantly responsible for the livelihood of the population" (Hershkovitz and Galili 1990:351).

Several problematic issues can be raised with regard to this conclusion. First and foremost, one possible diver and one possible net maker (both of indeterminate sex) are hardly resounding empirical support for their conclusion that men were primarily responsible for procuring marine resources. Second, they are either defining fishing very narrowly or ignoring an extensive ethnographic literature that describes women and children involved in fishing and acquiring other coastal resources (as one example, see Moss 1993). An oft-cited cross-cultural analysis of sexual labor divisions indicates that while hunting large aquatic fauna is mainly a male pursuit, fishing and gathering small aquatic fauna are activities often performed by both sexes (Murdock and Provost 1973:207–209).

The authors are to be commended for presenting their findings in such detail. This presentation enables the reader to identify several interesting musculature patterns that, unfortunately, are not pursued. As one example, four individuals (one female, one male, two of indeterminate sex) exhibit pronounced lateralization at the pronator quadratus insertion site on the ulna, with the left side showing more marked development (Hershkovitz and Galili 1990:336–338). This suggests a unilateral activity(ies) pattern that is shared by males and females.

The authors' choice of which patterns to explore and which to ignore highlights the influence that both personal outlook and theoretical bias can have in exploring sexed labor patterns. The observations from MSM, pathology, and dental wear are welcome and quite thought provoking. Yet the single potential labor scenario envisioned, which ignores any possible contribution of females, relegates the reconstruction to the stereotypical. As excavations at Atlit Yam are ongoing, we can hope for both a larger sample and future opportunities to expand the scope of sexual labor interpretations.

Smith (1989b, 1995)

Historically, human skeletal collections from ceramic-era sites in the Near East are less well studied. This is certainly true of the Chalcolithic and EBI periods in the southern Levant. Patricia Smith notes these circumstances and sets out to synthesize the current state of knowledge. The paucity of human osteological research is unfortunate because, in the absence of substantial Pottery Neolithic samples, these groups represent the earliest fully developed farming economies (Smith 1995:69). By "fully developed," she is referring to sedentary agricultural groups who make ceramics and use both primary and secondary domestic animal products. The overall portrait that Smith paints is one of increased environmental stress during the EBI compared to the Natufian and Neolithic. Smith (1995:69) suggests poorer nutrition and increased disease load as possible causes. Monitors of increased stress include a reduction in mean stature (Smith 1989b:308) and increased frequency of enamel defects on teeth affecting some 90 percent of the population (Smith 1995:69). Increases in both caries and tooth loss suggest that the carbohydrate content of the diet was increasing to the detriment of overall health (Smith 1989b:309).

To bolster the case that increased stress is responsible for these changes, Smith states that there are no pronounced morphological (particularly cranial) changes seen when comparing Chalcolithic/EBI populations with earlier groups. This supports a notion of genetic continuity through time; that is, the EBI groups are not immigrants from outside the southern Levant.

According to Smith, escalating health problems did not manifest themselves in interpersonal aggression. She maintains that the EBI sample contains no cases of trauma from blows or fractures (Smith 1989b:308). This is a curious statement since, in making it, she disagrees with Ortner's earlier analysis of the Bab edh-Dhra material (see the following section).

There are no studies that specifically address occupation or activity. Nor is sexual labor patterning discussed. However, Smith's summary has implications for activity pattern reconstructions. She alerts us to changing nutrition and health conditions that may make MSM comparisons between the EBI and the other time periods more complex.

Ortner (1979, 1981, 1982)

Tomb and charnel houses excavations at Bab edh-Dhra have produced skeletal remains from more than 300 EBI individuals. Most of the well-preserved material came from multichambered shaft tombs that typically included mixed, secondary burials of multiple individuals (approximately 150, or roughly half the excavated sample) (Frolich and Ortner 1982; Ortner 1979, 1981). The other half came from an aboveground charnel house. Burning and fragmentation make this material less informative overall (Ortner 1982). Detailed analysis is predicated on the laborious and time-consuming task of identifying and sorting these mixed materials into individuals that can be aged and sexed.

Beyond preliminary reporting, which includes a discussion of methodology and grave goods (Frolich and Ortner 1982), there are several detailed osteological reports from the site. These studies focus on paleopathology and provide complementary data to the nutritional and stature observations made by Smith (1989b, 1995). While these reports do not address sexual labor or activity patterns directly, the demographic and pathological information they contain is essential to any occupational assessment.

Analyses of cranial morphology suggest that the inhabitants were genetically similar to contemporaneous groups throughout the southern Levant (Krogman 1989). Despite high subadult mortality, many adults lived beyond fifty years of age. Dental wear is pronounced, suggesting a diet high in coarse, abrasive particles (Ortner 1981:132). This strengthens Smith's claim that carbohydrates (ground on stone tools that introduce abrasive material) made up a significant part of the EBI diet.

Contrary to Smith's observations, Ortner describes the first substantial evidence for traumatic injury. An EBI charnel house contained three individuals with healed head injuries. The wounds seem to have been caused by ax blows. Of the three injured, one was identified as an adult male and another a probable young adult male (Ortner 1982:94). Among the shaft tombs, Tomb A 100N differed from many of the other tombs in that it contained a primary burial dominating the central part of the chamber. The chamber was unusual in that it was paved with several large, flat stones. The adult male was about forty-five years old, and his skull exhibited two healed depressed lesions, seen as the probable results of blows to the head (Ortner 1981:126). Of the more than 300 EBI individuals at Bab edh-Dhra, at least four exhibit head wounds. At least three of them are adult and, probably, male. This pattern suggests that at least some of the male site inhabitants are involved in violent activities (raiding, warfare, competitions, and so on) that resulted in trauma to the head.

Since most diseases leave no skeletal signature, it is no surprise that there is little evidence of disease among the Bab edh-Dhra collection (Ortner 1981:132). However, there are two individuals who have lesions indicative of tuberculosis (Ortner 1979, 1981). This may represent the spread of bovine tuberculosis as animal husbandry and milk utilization increased (Smith 1989b:309).

Chronological Summary

Natufian

Natufian human remains are the most numerous and best studied of the time periods. The total count of Natufian skeletons numbers more than 400, although some of the remains have yet to be published in detail. Most of the extant literature takes the form of site-specific summaries (Arensburg 1985; Crognier and Dupouy-Madre 1974; Keith 1931; Perrot and Ladiray 1988; Soliveres-Massei 1988; Vallois 1937). Several comparative articles have sought to describe the Natufian population as a whole. Some of these focus on identifying patterns of internal variability/homogeneity with reference to either space (different sites/regions) or time (Early and Late phases) (Belfer-Cohen et al. 1991; Ferembach 1976; Lipschultz 1996; Smith 1991). Others have used composite Natufian samples in the context of longer-term diachronic study of human biological variability during the Pleistocene and the Holocene (Rathbun 1984; Smith, Bar-Yosef, and Sillen 1984; Smith, Bloom, and Berkowitz 1984).

Dental evidence supports the notion that Natufian groups incorporate large quantities of ground cereals in their diets (Smith 1972, 1991; Smith, Bar-Yosef, and Sillen 1984). Patterns of dental disease suggest that the diet was relatively high in abrasive, caries-producing matter. Strontium-to-calcium ratios also support the conclusion that Natufian diets were omnivorous, containing substantial amounts of vegetable foods (Sillen and Lee-Thorp 1991).

A consensus about relatively pronounced sexual dimorphism in long-bone robusticity seems to be emerging. The data concerning differences in male and female stature are less widely agreed on. The occupation inferences offered by Smith, Bloom, and Berkowitz (1984) relate to the rather standard ethnographic reconstruction of male hunting as responsible for elevated male robusticity.

There is an overall lack of evidence for traumatic injury from accident or violence (Belfer-Cohen et al. 1991). From El Wad, Arensburg described a large depression with no signs of healing on the skull (endocranium) of a young adult of indeterminate sex (cited in Belfer-Cohen 1995:12). Two individuals (no sex designations available) from Hayonim Cave also exhibit signs of trauma: one possible healed fracture on a femur and one mandible with new bone growth (a subperiosteal formation of new bone on the lower margin). With such sporadic occurrences, a population-based study of patterns of activity-induced trauma is not possible or warranted.

Arthritis is a relatively rare phenomenon, related in part to the underrepresentation of elderly (Belfer-Cohen et al. 1991). Because MSM are correlated with age, elevated scores in a relatively young population would be even more impressive.

Neolithic

Human remains from the PPN are generally more poorly preserved and occur in fewer numbers per site. The osteological collections from several large sites await final publication and were not available for my MSM study. For example, Jericho has the largest known number of PPN skeletons (Kurth and Rohrer-Ertl 1981), and the site of Basta also has forty-two individuals reported from two of the three completed field seasons (Schultz 1987; Schultz and Scherer 1991). Ongoing excavation at several other significant sites will boost the PPN sample (Atlit Yam, 'Ain Ghazal, Ghwair, and so on).

In general, neither abrupt dietary change nor an influx of outsiders characterize this initial period of domestication. Amid this apparent continuity, however, a dramatic increase in male stature offers tantalizing evidence that labor is changing (Smith, Bloom, and Berkowitz 1984). Molleson's (1994) work suggests that females may have been the primary grinders of grain as well as household craft specialists. Since hunting appears to decrease in importance, judging from faunal remains, what are the males up to?

At Basta, the analysts describe pronounced and sometimes severe degeneration in the shoulder joints of three adult males. The publication is a brief, preliminary report with no complete inventory or quantified data presentation (Schultz and Scherer 1991). Six cases of severe arthritis are noted among PPN adults at 'Ain Ghazal (Grindell 1998; Rollefson, Simmons, and Kafafi 1992; Rollefson et al. 1984). Five are adult males, and the sex of the sixth is indeterminate. Degenerative changes in the vertebra are noted in five. Are PPN males engaged in activities that produce different stresses on the back and shoulder than females? It should be mentioned that several of the individuals from 'Ain Ghazal with spinal pathologies have been described as possible cases of tuberculosis (El-Najjar, Al-Shiyab, and Al-Sarie 1997). If true, these cases represent the earliest evidence for this disease in the Old World. No other cases of tuberculosis have ever been suggested from PPN sites, which exhibit little evidence for pathology overall.

Traumatic injuries do not appear to be widespread. Three examples are identified from the large PPN population at Jericho (Kurth and Rohrer-Ertl 1981). During the 1995 field season at 'Ain Ghazal, excavators discovered one individual whom they described as having succumbed to a violent death. One male individual, found buried in a trash heap, had apparently died from a thin flint blade embedded into the left side of his skull. The projectile was delivered with enough force to push a 3-centimeter piece of the inner skull into the brain (Rollefson and Kafafi 1996). The site of Basta stands out from the overall PPN trauma pattern as having a relatively large number of traumatic injuries reported. Three adult males have depressed fractures in their skulls that, because of patterns of bone healing, do not appear to have been fatal (Schultz and Sherer 1991). These three individuals constitute roughly 33 percent of the adult male population and 14 percent of the adult population based on reports from the 1987 and 1988 field seasons (Schultz 1987; Schultz and Sherer 1991). An eight- to nine-year-old child was not as lucky. A blow to the occipital caused trauma that was likely fatal, this after suffering an earlier fracture as the result of a perforation wound to the left frontal (Roehrer-Ertl, Frey, and Newesely 1988).

Ideally, I could include examples of Pottery Neolithic skeletal analysis in this discussion. However, to date, Pottery Neolithic sites are relatively rare in the southern Levant and have not yielded significant amounts of well-preserved osteological material (Banning et al. 1996; Gopher and Orrelle 1995; Kafafi 1988a, 1988b, 1998). Efforts to expand our understanding of this important time period should rightly be viewed as a somewhat urgent challenge to Near Eastern prehistorians.

Early Bronze I

There is a dearth of osteological research from the EBI, with the work at Bab edh-Dhra as a notable exception. There are reporting problems that hamper the utility of many published reports. Site-specific reports often lump various Chalcolithic and Bronze Age phases together. The "lumped" data reporting renders assessments of change through time, at anything beyond a very gross scale, impossible. Overview articles often incorporate "eyewitness" accounts of assemblages for which there is no detailed publication. This reporting poses problems for both the independent assessment of the data and comparative study.

Much of the EBI osteological research has focused on cranial morphology. In part, this is due to the practical consideration that measurements can typically be taken from fragmentary remains. The nature of the research questions currently in vogue has also been influential. Many studies have focused on establishing biological affinities that are used to identify regional/ethnic differences and similarities—an appropriate venue for craniometrics.

It is significant that the cereal component of diet appears to increase during this period to the point where it compromises health. Proximity to livestock is suggested by the first possible cases of tuberculosis. From the sample at Bab edh-Dhra, we also have a pattern of trauma suggesting that violent activities affected males disproportionately.

Conclusion

Explicit connections between human remains and activity, let alone sexual labor patterns, are rare. Instead, it is our job as social scientists to tease out pertinent details from the literature. Sexual dimorphism in both stature and limb robusticity is one interpretive measure that can be gleaned from a number of reports. Certainly, stature and limb robusticity reflect genetic factors influenced by long-term adaptive changes due to selective pressures. Inasmuch as those selective pressures might differ between the sexes, we can expect sexual dimorphism to exhibit a genetic component (Frayer and Wolpoff 1985). But stature and limb robusticity are also susceptible to what Smith (1989a) describes as "plastic" changes. Plastic changes are those reflecting an individual's experiences during growth and development—among them, nutrition, disease, and activity. The changing lifestyle, from foraging to farming, certainly entailed potentially marked alterations in these variables affecting plastic change. Thus, the degree of sexual dimorphism can be used as a partial indicator of activity differences (Belfer-Cohen et al. 1991:415).

The evidence for nutrition, disease, trauma, degenerative changes, and dental modification has also led researchers to advance activity reconstructions. Ideally, the various markers of occupational stress can be integrated to illuminate the activity realm. In the past, integrative studies focused on activity and labor organization have been relatively rare. Molleson's work with the Abu Hureyra populations is one welcome exception, as is the analysis of the Atlit Yam material by Hershkovitz and Galili. With an explicit focus on activity and sexual labor patterns, we now turn our attention to the detailed analysis of MSM data from a number of sites from the southern Levant.

New Musculoskeletal Stress Markers   5

⊞

T
HE PREVIOUS CHAPTERS present the context in which my interest in labor organization and the transition to agriculture grew. My decision to focus on musculoskeletal stress markers (MSM) reflects personal, professional, and practical considerations. I was curious about exploring the potential for MSM analysis to investigate sexual labor patterns, and MSM seemed like a viable monitor of occupational stress given the size of available collections and the published accounts expressing a paucity of some other indicators of stress. My colleagues at Arizona State University had spearheaded some of the seminal research in this field and, most important, were willing to spend time providing practical training and advice. And while studies of cross-sectional geometry had yielded some interesting results in the context of sexual labor patterns, access to the necessary technology was not available in all the collections' settings.

Materials

A total of 158 skeletons from fourteen sites were included in the study (see Table 1.2). I examined each specimen and also read collection inventories, field notes, and published accounts describing the human skeletal material. The Natufian sites represented are Kebara, El Wad, Nahal Oren, Hayonim Cave, and 'Ain Mallaha. The first four of these are located in the hilly piedmont just east of the narrow coastal plain of present-day Israel. 'Ain Mallaha is located in the northern Jordan Valley, in the now dry Houleh Basin. The Neolithic sites come from a variety of locations in the southern Levant, concentrated in the northern portions of Jordan and Israel (see Figure 1.1). Bab edh-Dhra, the single Early Bronze I (EBI) site, is located on the Lisan peninsula overlooking the Dead Sea in central Jordan.

The sample consists of ninety-three males and sixty-five females. Sex determinations were based on previous osteological analyses that appear in

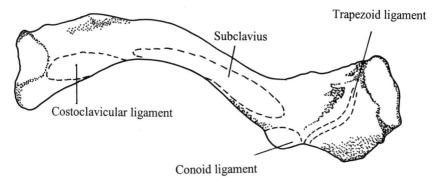

Trapezoid ligament

Subclavius

Costoclavicular ligament

Conoid ligament

Figure 5.1   Muscle and ligament attachment sites on the inferior surface of the left clavicle.

published accounts or as inventory lists on file at the museums and universities where the collections are housed. In general, my own sex assessments concurred with the earlier determinations. However, in several cases, the diagnostic elements used to approximate sex (typically the innominate) had been removed or substantially damaged. In these cases, I was not able to corroborate published sex determinations. When cortical preservation was insufficient to make accurate MSM assessments, those muscle and ligament sites were excluded. Neither does this sample include individuals showing evidence of healed fractures or severe degenerative joint disease on the elements being examined.

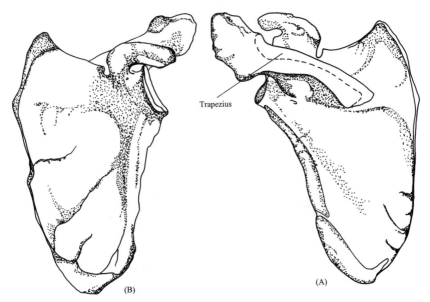

Trapezius

(B)

(A)

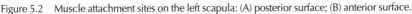

Figure 5.2   Muscle attachment sites on the left scapula: (A) posterior surface; (B) anterior surface.

Five elements of the upper arm and shoulder were examined with reference to sixteen muscle insertion sites, two common muscle origin sites, and three ligament insertion sites (Figures 5.1 to 5.4). These particular sites were chosen because of an assumption that changes in subsistence activities across the

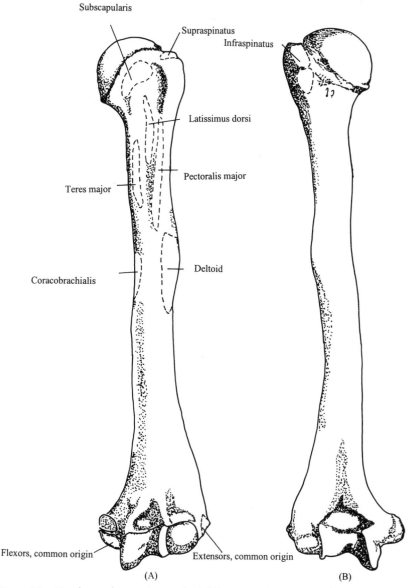

Figure 5.3   Muscle attachment sites on the left humerus: (A) anterior surface; (B) posterior surface.

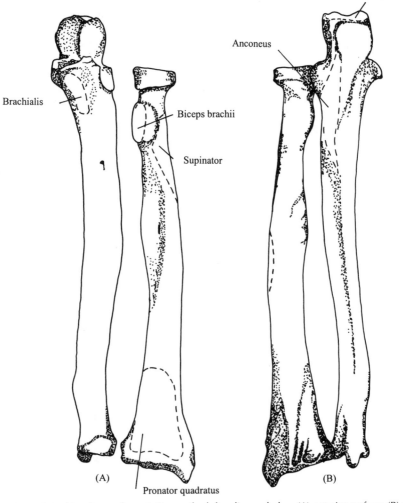

Figure 5.4   Muscle attachment sites on the left radius and ulna: (A) anterior surface; (B) posterior surface.

hunter-gatherer-to-farmer spectrum can reasonably be expected to influence upper-appendicular musculature. In addition, many of the MSM sites on these elements had proven useful in other studies (Hawkey 1988; Hawkey and Merbs 1995; Robb 1994). Insertion sites were emphasized because muscle contraction generally produces the most "pull" at insertion sites (Kennedy 1989) and therefore would leave the most noticeable traces there.

Methods

Two features of MSM expression were scored: robusticity (Figures 5.5 to 5.8) and stress lesions (Figure 5.9). Robusticity refers to roughening or rugged markings at the sites of muscle and ligament attachment on the cortical surfaces of bones. Stress lesions are characterized by pitting, or "furrowing," in the cortex (Hawkey 1988). The MSM scores were derived using a visual reference system devised by Diane Hawkey that identifies threshold criteria and standardized qualitative descriptions of each grade. This system accounts for the unique and complex morphology of each individual MSM site (Hawkey 1988; Peterson 1994).

In a number of studies using Hawkey's scoring method for MSM on human skeletal remains, results suggest that different observers can obtain highly standardized results. Specifically, the margin of inter- and intraobserver error consistently fell below 5 percent (Hawkey 1988; Hawkey and Street 1992; Nagy and Hawkey 1993; Peterson 1994)

The total MSM score for each attachment site was assigned on the following scale: 0 = no expression (neither robusticity nor stress lesion), 1 = faint robusticity, 2 = moderate robusticity, 3 = strong robusticity, 4 = faint stress lesion combined with strong robusticity, 5 = moderate stress lesion, and 6 = strong stress lesion. As

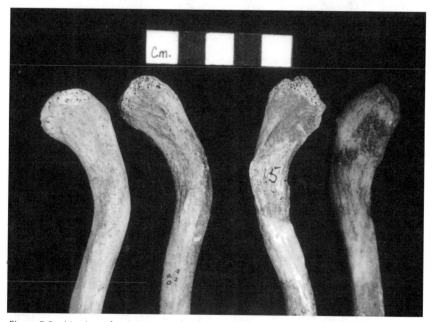

Figure 5.5   Varying robusticity scores for the conoid ligament insertion site. From left to right: 1.0, 1.5, 2.5, and 3.0.

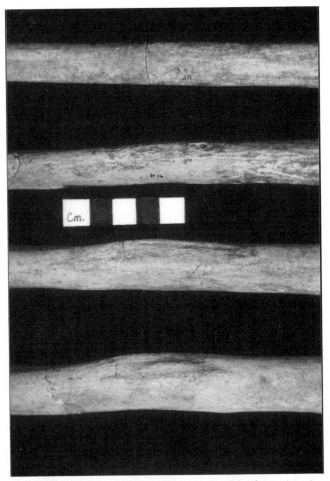

Figure 5.6   Varying robusticity scores for the deltoid insertion site.
From top to bottom: 1.0, 2.0, 2.5, and 3.0.

scoring proceeded, intermediate scores were added for expressions that fell between
the visual and descriptive characterizations for the original, standardized scores (0.5,
1.5, and 2.5).

   This ordinal scale reflects several current assumptions. First, I assume that increases in robusticity reflect increases in activity level and not, for instance, differences in body size. Of particular concern here are issues of sexually dimorphic
differences in body size. Preliminary evaluations of the relationship between body
size and MSM, however, suggest that MSM vary as a function of activity
(Churchill and Morris 1998). Second, the scale suggests that stress lesions represent a continuum of stress beyond the robusticity reaction (Hawkey and Merbs

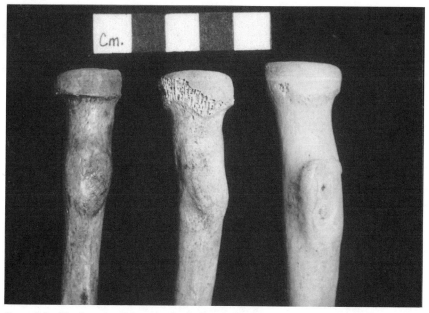

Figure 5.7 Varying robusticity score for the biceps brachii insertion site. From left to right: 1.5, 2.5, and 3.0.

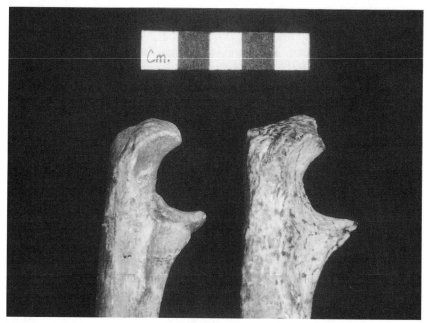

Figure 5.8 Varying robusticity scores for the triceps brachii insertion site. From left to right: 1.0 and 2.0.

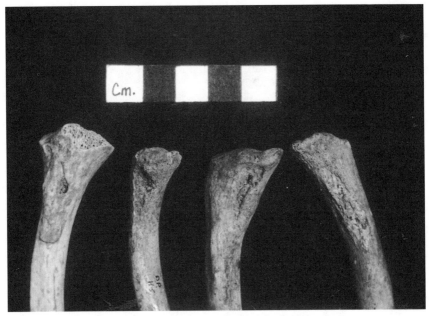

Figure 5.9   Examples of stress lesions at the costoclavicular ligament site.

1995). Future research in the relatively new field of MSM can productively focus on demonstrating that morphological changes at the muscle attachment sites are related to increased muscle use under controlled conditions. It should be noted that stress lesions were very rare in these samples. Strengthening these assumptions is a commonly agreed-on goal of researchers using MSM data (Peterson and Hawkey 1998).

As discussed in Chapter 3, age has been relatively well established as a factor contributing to MSM development. Studies from both Old and New World populations demonstrate the increasing severity of MSM as individuals age (Hawkey 1988; Robb 1994). Unfortunately, obtaining accurate demographic data from the southern Levant can be challenging (Hershkovitz and Gopher 1990). For example, most of the age estimates provided for individuals I used in the MSM study consist of generic "adult of indeterminate age" categorizations. More specific age estimations were often impossible to determine. This lack of demographic control stems from a number of sources.

In the case of the Natufian sample, Belfer-Cohen, Schepartz, and Arensburg (1991) note that even among the relatively numerous Natufian skeletons, 56.5 percent of the adults are assigned to an "indeterminate adult" category. Poor preservation seems to be the primary cause. The remains from Hayonim Cave are an important exception, with more specific age estimates available for a number of individuals. For these remains, I concurred with the estimates provided by the original analyst (Belfer-Cohen 1988).

Of the Natufian individuals with finer age estimates, very few live past thirty-five years (Belfer-Cohen et al. 1991). By looking at other prehistoric and ethnographic hunter-gatherer groups, we have an idea of what their "normal" age distribution curves might look like. Low numbers of both children and older adults in the Natufian sample suggest that the skewed age distribution reflects cultural factors more than a real assessment of life expectancy.

Aging the Neolithic remains beyond "indeterminate adult" was difficult because of poor preservation and the practice of skull removal. More specific age estimates were established for ten individuals from hands-on analysis, published descriptions, museum inventory lists, and available field notes.

The museum inventory list for the EBI skeletal material from Bab edh-Dhra used the designations prenatal, infant, child, adolescent, and adult. Ortner provides more specific age estimates for some adults in his 1981 publication. I did not attempt any finer age grading of the Bab edh-Dhra material, which in retrospect is problematic.

To compensate partially for the lack of age control, no Bab edh-Dhra individuals described as "adolescent" were included in this study because of the likely skewing effects of less robust expressions of MSM on younger individuals.

The lack of detailed age estimates for many of the adults used in my MSM study is a shortcoming that must be borne in mind until a time when samples improve or restudy provides improved data. For example, if male and female groups sampled within a particular time period have dissimilar age profiles, mean score comparisons could influence interpretations of sexual patterns. In the same vein, changes in single sex patterns through time (how male labor patterns changed from the Natufian through the Early Bronze Age) could also be influenced if between-period age profiles differ.

Analytical Techniques

Hypotheses and models in archaeology are typically built up incrementally from a variety of analytical procedures. Redundant patterns in results across various statistical tests are more powerful and convincing at explaining variability in the data, and so I relied on a number of techniques—univariate, bivariate, and multivariate—to illuminate the occupational significance of the MSM examined.

Cluster Analysis

One situation I wanted to avoid in my examination of sexual activity patterns was to presuppose that differences exist between male and female groups—assuming that a sexual division of labor was in place. Analytically, relying on techniques that begin by dividing the sample into male and female groups and looking for differences tacitly express just that assumption—that the differences between groups are more salient than the similarities. The ethnographic record clearly shows that the nature and extent of labor divisions should never be assumed. Too often, prehistorians have begun the discussion of sexual roles by accepting naturalistic assumptions that translate biological differences wholesale into a narrow range of culturally constructed sex roles (Peterson 1994). Cluster analysis, used as a starting point, avoids that assumption by allowing us to explore patterning at the level of the individual (Robb 1994, 1998).

However, cluster analysis has data requirements that often make it difficult to apply to MSM data. Specifically, cluster analyses require a complete data matrix (e.g., no missing data). My MSM data reflected the archaeological reality of bones that were sometimes more than 10,000 years old—few individuals could be scored for all MSM sites.

To accommodate this tension between preferred technique and data shortcomings, I identified subsets of relatively complete MSM scores for individuals from Natufian and EBI contexts. The sample size suffers considerably, but the cluster results are suggestive and, when viewed as essentially exploratory "first steps," deemed worthwhile. I employed a clustering algorithm using squared Euclidean distances (Norusis 1990). The particularly fragmented nature of the Pre-Pottery Neolithic (PPN) sample precluded using cluster analysis.

Rank Ordering

Some researchers have found it informative to use rank orders of mean MSM scores, from high to low or vice versa, as a way of exploring differential utilization of specific muscles and sets of synergistic muscles between subsets of a study population, particularly males and females (Hawkey 1988). Here, MSM mean values were assigned a rank of 1 to 21 in descending order for each sex. The analysis involves comparing the rank orders rather than the mean score values. Right-side mean MSM scores are reported in rank order profiles and mean rank sum comparisons.

Significant Rank Sum and Mean MSM Differences

Patterned differences among sex groups were also identified using the nonparametric Mann–Whitney U-test (also referred to as the Wilcoxon rank sum test). Since this test requires fewer assumptions about the size, distribution, and variance of samples than a two-sample t-test (Norusis 1990), it is particularly appropriate for use with ordinal data.

Since the Natufian and Neolithic aggregate samples included multiple sites, steps were taken to ensure that patterns of variability did not reflect site-specific differences but instead were generally applicable to the sample as a whole. I used the nonparametric Kruskal–Wallis test and the H-statistic it produces to test hypotheses that there were no significant differences identified between various sites with respect to each MSM rank sum. Sample size problems, however, sometimes made it difficult to rule out the influence of intersite variation completely. For each MSM site, all cases from each site are combined and ranked, and average ranks are assigned in the case of ties. Ranks are summed, and the H-statistic is calculated, which has approximately a chi-square distribution, with an observed significance level (Norusis 1990). In general, the Natufian sample seems to be fairly homogeneous, with intersite variability not influencing MSM patterning significantly (Peterson 1994). For several MSM, El Wad seemed to be an outlier. This material was, overall, in the worst state of preservation. Due consideration is given to this in the following analyses. Intersite variability was far more difficult to assess for the Neolithic collections, as sample size typically prevented using the rank comparisons with much confidence.

In the diachronic analysis, I again used the nonparametric Kruskal–Wallis procedure with the H-statistic. While generally less powerful, Kruskal–Wallis is generally considered more appropriate when the data are ordinal (Norusis 1990:219). For those MSM with significance levels less than or equal to 0.05, a parametric analysis-of-mean-variance procedure (one-way) was employed with the Scheffé multiple comparison procedure. Mean variance patterns typically mirrored the multiple rank comparisons but provided additional insights by identifying the mean pairs that were significantly different at the 0.05 level. This helped elucidate the nature of diachronic differences between the multiple MSM samples.

In these analyses, I share the position with a number of other researchers that MSM data are ordinal in nature and amenable to certain numeric manipulations during exploratory data analysis (Churchill and Morris 1998; Hawkey and Merbs 1995; Peterson 1998; Robb 1998; Steen and Lane 1998). This is not, however, a universally shared opinion (Stirland 1998). At the root of this debate is an ongoing controversy among statisticians over the applicability of using numeric-based statistics (such as mean scores of central tendency) on this type of data. Some argue that statistical measures using ordinal data often correspond closely to continuous variability that underlies those scores and are thus reasonable tools. Others express concern that results based on integer scoring could be substantially different from the underlying data structure (for details, see Weisberg 1992).

As with any new technique, there are methodological refinements to be made in MSM analysis. Establishing the presence of patterns in MSM data provides the incentive for these further explorations. Calculating and manipulating mean MSM scores ultimately facilitates identifying those patterns. So, for now, I side with the statisticians that advocate using numeric-based statistics with ordinal data.

Natufian Results

Analysis

My analyses of the Natufian sample provided the most consistent results across the spectrum of techniques utilized. As a result, this is one case where I felt comfortable suggesting a specific activity reconstruction for some of the MSM patterning. Specifically, the results of the MSM analysis suggest that killing game during the Natufian was accomplished primarily by men using hand- or atlatl-delivered projectiles. This specific result and a more general reconstruction of both male and female labor patterns were derived from the following analyses.

Cluster analysis provides the least biased analytical starting point as previously described. I selected nineteen individuals who all had right-side scores for nine MSM sites: pectoralis major, latissimus dorsi, teres major, deltoideus, coracobrachialis, flexors, triceps brachii, anconeus, and biceps brachii. This sample was deemed, subjectively, large enough to provide an interesting cross section of the Natufian individuals. All archaeological sites were represented. Complete and average methods for combining clusters produced similar results. The results discussed are derived from the average linkage method. The distance coefficient and agglomeration schedule suggest that a five-cluster solution produced a reasonable "fit" with the Natufian data. Figure 5.10 displays cluster composition.

Cluster 1 is composed of six individuals: four females and two males. Comparing the mean scores for the various MSM, cluster 1 is a "middle of the road" cluster, not scoring particularly high or low with respect to any one MSM. Cluster 3 is composed of seven males. Mean MSM scores for triceps brachii and anconeus are noticeably higher for this cluster. Cluster 5 contains two males and two females and is characterized by the highest mean scores for pectoralis major MSM and notably elevated score for teres major. Clusters 2 and 4 are composed of single individuals, both females. These specimens seem to represent outliers in that they have low to average scores for most MSM, with higher spikes for specific muscle attachments: teres major in the case of specimen 10256 from El Wad and latissimus dorsi and to a lesser extent coracobrachialis for specimen 10353 from Kebara.

Lateralization and available age information can also be examined in conjunction with the cluster results as interpretive aids. The clustering algorithm was performed using right-side scores only. But patterns of symmetry or asymmetry between cluster-characterizing MSM yielded another interpretive perspective (Table 5.1). When both right and left scores were present, for example, the seven indi-

Cluster	Individuals (Inventory#, Site, Sex)		
Cluster 1 Low MSM mean scores Low variability	H91 H11 10261 H20 10255 10253	M HC EW HC EW EW	F M F M F F
Cluster 2 Low MSM mean scores Moderate variability High teres major	10256	EW	F
Cluster 3 Moderate MSM mean scores Moderate variability High triceps brachii & Anconeus	H43 H29 H25 H27 H8 10349 10351	NO HC HC HC NO K K	M M M M M M M
Cluster 4 Moderate MSM mean scores Moderate variability High teres major & latissimus dorsi	10353	K	F
Cluster 5 Moderate MSM mean scores Moderate variability High pectoralis major	H9 H33 H19 H93	HC HC HC M	F M M F

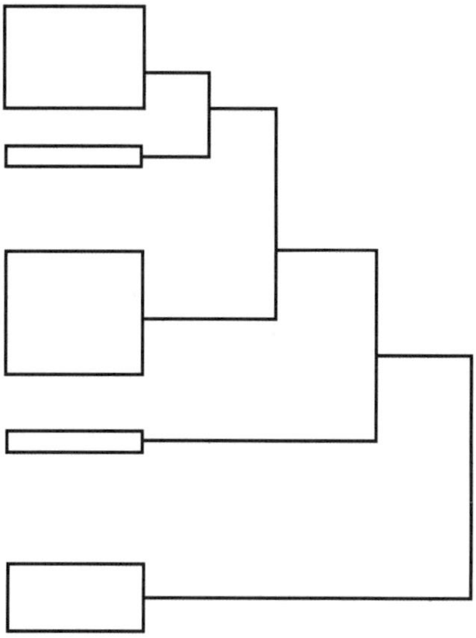

Key: Sites: M = 'Ain Mallaha; HC = Hayonim Cave; EW = El Wad; NO = Nahal Oren; K = Kebara

Figure 5.10   Five-cluster solution for Natufian sample.

viduals in cluster 1 display a marked degree of symmetry or bilateralization in MSM scores. That is true of the females as well as the males.

Could the "middle of the road" cluster be age dependent? In other words, are the individuals in cluster 1 intermediate in age rather than activity? Body HC11 is aged seventeen to nineteen years, and HC 20 is aged twenty-five to thirty years (Belfer-Cohen 1988). When I examined the individuals in the other clusters for whom I have age data, the argument that this cluster represents more middle-aged individuals is not substantiated. One final potentially significant variable comes from the overrepresentation of individuals from El Wad. Cluster 1 contains three (50 percent) of the four individuals included in the entire Natufian cluster sample (21 percent).

The all-male cluster 3 stands out by virtue of its high scores for triceps brachii and anconeus MSM. Both of these muscles are heavily involved in motions of forearm extension. Unfortunately, left scores for the cluster-defining MSM were absent from many individuals, hampering the assessment of symmetry. If we expand our investigation of lateralization to include all twenty-one observed MSM, however, there is evidence for unilateral muscle development in

Table 5.1 MSM Lateralization Profile[1] for Natufian Individuals from Cluster Analysis

Cluster	Individual	Site	Sex	PM	LD	TM	DT	CC	FL	TB	AN	BB
							MSM Site[2]					
1	H91	Mallaha	F	100	—	—	100	100	—	—	—	—
1	H11	Hayonim Cave	M	100	100	100	100	100	100	—	—	—
1	10261	El Wad	F	100	100	100	100	100	—	—	—	100
1	H20	Hayonim Cave	M	100	100	100	100	—	100	—	100	100
1	10255	El Wad	F	80	100	100	100	100	100	—	—	—
1	10253	El Wad	F	80	100	100	125	100	100	100	100	100
2	10256	El Wad	F	100	100	100	100	100	100	100	100	100
3	H43	Nahal Oren	M	—	—	—	—	—	—	—	100	—
3	H29	Hayonim Cave	M	100	100	100	100	100	—	100	100	100
3	H25	Hayonim Cave	M	60	100	100	100	100	100	—	—	—
3	H27	Hayonim Cave	M	—	—	—	—	—	100	—	—	—
3	H8	Nahal Oren	M	100	100	167	100	100	100	—	100	100
3	10349	Kebara	M	100	100	100	100	100	100	100	100	125
3	10351	Kebara	M	—	—	—	—	—	—	100	100	80
4	10353	Kebara	F	—	—	—	100	100	100	100	100	—
5	H9	Hayonim Cave	F	—	—	—	—	—	—	—	—	—
5	H33	Hayonim Cave	M	—	—	—	100	100	—	—	100	100
5	H19	Hayonim Cave	M	100	—	100	100	100	100	100	100	100
5	H93	Mallaha	F	100	—	—	100	100	—	—	—	—

[1]Computed by $(X_L/X_R) \times 100$, including individuals where paired right and left side MSM scores exist.
[2]PM = pectorialis major, LD = latissimus dorsi, TM = teres major, DT = deltoideus, CC = coracobrachialis, FL = flexors, TB = triceps brachii, AN = anconeus, BB = biceps brachii.

several of the individuals (Peterson 1994). KB 10349 and KB 10351 demonstrate pronounced right-side lateralization. Again, by virtue of ages assigned to some of the Hayonim Cave individuals, I can make the tentative case that high scores do not reflect older individuals. HC 25 and 27 fall in the twenty-five- to thirty-year-old age category, while HC H29 is described as seventeen to eighteen (Belfer-Cohen 1988).

Pectoralis major and teres major are responsible for pulling the arm across the chest (adduction), and high scores for these MSM characterize the mixed-sex cluster 5. At the pectoralis site, all individuals exhibited grooving to varying degrees. For some females and males, the pattern is bilaterally expressed on right and left humeri, suggesting that both arms are involved in the movements responsible for such pronounced MSM. Again, age does not appear to be a definitive factor in cluster membership since the two individuals from Hayonim Cave are relatively young. Specimen H9 is estimated to be sixteen to nineteen years old and HC H19 twenty to twenty-five years old (Belfer-Cohen 1988). What I can say with some certainty is that these males and females were involved in some activity that subjected their pectoralis major and teres major muscles to high levels of stress. If a single activity is assumed responsible for the pattern, then at least one strenuous activity was shared by males and females.

The unique individual composing cluster 2 has pronounced teres major muscle attachments on both her right and her left humeri. As previously described, this muscle functions to pull the arm across the chest, pull raised arms down, and/or pull the trunk toward arms when the arms are fixed. The teres major muscle and most of her other muscles were developed bilaterally. In this respect, the female in cluster 2 shares some important attributes with cluster 5's members.

Cluster 4 also contains a single female individual with clear bilateral symmetry in terms of overall MSM profile. Unfortunately, only right-side scores are available for the high-scoring latissimus dorsi that set this individual apart.

When we look at the Natufian cluster results in total, we can speak alternatively of similarities and distinctions with reference to sex-specific patterning. Two of the groups (clusters 1 and 5) consist of mixed-sex groups. This pattern indicates that some activity patterns (specific tasks, level of work intensity, or both) were shared by males and females. Three of the clusters that are composed of either mixed sex (5) or single females (2, 4) are characterized by pronounced muscle activity involving adducting the arm, most typically expressed bilaterally. This stands in stark contrast to the large all-male cluster (3), which is characterized by high scores in muscles responsible for extending the forearm that tend to be expressed unilaterally. The majority of Natufian males exhibit this pattern, suggesting a widespread pattern of activity that is distinctively male.

Given that the preliminary cluster results suggest that some important sexually dimorphic patterning occurs in the Natufian musculature, the rank order profile of the twenty-one MSM scores provides some additional information. Males and females have similar MSM rank order profiles with respect to many muscles active in lifting, for example, pectoralis major, deltoideus, biceps brachii, and so on (Table 5.2). However, there are also muscles that stand out as quite different in rankings between males and females. Among those muscles, coracobrachialis and teres major have higher rankings among females, while triceps brachii and anconeus rank higher in males.

Functionally, these rankings reinforce the notion that habitual activities involving adduction contribute more substantially to many females' workloads (and

Table 5.2   Rank Order of Natufian Mean MSM Scores by Sex and Largest Differences in Rank Order Scores by Sex

Female Mean MSM (n)	Ranking	MSM Site	Male Mean MSM (n)	Ranking
1.07 (14)	16	Subclavius	1.25 (24)	18
2.50 (11)	2	Costoclavicular ligament	2.58 (18)	2
1.54 (11)	8	Trapezoid ligament	1.60 (19)	9
2.00 (12)	6	Conoid ligament	1.83 (23)	6
1.33 (3)	10	Trapezius	1.45 (10)	12.5[1]
1.37 (4)	9	Subscapularis	1.70 (10)	7
0.62 (4)	21	Supraspinatus	1.17 (6)	19.5[1]
2.89 (9)	1	Pectoralis major	2.90 (21)	1
1.17 (6)	13	Latissimus dorsi	1.36 (14)	15
2.19 (8)	4	Teres major	1.67 (15)	8
2.14 (14)	5	Deltoideus	2.43 (23)	3
1.18 (14)	12	Coracobrachialis	1.17 (20)	19.5[1]
1.11 (9)	14	Extensors, common origin	1.45 (19)	12.5[1]
0.91 (11)	19	Flexors, common origin	1.30 (20)	17
0.75 (2)	20	Infraspinatus	0.94 (8)	21
1.91 (11)	7	Brachialis	2.02 (20)	5
0.94 (9)	17.5[1]	Triceps brachii	1.57 (20)	10
1.10 (10)	15	Anconeus	1.53 (18)	11
2.22 (9)	3	Biceps brachii	2.24 (20)	4
0.94 (8)	17.5[1]	Supinator	1.32 (11)	16
1.19 (8)	11	Pronator quadratus	1.41 (11)	14

Rank Score			
F	M	MSM Site	Rank Difference
12	19.5	Coracobrachialis	7.5
17.5	10	Triceps brachii[2]	7.5
4	8	Teres major	4
15	11	Anconeus[2]	4

[1]Two-way tie in mean scores.
[2]Significant differences.

Table 5.3   Significant Differences in Natufian Mean MSM Scores by Sex: Results of Mann–Whitney Tests

MSM Site	U	Z-statistic	Two-tail p[1]	Comment
Deltoid	99.5	−2.05	.04	Male score higher
Flexors	58.5	−2.22	.03	Male score higher
Triceps brachii	30.0	−2.98	.002	Male score higher
Anconeus	47.0	−2.16	.03	Male score higher
Supinator	23.5	−1.89	.05	Male score higher

[1]Corrected for ties.

some males'), while for males, the same can be said of activities involving forearm extension.

The MSM rank sum comparisons between males and females strengthen the patterning previously observed (Table 5.3). The significant differences listed are those that measured at or below the $p \leq 0.05$ level. All five of the significant differences—deltoideus, triceps brachii, anconeus, supinator, and the flexors—involve higher mean scores among males. These muscles represent actions of forearm and hand flexion and extension as well as forward movement of the arm with the lower arm twisting the palm forward (clockwise).

Interpreting Natufian MSM

I propose that the Natufian males in cluster 3 were participating in habitual hunting activities, preparatory target practice, as well as ritual displays of prowess and/or reenactments (Peterson 1998). Hunting with an atlatl or a spear requires an overhand throwing motion. In the case of the atlatl, the length of the arm's fulcrum is extended with the throwing stick to enhance projectile distance and penetration. Throwing motions involve displacement of the forearm resulting from medial rotation of the arm at the shoulder, shoulder and arm extension, and sudden shifts from forearm supination to pronation (turning inward).

Muscle signatures on bone associated with hunting are among the most often studied. Among Pleistocene hunter-gatherers in central India, Kennedy (1983) correlates robusticity at the supinator, anconeus, and triceps brachii muscle insertion sites specifically with supination and hyperextension of the arm. Dutour's (1986) study of Neolithic Saharan populations describes the involvement of the wrist and hand flexors. Obviously, pronounced unilateral expression in this musculature would also be an important association between the muscle pattern and throwing. These same patterns are repeated among the Natufian males in cluster 3. The rank order differences and the significant differences in mean scores between males and females lend further support to the notion that a subset of Natufian males were habitually throwing things. And I presume that some of this throwing activity involved weapons used in hunting, a well-documented archaeological activity.

The Natufians appear to correspond to a pattern, derived from both ethnographic data and evolutionary ecology perspectives, wherein males are responsible for killing medium to large game animals. A logical correlate of the MSM data is, perhaps, more controversial. The results indicate that hand- or atlatl-delivered technology continued to play an important role in hunting well into the Epipaleolithic and that the bow and arrow did not replace technologies involving overhand throwing.

The question as to what weapon system or systems were being used in the Levant of southwestern Asia at this time has confounded archaeologists for some time. The material culture associated with hunting technologies is equivocal because of the vagaries of preservation and tool function assignments. Despite the lack of definitive data—examples of stone tools hafted in arrow shafts—many researchers have nonetheless argued that circumstantial evidence points to Natufian utilization of bow-and-arrow technology (Anderson-Gerfaud 1983; Olszewski 1993; Valla 1987b). Cumulatively, the artifactual data indicate that Natufian craftspeople had the requisite skills in lithic manufacture, woodworking, and hafting technology necessary for archery. But the results of the MSM analysis suggest that Natufian hunters used these skills to continue hunting using hand- or atlatl-delivered weapons (Peterson 1998).

What about other activity patterns, specifically those involving female labor and mixed labor groups? Teres major and latissimus dorsi are two muscles that stand out in several lines of analysis for contributing substantially to the female MSM profile. Teres major assists latissimus dorsi in drawing the humerus down and backward, when previously raised. Importantly, when the arm is in a fixed position, these muscles work in tandem, along with pectoralis major, to draw the trunk forward (Gray 1974).

High teres major scores have been associated with grinding maize using a mano and metate among proto- and prehistoric Native American women (Hawkey 1988; Hooton 1930). Reciprocal grinding is one activity that involves repetitive, habitual adduction. However, querns and hand stones occur only sporadically in Natufian ground stone assemblages. Only Hayonim Cave and Mallaha, among the sites examined in this study, had reciprocal grinding equipment (Wright 1992). The mean MSM differences between sexes for latissimus dorsi and teres major become more pronounced moving from the total Natufian sample to just those individuals from Hayonim Cave and Mallaha (Peterson 1994). Interestingly, both males in cluster 5 are from Hayonim Cave. This raises the possibility that a shared male and female activity spectrum may have been present at certain sites where plant-processing equipment was found.

However, the elevated latissimus dorsi and teres major scores are maintained at all sites, not just those with reciprocal grinding tools. This suggests the very real possibility that other tasks involving the synergistic combination of muscles involved in adduction may contribute to the pattern. The archaeological record provides some direction in our exploration for other habitual, labor-intensive activities that might be contributing to this pattern.

Bone tools described as spatulas, spatulates, or *lissoirs* are also fairly common during the Natufian. They are widely distributed among Natufian sites, including Kebara, El Wad, Mallaha, and Hayonim Cave (Campana 1989; Garrod and Bate 1937; Perrot 1966; Turville-Petre 1932). These objects have been described as skin or hide rubbers. The tools have broad, uniformly curved wear surfaces that are well polished and have faint striations (Campana 1989). Experimental evidence demonstrates that axial strokes applying compressive force against a yielding surface such as animal skin or leather produces similar wear (Campana 1989). Ethnographic accounts of the tools and motions associated with hide processing suggest that it might be a second activity resulting in the bilateral MSM patterning among some Natufian males and females.

To add nuance to the interpretations, we should make final note of the individuals in cluster I, both males and females that had musculature patterns that were described as "middle of the road." The lack of distinctive patterning in MSM for this group can point us in a number of directions. They may represent an MSM baseline in a cultural system where tasks and activity level among many adult men and women are quite similar. The village reconstruction presented in Figure 5.11 is an attempt to put a "human face" on some of the MSM interpretations.

Figure 5.11   Daily life at a hypothetical Natufian village.

In short, the analyses support a weakly developed sexual division of labor during the Natufian in terms of habitual activities. Each of these hypotheses can clearly benefit from further delineation and testing. Research looking at cross-sectional geometry of Natufian long bones from the southern Levant is currently under way (Sally Casey, personal communication). Casey's results represent a welcome addition to integrative occupational reconstructions.

Neolithic Results

Analysis

Investigations of Neolithic MSM patterns yield additional occupational insights. In general, current evidence warrants fewer specific activity reconstructions yet suggests profound changes in workload and new patterns of synergistic muscle activity. Comparisons with the Natufian prove especially interesting. In general, small sample size haunts many interpretations and limits analyses. To reiterate, without cluster analysis to compare individual MSM profiles, we begin by separating the sexes and looking for differences between sex groups. Thus, the potential danger for imposing labor scenarios that overemphasize sexual dichotomies looms larger here.

Our initial impression when glancing at the MSM rankings for the Neolithic seems to indicate a number of MSM scores with wide rank disparities (Table 5.4). However, several large rank differences result from samples that are too small to be meaningful (trapezius, pectoralis minor, and subscapularis). More meaningful rank order differences occur for three MSM sites: latissimus dorsi, costoclavicular ligament, and extensors. Males have higher rank order and mean scores for the first two MSM. Only the extensors correspond to higher rank and mean score for Neolithic females. Interestingly, the pattern of higher score for female extensors and higher score for male latissimus dorsi represents a substantial inversion of the Natufian profile.

Looking at the overall symmetry profile, we can characterize the Neolithic sample as fairly symmetrical (Table 5.5). This pattern in the generalized population is particularly noticeable in the forearm elements. And even among the MSM on the clavicle and humerus, the Neolithic males exhibit more pronounced symmetry than the Natufian predecessors (Peterson 1994). The muscles earmarked from rank score comparisons clearly reflect this trend. Males and females were completely symmetrical (scoring the same for right and left in every instance when paired skeletal elements were present) for latissimus dorsi and the extensors. Only the costoclavicular ligament indicates some right-side asymmetry, particularly pronounced among the males.

Generally, then, we can characterize the sexual patterns of lateralization as converging during the Neolithic. The habitual activity spectrum for both Ne-

Table 5.4   Rank Order of Neolithic Mean MSM Scores by Sex and Largest Differences in Rank Order Scores by Sex

Female Mean MSM (n)	Ranking	MSM Site	Male Mean MSM (n)	Ranking
0.93 (7)	20	Subclavius	1.35 (13)	17
1.92 (6)	7[1]	Costoclavicular ligament	2.64 (11)	3
1.92 (6)	7[1]	Trapezoid ligament	1.83 (9)	8
1.67 (6)	10	Conoid ligament	1.72 (9)	11
2.00 (2)	4	Trapezius	1.50 (3)	14.5[2]
1.25 (2)	16.5[2]	Subscapularis	1.75 (2)	10
1.25 (2)	16.5[2]	Supraspinatus	1.50 (2)	14.5[2]
2.42 (6)	2	Pectoralis major	2.86 (7)	1
1.50 (3)	13	Latissimus dorsi	2.10 (5)	7
1.92 (6)	7[1]	Teres major	2.36 (7)	6
2.43 (7)	1	Deltoideus	2.50 (10)	4
1.00 (7)	18.5[2]	Coracobrachialis	1.17 (9)	20
1.30 (5)	15	Extensors, common origin	1.25 (6)	19
1.00 (5)	18.5[2]	Flexors, common origin	1.30 (5)	18
0.75 (2)	21	Infraspinatus	1.00 (2)	21
1.94 (9)	5	Brachialis	2.38 (13)	5
1.36 (7)	14	Triceps brachii	1.44 (8)	16
1.72 (9)	9	Anconeus	1.70 (10)	12
2.33 (9)	3	Biceps brachii	2.71 (12)	2
1.62 (8)	11	Supinator	1.62 (12)	13
1.58 (6)	12	Pronator quadratus	1.83 (12)	9

Rank Score			
F	M	MSM Site	Rank Difference
13	7	Latissimus dorsi	6
7	3	Costoclavicular ligament	4
15	19	Extensors, common origin	4

[1]Three-way tie in mean scores.
[2]Two-way tie in mean scores.

olithic males and Neolithic females involved a number of strongly bilateral tasks. For females, this appears to be a continuation of the bilateral symmetry present during the earlier period. For the Neolithic males, the trend represents a more significant reorientation. Specifically, the bilateral MSM in Neolithic males is a noticeable deviation from the strongly unilateral muscle development among the proposed Natufian hunters. The earliest farming lifestyle, then, entailed greater changes in the habitual activities of males compared to that of females.

Turning to the examination of significant differences in rank sum comparisons, another conversion between males and females is found (Table 5.6). Here one muscle, brachialis, scored significantly higher for Neolithic males. Brachialis

Table 5.5   Aggregate MSM Lateralization[1] Profile for the Neolithic

MSM Site	Male (n)		Female (n)	
Clavicle				
Subclavis	92	(10)	100	(5)
Costoclavicular ligament	72	(8)	95	(5)
Trapezoid ligament	90	(2)	80	(4)
Conoid ligament	100	(6)	100	(4)
Scapula				
Trapezius	100	(3)	100	(1)
Humerus				
Subscapularis	100	(1)	—	—
Supraspinatus	100	(1)	—	—
Pectoralis major	109	(6)	100	(1)
Latissimus dorsi	100	(5)	100	(1)
Teres major	100	(6)	100	(1)
Deltoideus	102	(8)	100	(2)
Coracobrachialis	112	(8)	100	(2)
Extensors	100	(4)	100	(3)
Flexors	100	(3)	100	(2)
Infraspinatus	100	(1)	—	—
Ulna				
Brachialis	100	(10)	100	(5)
Triceps brachii	100	(6)	100	(4)
Anconeus	100	(10)	100	(5)
Radius				
Biceps brachii	100	(8)	92	(3)
Supinator	100	(8)	100	(2)
Pronator quadratus	100	(5)	100	(3)

[1]Computed by $(X_L/X_R) \times 100$, including those individuals where paired and left MSM scores exist.

flexes the forearm. Importantly, brachialis was used bilaterally in Neolithic males as well as females.

To summarize, brachialis and latissimus dorsi are both high-ranking MSM sites in males, and they are bilaterally expressed. In various synergistic combinations, they account for forearm flexion, supination/turning arm inward/hand turning clockwise, and adduction/drawing arm down.

The costoclavicular ligament is the only MSM that these analyses point to that constitutes a unilateral muscle development. Again, it is more strongly developed

Table 5.6   Significant Differences in Neolithic Mean MSM Scores by Sex: Results of Mann–Whitney Tests

MSM Site	U	Z-statistic	Two-tail p[1]	Comment
Brachialis	25.0	−2.41	.01	Male score higher

[1]Corrected for ties.

in males. The costoclavicular ligament limits elevation of the clavicle, as in shrugging motions.

The common origin site of the extensors ranks higher among Neolithic females than males. The MSM are bilaterally expressed. The extensor muscles, which have a common origin site on the lateral epicondyle of the humerus, are associated with elbow extension, abducting (raising) the wrist, and dorsal extension of the hand.

Interpreting Neolithic MSM

Accounting for the effects of age is a concern with the Neolithic skeletal sample. Are the differences between Natufian and Neolithic males related to different age profiles? Are the patterns between Neolithic sex groups a result of comparing an older male population to a younger female population? Unfortunately, we cannot address these concerns with much empirical certainty at present. Belfer-Cohen, who has examined a number of Natufian and PPN samples, states that individuals over age forty-five are relatively scarce (0–15 percent) in both groups (Belfer-Cohen, cited in Hershkovitz and Gopher 1990:23). If the samples included here broadly reflect Belfer-Cohen's composite description, perhaps age differentials between time periods are not problematic.

Within the Neolithic sample used here, I was able to compile age information beyond a generic "adult" characterization for ten individuals from either published accounts, field notes, or personal observations. Belfer-Cohen's age profile impression is substantiated here, as only one individual falls into the forty- to fifty-year range. All five of the females fall in a range between seventeen and thirty-five. Three of the five males fall into this same range (assuming that "middle aged" fits here). The last two male individuals fall into a thirty-five- to fifty-year category. This may hint at some age-based discrepancies in the Neolithic MSM sample. But a majority of the individuals still fall into the "adult of indeterminate age" category.

It appears that both male and female musculature is associated with some habitual, bilateral activities during the Neolithic. The male muscle group we have identified corresponds to the motions of flexion, supination, and adduction. Neolithic females experience increased stress at the extensor sites. What are the tasks or sets of tasks suggested by these synergistic muscle groups?

That the male MSM patterns are related to hunting seems unlikely. Spear, atlatl, or bow and arrow use all involve profound asymmetrical stresses. One arm of an archer is for drawing back the bowstring and the other for bracing and extending the bow itself (Dutour 1986; Hawkey 1988; Stirland 1993). Dutour (1986) describes how the MSM of the right arm would reflect flexion at the elbow and external rotation of the shoulder. The MSM of the left arm would respond to extension at the elbow with compressive force, specifically at triceps brachii. Hawkey and Merbs (1995) further associate trapezius and latissimus dorsi with the action of drawing the right shoulder back during flexion. Neither this pattern nor ones associated with overhand throwing are in evidence during the Neolithic.

We can turn to the archaeological records for suggestions of activity realms that required increased labor inputs during the Neolithic. Since our sample includes sites with known chronological and geographic variation, these observations are often general in nature. While we can be confident that an increasing reliance on domestic cereals placed new demands on the time and energy of Neolithic groups, it is premature to assume the exact types and intensity of these new agricultural chores.

Nonetheless, there is evidence—in the form of large ground and bifacially chipped implements described variously as hoes, picks, celts, adzes, and axes—that tilling the soil and/or timbering were increasingly important tasks. Tilling is defined broadly here to signify a range of activities from preparing the soil for planting (turning, harrowing, and so on) to the actual planting and covering of seeds. Timbering refers to land clearance activities to open areas for agriculture, procure fuel, acquire building materials, and chop wood.

Tilling the soil with hoe, digging stick, or adze would require repetitive downward blows involving forearm flexion and extension. The extensors, triceps brachii, and anconeus are important in conjunction with latissimus dorsi to make downward strikes or blows (Dutour 1986; Hawkey 1988). The trapezius is also brought into play with the pulling action associated with hoeing (Hawkey 1988). While both arms are typically involved in the downward stroke and pulling motions, Bridges (1985) expects an increase in bilateral asymmetry to be present if these activities comprise an increasing component of the habitual activity spectrum, as they are often performed emphasizing one arm. Timbering and chopping wood involve the same sort of repetitive striking motions and use some of the new tool forms previously described. Without the benefit of experimental kinesiological studies focused at differentiating the two activities, I think it is safe to assume a broadly similar muscle development pattern from the two types of activities.

Village size increases from Natufian through PPNB times (Bar-Yosef and Belfer-Cohen 1991). With this, the demand for wooden beams, fuel for lime plaster production, and fuel for cooking and heating increased. Cutting and hauling timber and hauling fuel would have involved relatively more effort during the Neolithic than the Natufian.

One of the muscle patterns discerned from the Neolithic analysis supports male participation in timbering or tilling. Among the high rank-order MSM for Neolithic males are latissimus dorsi (involved in making downward striking blows). Using ax, hoe, or adze involves substantial forearm flexion that may also account for the significant-difference MSM rank sums between males and females for brachialis. While bilateral activities contributed substantially to the MSM development of Neolithic males, there are still some assymetries present (Table 5.5). Tilling and timbering are tasks consistent with this pattern.

Lifting and hauling loads can involve any number of synergistic muscle combinations, depending on the container technology and habitual posture used. Options to be considered include tumpline, backpack, travois, balancing load on head, and so on. Supporting heavy loads and lifting using the arms involve pectoralis major and biceps brachii specifically. These muscles rank quite high for Neolithic males and females. Balancing the weight of a load may encourage the muscle stress to be exerted bilaterally as well. Perhaps an increase in burden bearing is contributing to the muscle profile of Neolithic males and females.

In the realm of plant food processing, the PPN is characterized by another jump in the proportion of sites containing ground stone artifacts, now more than 70 percent for both PPNA and PPNB (Wright 1993). The number of querns (reciprocal grinding tools) relative to mortars also increases (Wright 1993). The changing nature of the grinding tools indicates widespread use of a more intensive and efficient processing technology, now typically involving multiple processes of dehusking, crushing, and grinding. The labor output involved in producing ground cereals through these three stages increases.

Pronounced teres major and latissimus dorsi MSM have been linked to reciprocal grinding among puebloan groups in the American Southwest (Hawkey 1988). To reiterate, the teres major assists latissimus dorsi in drawing the humerus down and backward, when previously raised. Increases through time in mean scores and rankings for both MSM during the Neolithic sample are apparent among males rather than females. This raises the possibility that males were significantly involved in plant-processing activities.

Weaving is another activity that involves repetitive, bilateral motions of the upper body. Textile evidence suggests that both flax and palm fibers were being manufactured by the PPN (Bar-Yosef, Schick, and Alon 1993). Ground looms are the norm for this part of the world (Barber 1991). Ground looms would be used in a seated or kneeling position, with arms repeatedly flexed and extended as one tamps down the weft. Weaving activities have not been substantially discussed in the MSM literature, nor are there parallels between weaving motions and the types of musculature described in the physiology literature.

Activities involved in the mining, preparation, and production of clay and ceramics may well contribute to the musculature patterns of Pottery Neolithic individuals. But since the vast majority of our Neolithic sample comes from pre-pottery contexts, it is not productive to explore those activities in detail.

The Neolithic MSM point toward an activity regime that was increasingly bilateral in terms of upper-body musculature. This constitutes a substantial change among the males in comparison with their Natufian counterparts. Fewer mean score differences seem to indicate that activity levels for males and females are more roughly similar than before. In conjunction with the archaeological record, changes in male musculature may be related to increased burden-bearing, agricultural, or cereal-processing activities. Overall, the activities associated with the adoption of farming apparently brought greater changes to the musculature of males than to that of females. Despite the coarse-grained nature of the Neolithic findings, I find it valuable to attempt to reconstruct a possible village labor scenario based on these results (Figure 5.12).

Figure 5.12   Daily life at a hypothetical Neolithic village.

Early Bronze I Results

Analysis

The data from EBI Bab edh-Dhra provide a glimpse into a fully established, mixed agropastoral community. By this time, the cumulative effects of technological, economic, and social changes from the Pottery Neolithic and Chalcolithic periods are fully expressed. The MSM patterns for the EBI inhabitants at Bab edh-Dhra indicate major shifts in both task spectrum and the sexual organization of those activities.

For the EBI sample, the clustering procedure used a total of nineteen individuals who were examined with respect to nine MSM. The choice of which MSM to use in the clustering algorithm reflects the requirements of the complete data matrix. And while there is substantial overlap between the sets of MSM used in the Natufian and EBI cluster analysis, they are not identical. The specific MSM sites used in the EBI analysis were pectoralis major, latissimus dorsi, teres major, deltoideus, brachialis, triceps brachii, anconeus, biceps brachii, and supinator.

In the EBI case, the distance coefficient and the agglomeration schedule suggested a two-cluster solution best described by the inherent variability in the MSM scores (Figure 5.13). Most noticeably, the majority of individuals ($n = 14$) fall into cluster 2, characterized by relatively low scores in each of the nine MSM categories. Males are slightly overrepresented, making up 71 percent of cluster 2 compared to 63 percent of the total sample. Conversely, more females than expected occur in cluster 1

Cluster	Individuals (Inventory #, Site, Sex)		
Cluster 1	A100 E1	M	
Moderately low MSM mean scores	A110 NE4	F	
Low variability	C11 3	M	
High pectoralis major, latissimus	A110 NE3	F	
dorsi, & biceps brachii	G4 2	F	
Cluster 2	A107 S3	M	
Low MSM mean scores	A80 S4	M	
Moderate variability	A80 S50	F	
	A107 S6	M	
	C11 2	F	
	A87 SE1	M	
	A110 SE1	M	
	A102 S2	M	
	A79 N2	M	
	A102 E3	M	
	G4 1	F	
	A110 NW1	M	
	G4 4	M	
	A111 E2	F	

Figure 5.13   Two-cluster solution for Early Bronze I sample.

(60 percent of cluster compared to 37 percent of sample). The three females and two males in the cluster exhibit consistently higher mean MSM scores, with pectoralis major, latissimus dorsi, and biceps brachii being most distinctive.

Those high-scoring muscles indicate more substantial muscle load demands on both the upper arm and the forearm for the members of cluster I. Looking at the patterns of lateralization between right- and left-side MSM for the five individuals revealed an interesting pattern (Table 5.7). Four of the five members of the cluster exhibited pronounced unilateral symmetry with reference to a number of MSM scores. Only one individual (female G4-2) was bilaterally symmetrical.

Before advancing any explanations, let's discuss the other novel MSM results from the rank order and rank sum comparison analyses that build on these cluster results (Table 5.8). In both number and kind, the EBI rank order and mean comparison patterns are also distinctive. In well over half the MSM sites, female scores exceed those of males. This is a novel pattern. Our initial impression is of a pronounced increase in female workload relative to males.

The number of rank order differences increases relative to both the Natufian and the Neolithic. Looking at those MSM with reasonable sample size, seven have rank order differences of four or greater. Four of the seven indicate higher MSM scores for females. The females' MSM that outrank those of males tend to focus on the muscles and ligaments inserting on the clavicle, acting to stabilize it and the scapula. The remaining three higher male mean rankings center on rotator cuff muscles, indicative of activities involving stability and mobility in the shoulder.

A consistent pattern of right-side asymmetry is expressed among the high female rank scores for the trapezoid, costoclavicular, and conoid ligaments. At the individual level, right-side asymmetry was also noted among the distinctive MSM defining cluster I. Unilateral MSM expression may well suggest an increase in tasks that require significantly higher muscle demands on one arm.

Pectoralis major is the only muscle exhibiting sexually dimorphic rank order differences that also stood out as a definitive criterion in clustering. Cluster I, composed of three females and two males, had relatively high pectoralis major MSM scores that were also unilaterally expressed.

During the Natufian and Neolithic, significant mean score differences always consisted of higher male scores. In this respect, the EBI MSM profile is again unique. The three MSM that have significant differences between sex groups are characterized by higher female scores: conoid ligament, brachialis, and biceps brachii (Table 5.9). Biceps brachii and brachialis are the two principal flexors of the forearm. Scores for forearm extensors, triceps brachii, and anconeus are also higher in females, although not significantly so. The conoid ligament limits rotation of the scapula and had previously been discussed in the context of rank order differences.

Interestingly, both biceps brachii and brachialis exhibit some left-side asymmetry among a reasonable sample of paired ulnae and radii. This deviation from the

Table 5.7 MSM Lateralization Profile[1] for Early Bronze I Individuals from Cluster Analysis

Cluster	Individual	Site	Sex	MSM Site[2]								
				PM	LD	TM	DT	BR	TB	AN	BB	SP
1	A100 E1	Bab edh-Dhra	M	100	100	100	83	100	100	100	—	—
1	A110 NE4	Bab edh-Dhra	F	100	100	100	100	75	100	100	67	100
1	C11 3	Bab edh-Dhra	M	100	100	100	100	75	100	100	67	100
1	A110 NE3	Bab edh-Dhra	F	80	100	100	80	100	100	100	—	67
1	G4 2	Bab edh-Dhra	F	100	100	100	100	100	—	100	100	100
2	A107 S3	Bab edh-Dhra	M	100	100	100	100	100	100	50	100	100
2	A80 S4	Bab edh-Dhra	M	100	100	100	100	—	—	—	100	100
2	A80 S50	Bab edh-Dhra	F	100	100	100	100	100	100	100	100	100
2	A107 S6	Bab edh-Dhra	M	100	100	100	100	100	100	100	100	100
2	C11 2	Bab edh-Dhra	F	100	100	100	100	100	100	100	100	100
2	A87 SE1	Bab edh-Dhra	M	100	100	100	100	100	100	100	—	—
2	A110 SE1	Bab edh-Dhra	M	100	100	100	100	100	100	100	67	100
2	A102 S2	Bab edh-Dhra	M	100	100	100	100	100	—	100	—	—
2	A79 N2	Bab edh-Dhra	M	—	—	—	100	—	—	—	100	100
2	A102 E3	Bab edh-Dhra	M	—	—	—	100	—	—	—	100	100
2	G4 1	Bab edh-Dhra	F	75	100	100	100	100	100	100	100	100
2	A110 NW1	Bab edh-Dhra	M	100	100	100	100	—	—	—	—	100
2	G4 4	Bab edh-Dhra	M	100	100	100	100	—	—	100	100	100
2	A111 E2	Bab edh-Dhra	F	100	100	100	100	100	100	100	100	100

[1]Computed by $(X_L/X_R) \times 100$, including only individuals where paired right and left MSM scores exist.
[2]PM = pectoralis major, LD = latissimus dorsi, TM = teres major, DT = deltoideus, BR = brachialis, TB = triceps brachii, AN = anconeus, BB = biceps brachii, SP = supinator.

Table 5.8   Rank Order of Early Bronze I Mean MSM Scores by Sex and Largest Differences in Rank Order Scores by Sex

Female Mean MSM (n)	Ranking	MSM Site	Male Mean MSM (n)	Ranking
1.30 (5)	9	Subclavius	0.89 (9)	15
2.17 (6)	1	Costoclavicular ligament	1.37 (4)	7
1.37 (4)	8	Trapezoid ligament	0.87 (8)	16
2.10 (5)	2	Conoid ligament	1.39 (9)	6
0.67 (3)	17	Trapezius	1.08 (6)	11
1.00 (7)	13.5[1]	Subscapularis	1.67 (6)	3.5[1]
0.64 (7)	19	Supraspinatus	0.75 (6)	20.5[1]
1.77 (11)	5	Pectoralis major	1.89 (14)	1
1.15 (10)	11	Latissimus dorsi	1.11 (14)	9
1.40 (10)	7	Teres major	1.25 (14)	8
1.71 (12)	6	Deltoideus	1.67 (18)	3.5[1]
0.58 (12)	20	Coracobrachialis	0.79 (17)	18
0.94 (9)	15	Extensors, common origin	0.90 (10)	14
0.64 (7)	18	Flexors, common origin	0.82 (11)	17
0.50 (7)	21	Infraspinatus	0.75 (8)	20.5[1]
1.91 (11)	3	Brachialis	1.53 (16)	5
1.06 (9)	12	Triceps brachii	1.04 (14)	12
1.00 (11)	13.5[1]	Anconeus	0.94 (16)	13
1.87 (4)	4	Biceps brachii	1.71 (14)	2
0.87 (12)	16	Supinator	0.77 (13)	19
1.20 (10)	10	Pronator quadratus	1.09 (11)	10

Rank Score			
F	M	MSM Site	Rank Difference
13.5	3.5	Subscapularis	10
8	16	Trapezoid ligament	8
17	11	Trapezius	6
9	15	Subclavius	6
1	7	Costoclavicular ligament	6
2	6	Conoid ligament[2]	4
5	1	Pectoralis major	4

[1]Two-way tie in mean score.
[2]Significant differences.

Table 5.9   Significant Differences in Early Bronze I Mean MSM Scores by Sex: Results of Mann–Whitney Tests

MSM Site	U	Z-statistic	Two-tail p[1]	Comment
Conoid ligament	7.0	−2.14	.03	Female score higher
Brachialis	42.0	−2.42	.01	Female score higher
Biceps brachii	69.5	−2.26	.02	Female score higher

[1]Corrected for ties.

right-side asymmetry among the shoulder-stabilizing ligaments suggests that multiple habitual activities are contributing to the female MSM profile. Contemplating the male musculature, one finds that higher scores are retained on a few of the humeral muscles, as in the case of coracobrachialis and pectoralis major. In addition, the wrist/hand flexors are nominally higher among males. And finally, as suggested by the rank ordering, all four of the rotator cuff muscles are higher among men.

Interpreting EBI Results

When I first examined the summary statistics from the EBI sample, I was startled by the results. Because of the pronounced changes between the EBI results and the earlier periods, I worried that my observations were skewed. My fears were enhanced because this was the first collection that I had examined. To allay these concerns, I returned to the Smithsonian Institution and reanalyzed the collection. After I reexamined each element, the original Bab edh-Dhra results remained unchanged. Not only were my initial results confirmed, but this consistency also speaks well for the standard visual reference system employed.

The majority of age information for Bab edh-Dhra individuals specifies only "adult" (eighteen or more years). In the search for correspondence between the museum's database records and published accounts, only two cases could be identified with more specific age data: one female (A80S50) at eighteen to twenty years and one male (A80S4) at fifty or more years (Ortner 1981). Without finer-grained age data, these analyses proceed under the assumption that male and female subsets are roughly equivalent in age. From the evidence for deteriorating health status during the EBI (Smith 1989b), one might expect that women would be more susceptible to health problems leading to decreased life expectancy given the rigors of pregnancy, childbirth, and lactation. It is at precisely this time, however, that we find female scores escalating relative to those of males. So, even if females have a shorter life expectancy, they are spending those years hard at work.

By EBI times, researchers agree that animal husbandry had become a very important aspect of village economy. This population is our first glimpse into a lifestyle from antiquity that made use of wool and milk secondary products as well. Might it be that some of the novel patterns relate to these changes?

Dairying tasks can be jointly described as labor intensive and habitual. Animals must be milked once, sometimes twice, a day. To increase the shelf life of fresh milk, those without the benefit of refrigeration rely on processing the liquid into a variety of semisolid forms that are less prone to spoil and more amenable to storage. Processing can also enhance the human "digestibility" of dairy products. Potential EBI milk-processing tools come in the form of elongated, almost cigar-shaped ceramic containers that were closed except for narrow central neck openings. Lug rings at either end suggest that the containers were probably suspended and rocked back and forth to churn the liquid into a semisolid state. Both milking and milk processing would have entailed significant forearm flexion and extension. An examination of the cervical vertebrae for signs of loading identified as "milker's neck" (Olin et al. 1982) might provide additional verification in future studies.

Hoeing, digging, and chopping tasks also require substantial flexion and extension of the forearm (Dutour 1986; Hawkey 1988) often accompanied by repetitive downward blows (latissimus dorsi). High rank order values for the clavicle and scapula stabilizers may be relevant here as well. When forearm flexion is carried out vigorously, with arms extended horizontally, flexion and extension would involve rotation at the sternoclavicular joint (costoclavicular ligament) with the shoulder being drawn forward (trapezoid ligament) and back (conoid ligament).

High biceps brachii scores have also been associated with burden bearing, as have deltoideus scores (Weineck 1986). The EBI case is the only one in which mean female deltoideus MSM surpass those of males. Latissimus dorsi and teres major muscles have been linked to grinding motions (Hawkey 1988). Both of these are elevated in the EBI women's sample as well. Whether the result of dairying, cultivation, or other activities, the left-side lateralization of the high-scoring biceps brachii and brachialis muscles is curious.

Lastly, there is evidence to suggest that specialized production of both ceramic vessels and Canaanean flint blades might begin in the EBI. Could the individuals in cluster 1 represent specialists? Flint knapping might encourage the unilateral musculature expressed by the individuals in this cluster, and so too could some aspects of ceramic production, for example, if one arm is used primarily to rotate the *tournette*, the slow wheel on which the vessels were built. If so, then we must entertain the notion that both females and males had specialized economic roles during the EBI. More specific age data for the individuals in cluster 1 would also be helpful, as the increased robusticity may also potentially be indicative of an older group.

What about the males? In arid environments, moving herds daily for water and fodder is a necessity during at least some seasons. Herding would seem to require, in itself, little in the way of habitual upper-body muscle demands. We can hypothesize, on the basis of the analyses presented here, that males may have had primary responsibility for these herding tasks. This might explain the reductions in male musculature relative to females. Herders, then, would be included in the low-muscle cluster 2, which, it should be noted, includes some females as well. Added insights may well be revealed from analyses that examine the structural changes and MSM patterns among the lower limbs.

The EBI results suggest fundamental shifts in the types of activities making up the daily, habitual task spectrum as well as the sexual organization of those tasks. A vision of what EBI village life may have resembled is offered in Figure 5.14. These

Figure 5.14   Daily life at a hypothetical Early Bronze I village.

results and interpretations become more meaningful when we examine them in light of long-term, diachronic change.

Diachronic Results

Analysis

So far, I have focused on reconstructing activities and workloads within specific time periods. I characterized the Natufian as a period when sexual divisions of labor were weakly developed, specifically with reference to male throwing and female processing. With the rise of farming, the workloads and, perhaps, activities of males and females converge in significant ways. Males experience more profound labor reorganization during the Neolithic, and distinctive sexual dichotomies appear far less frequently. Labor patterns undergo a second significant transformation during the EBI. Females are participating differentially in activities involving the muscles of the upper body, often unilaterally. The habitual activities of males demonstrate less upper-body involvement. During the EBI, a pattern of more sexually divided labor seems warranted.

Analyses that examine those same three time periods simultaneously lead us into a discussion of changing labor patterns through time. The strongest pattern that comes to light comparing the three time periods simultaneously is the repeated low ranking of the EBI sample from Bab edh-Dhra (Table 5.10). Significant differences

Table 5.10 Results from Multiple Mean Comparisons for Three Time Periods: Significant Differences in Kruskal–Wallis Tests[1]

Sex	MSM Site	Pattern
Females	Pectoralis major[2]	Early Bronze significantly lower than Natufian
	Coracobrachialis[2]	Early Bronze significantly lower than Natufian
	Deltoid[2]	Early Bronze significantly lower than Neolithic
	Supinator	Early Bronze significantly lower than Neolithic
Males	Pectoralis major[2]	Early Bronze significantly lower than Natufian
	Coracobrachialis	Early Bronze significantly lower than Natufian
	Extensors[2]	Early Bronze significantly lower than Natufian
	Triceps brachii[2]	Early Bronze significantly lower than Natufian
	Latissimus dorsi[2]	Early Bronze significantly lower than Neolithic
	Teres major[2]	Early Bronze and Natufian significantly lower than Neolithic
	Trapezoid ligament[2]	Early Bronze significantly lower than Natufian and Neolithic
	Deltoid[2]	Early Bronze significantly lower than Natufian and Neolithic
	Brachialis[2]	Early Bronze significantly lower than Natufian and Neolithic
	Anconeus[2]	Early Bronze significantly lower than Natufian and Neolithic
	Biceps brachii[2]	Early Bronze significantly lower than Natufian and Neolithic
	Supinator[2]	Early Bronze significantly lower than Natufian and Neolithic

[1] Significance value of 0.05 or less.
[2] Indicate groups deemed significant using the parametric one-way Scheffé test (at value of 0.05 or less).

in rank sums reflect cases of lower EBI scores relative to the Natufian, the Neolithic, or sometimes both. The low scoring pattern for EBI is consistent among both males and females, although the number of differences among the members of the male group is considerably higher. This higher number of low EBI male scores corresponds to the inverted sex patterning noted earlier in the chapter. These results suggest a significant realignment of activity and labor between the EBI and the two earlier periods, which is particularly pronounced for males.

Comparing the three periods simultaneously, only a single MSM was identified as significantly different in both rank sum and mean between the Natufian and Neolithic periods: The Neolithic males outscore the Natufian for teres major (Table 5.10). Somewhat concerned that the large discrepancies between EBI scores and the earlier periods were swamping out variability between Natufian and Neolithic samples, I ran a series of Mann–Whitney comparisons looking at individual MSM between those of just the Natufian and Neolithic periods.

A total of four cases of significant differences occurred, three of them when comparing male samples (latissimus dorsi, teres major, and anconeus) and one comparing females (supinator) (Table 5.11). In every case, the Neolithic rank sums were significantly larger than the Natufian. These results suggest that the Neolithic lifestyles were slightly more strenuous than the previous Natufian in terms of habitual upper-body activities and that males may have borne these increases slightly more than females.

Interpreting Diachronic Patterns

Let's first try to understand the depressed scores among such a variety of MSM for the EBI period. The overall impression from reports and conversations with analysts who have worked with the material from Bab edh-Dhra indicated that the EBI adults had little pronounced musculature and were generally quite "gracile" (Ortner 1982 and personal communication; Smith 1989b). Physical anthropologists have argued (see Chapters 2 and 4) that EBI populations were negatively affected by nutritional and health problems not evident in the preceding periods. So

Table 5.11   Results from Mean Comparisons for Natufian and Neolithic Periods: Significant Differences in Mann–Whitney Tests[1]

Sex	MSM Site	Pattern
Females	Supinator[2]	Natufian significantly lower than Neolithic
Males	Latissimus dorsi[2]	Natufian significantly lower than Neolithic
	Teres major	Natufian significantly lower than Neolithic
	Anconeus[2]	Natufian significantly lower than Neolithic

[1]Significance value of 0.05 or less.
[2]Indicate groups deemed significant using the parametric t-test (at value of 0.05 or less).

perhaps the EBI adults are not living as long and not acquiring the MSM robusticity of their Natufian and Neolithic predecessors. However, published accounts give exactly the opposite impression—making this conclusion unlikely. Ortner (1981:132) tells us that despite high subadult mortality, many adults at Bab edh-Dhra lived beyond fifty years. In contrast, Belfer-Cohen states that individuals over age forty-five are relatively scarce in both Natufian and PPN samples (Belfer-Cohen, cited in Hershkovitz and Gopher 1990:23). If our samples for the MSM study broadly reflect these composite descriptions, age-related discrepancies cannot be the main variable in the decreased MSM robusticity for the EBI sample.

Another potential scenario depicts EBI populations as unable to maintain the same levels of activity during the lifetimes because of poor health. This is more difficult to assess. But we should bear this factor in mind and be cautious not to interpret the diachronic MSM results exclusively through a lens of activity change.

Looking to activity patterns, several developments in the realm of animal husbandry are worth revisiting. Evidence from statuary suggests that from the Chalcolithic onward, donkeys were used as a form of transport (Epstein 1985). Figurines of donkeys, laden with large jars or baskets, have been found in ossuary caves at Giv'atayim and Azor (Kaplan 1969, 1976). Laden donkey figurines continue to occur in Early Bronze Age contexts (Epstein 1985). Donkey remains were found in excavation areas across the site at Bab edh-Dhra (Finnegan 1981). This development has implications for activities of burden bearing. Transporting water and fuel to villages, fodder to animals, agricultural products from the fields, and a variety of industrial raw materials to the site are just a few of the tasks that would have been facilitated by animal transport.

The diminution in both EBI male and female MSM relative to other time periods may attest to the introduction of ancillary transport by donkeys, the quintessential "beast of burden." Given the ubiquitous role of burden bearing and variety of contexts in which it would be performed, it seems likely that the use of donkeys may well cause decreases in muscles among both men and women. MSM from some of the major weight-bearing muscles of the arm support this. Biceps brachii MSM for EBI males, for example, rank significantly lower than those for both Natufian and Neolithic males (Table 5.10). Pectoralis major MSM scores are lower also in both males and females relative to the Natufian counterparts.

The trend over time in the southern Levant is for the increased use of domestic animals and their secondary products in the subsistence realm. The pastoral part of the economy in this part of the world typically involves moving animals almost constantly in search of water and fodder. Herding activities are likely to have increased during the EBI. Herding activities in and of themselves do not require much upper-body muscle use, particularly in conjunction with donkeys/mules as porters. Some segment of the community at Bab edh-Dhra was likely involved in an activity that, based on ethnographic examples, took them away from the village and village-based tasks on a daily basis (if not for longer periods of time). A decrease in upper-body musculature could be expected among individuals or groups spending substantial periods of time herding in that this activity would remove them from the labor pool concerned with other more strenuous agropastoral tasks. Perhaps male involvement in herding helps us understand the substantial decreases in EBI males' MSM relative not only to EBI females but also to males from the earlier time periods.

And what of those other agropastoral tasks? Daily village life at Bab edh-Dhra clearly involved cultivation and processing of domestic products, the construction of houses and facilities, and so on (Rast 1981; Schaub and Rast 1984). While much of the primary land clearance may have been accomplished by earlier peoples, preparing the soil for planting, attending to crops while growing, harvesting, and processing would still be regular, laborious parts of the agriculture cycle. Milking and churning activities can be added to the list of habitual activities. If a pattern of high female participation in these activities is posited, this might explain the increases in EBI robusticity relative to males as well as continuity with women from other agricultural contexts.

Turning to the two-period diachronic comparison of Natufian and Neolithic individuals, a pattern of continuity through time among females is evident. Only the supinator, responsible for twisting and extending the elbow, shows a significantly higher MSM rank sum during the Neolithic. Increases in forearm extension involving the supinator are mirrored in a higher rank ordering through time as well. The pattern has a parallel in Neolithic males, although it is less pronounced. Male mean MSM scores and rank ordering for supinator indicate an increase in activities involving this muscle. This convergence suggests either shared activities or similar synergistic muscle demands that focus increasingly on forearm extension among both males and females.

For males, the latissimus dorsi, teres major, and anconeus MSM rank sums are all significantly higher during the Neolithic. Interestingly, teres major MSM not only becomes more sexually dimorphic through time but also shows an inversion in rank ordering. During the Natufian, females had a higher MSM mean score and higher ranking for the muscle. During the Neolithic, males' teres major indicates a higher mean score and a slightly higher ranking. This suggests a major functional shift between periods between some activity(ies) involving teres major. Males used it more, females less. Latissimus dorsi also shows a big jump in rank order through time, moving from fifteenth during the Natufian to seventh during the Neolithic. No similar diachronic pattern for females appears.

Functionally, latissimus dorsi and teres major work synergistically to pull a raised arm down, while anconeus is an important muscle in forearm extension.

Synergistically, these muscles can be associated with either reciprocal grinding (Hawkey 1988; Hooton 1930), tree felling (Dutour 1986; Hawkey 1988), and/or soil preparation (Bridges 1985). However, to assign increased male activity levels to any one of these realms is premature without some corroborating evidence.

In contrast with the profound diachronic changes noted for the EBI, there are fewer pronounced differences between the single-sex groups during the Natufian and Neolithic. In all cases, they involve higher MSM rank sums, presumably reflecting higher activity levels among the early farming groups. This supports the hypothesis that there is an increase in activity level involving upper-body musculature during the first agricultural periods.

Conclusion

During the Natufian, some sexually dimorphic MSM patterns occur. Divergent patterns of symmetry, rank order differences, and cluster composition all suggest that an overhand throwing motion, presumably related to hunting with spear or atlatl, is one activity reconstruction that explains the MSM profile for a subset of Natufian males. Female musculature is more tentatively linked with processing tasks involving bilateral motions. Importantly, many strenuous activities or similarly rigorous activities were shared by the sexes. Similarities in rank order profiles as well as mixed-sex clusters attest to this. I would characterize the sexual division of labor as weakly developed at this time, focusing on a limited subset of daily tasks.

There is evidence for some reorganization of daily labor patterns during the Neolithic. Male musculature becomes increasingly bilateral and resembles the female pattern in this respect. The number of muscles showing significant differences between the sexes decreases. These MSM monitors of muscle use suggest unprecedented convergence in activity and activity level between the sexes. At the same time, activity levels for males and females increase during the Neolithic. This certainly suggests that emergent farming economies meant more strenuous workloads for adults compared to their hunter-gatherer predecessors. Similarly, the MSM analysis suggests that these tasks were shared, with neither males nor females being responsible for the majority of the new labor inputs. Male musculature appears to undergo more profound changes than that of females, which can be characterized as fundamentally more stable. So I conclude that male labor experiences more significant shifts over the course of this first stage in the transition to domestication economies. Overall, there is little available data that suggest significant differences in workload or activity between males and females during the Neolithic.

The EBI period at Bab edh-Dhra can be characterized as entailing major shifts in MSM patterns. Female activity levels increase notably compared to males as examined through a number of indices. Male musculature diminishes substantially compared to males from the previous time periods. I tentatively explain these inversions by suggesting that EBI males and females had distinctive yet complementary tasks related to increased dependence on domestic animals and their products. These tasks place very different demands on the upper-body musculature of males and females (herding vs. processing, respectively). The evidence for declining health status, while apparently not resulting in shorter life expectancy, should be borne in mind when interpreting depressed EBI MSM scores. At EBI Bab edh-Dhra, the portrait of a more sexually segregated labor system, with females experiencing greater muscle demands in the upper body, emerged.

The primary goal of this chapter was to establish the basis for some preliminary conclusions about activity levels and sexual divisions of labor. Different levels of success were attained, depending on the nature of the skeletal sample as well as the degree to which certain tasks have been discussed and outlined in the anatomical/kinesiological literature. These data provide the evidence for the empirically based, working model of changing labor organization and sexual task divisions developed in Chapter 6.

Modeling Changing Labor Scenarios 6

I N THE FIRST chapter of this book, I made the point that social changes must
be viewed as essential variables in our understanding of the development of
agricultural economies. Choosing to focus on the social organization of labor led me inexorably to questions of sexual divisions of labor. Many influential
anthropologists, historians, and feminists have assumed not only that sexual divisions of work were universal in the past but also that tasks were always highly
segregated into mutually exclusive realms of "men's work" and "women's work."
Another common assumption has been that, while not entirely static, the organization of daily tasks marched inexorably toward more dichotomous, polarized
systems through time. Recently, these assumptions have been challenged by researchers who view the social dynamics of prehistoric labor systems as worthy of
systematic investigation (cf. Dobres 1995; Gero 1991; Kehoe 1990, 1991; Nelson 1997).

This new perspective has been relatively slow arriving among researchers working in the southern Levant (for an exception, see Crabtree 1991). The musculoskeletal stress marker (MSM) study provides data relevant to both of these assumptions. For example, the current evidence does not support strongly defined
sexual divisions of labor during either the Natufian (12,000–10,000 B.P.) or the
Neolithic (10,000–7,700 B.P.) period. Neither does labor grow more segregated
by sex through time in any linear or progressive fashion. In fact, the Neolithic data
point to male and female workloads and, possibly, activities that are more broadly
similar than they were in either the earlier or the later period.

Having challenged these popular labor preconceptions, in this chapter I en-
large the scope of the MSM analyses by examining them within a variety of contexts. First, how do the MSM results correspond with previous studies of occupational reconstructions in the Near East? In general, I find that the MSM results

lend credence to several occupational trends identified by previous bioarchaeologists. Occupational conclusions are further elaborated by examining them in spatial contexts. Specifically, how do postulated workloads and activity patterns "play out" within sites and settlement regions? And what does this tell us about the social context of sexual labor patterns? Finally, I ask, How do the patterns of sexual labor derived here correspond with extant models for labor changes across the foraging-to-farming spectrum? Models are drawn from archaeological, ethnographic, and feminist literature. An engendered view of changes in labor organization spanning the development of mixed farming economies in the southern Levant is offered in conclusion.

Integrating MSM with Previous Activity Reconstructions

The study of humeral robusticity by Smith, Bloom, and Berkowitz (1984) concluded that the Natufian sample had consistently higher cortical thickness values than the Middle Bronze, Roman/Byzantine, and Early Arab period samples. Furthermore, the Natufian sample exhibited the most sexual dimorphism. Two conclusions derived from these results are directly supported by the MSM analysis in the previous chapter: (1) that the pronounced robusticity patterns among Natufian males could be influenced by hunting activities and that furthermore (2) males as a group tended to experience more change in upper-body musculature through time than females as they moved from hunting and gathering to agropastoral settings.

Rathbun's diachronic examination of stature changes through time led him to conclude that female stature tended to be more stable compared to male stature in a sample drawn from sites in Iran and Iraq (Rathbun 1984:146–147). Second, within-period comparisons between males and females indicated significant differences for all periods except the Neolithic (Rathbun 1984:146). While activity is only one variable influencing stature, it is interesting to note the close parallels between these findings and the MSM results with respect to convergence of male and female activity indicators between southern Levantine Natufian and Neolithic samples. One might posit an emergent regional pattern for the Near East with reference to Neolithic labor patterns.

So if male labor is being substantially reoriented during the Neolithic, what types of activities are becoming habitual? The limited evidence for degenerative joint change in Pre-Pottery Neolithic (PPN) skeletons suggests that at least some males from Basta and 'Ain Ghazal are participating in tasks that place significant demands on upper-body musculature. And I argue that while bilateral MSM development increases, some unilateral activities were still habitual among males. Tilling the soil, timbering, and burden bearing are activity realms that were increasingly demanding of human time and muscle power.

Abu Hureyra's skeletal series provided Molleson the opportunity to explore activity among Neolithic inhabitants along the Euphrates River. She integrates observations from the lower limbs, spine, and teeth to advance specific activity reconstruction that I did not attempt using MSM alone. Specifically, she characterizes a group of Neolithic individuals, primarily women, as having spent significant periods of time kneeling on the ground, probably to grind grain on querns (Molleson 2000). I feel comfortable extrapolating from Molleson's well-supported behavioral reconstruction that at least some of the muscle patterning among the Neolithic MSM drawn from Jordan and Palestine is likely derived from grinding activities as well. But even with the finer-grained activity conclusions that Molleson achieves with an integrated skeletal examination, the issue of the degree to which remaining tasks were sexually divided remains ambiguous. Based on the joint findings of Molleson and the MSM analysis, it is still premature to suggest any strictly dichotomous division of specific activities. Male and female scores are increasingly converging, and male MSM profiles show increases in bilateral symmetry of muscle use. If women are, in fact, the primary grinders, then men are doing some similar activity(ies) with both hands that influences similar muscles of the upper body.

Discussion of Early Bronze skeletal evidence with reference to activity and occupation is quite limited. Ortner (1981, 1982) does describe four individuals at Bab edh-Dhra with head wounds that seem to have been caused by ax blows. The three for whom sex could be determined are male. The cluster analysis performed as part of the MSM study does not, however, suggest any subset of individuals who may have participated differentially in activities involving weapon use.

In general, the extant occupational literature for Near Eastern groups supports and strengthens many of the conclusions derived from MSM analysis.

Activities and Performance Spaces

For each time period, the intra- and intersite spatial issues that could be addressed vary considerably. This eclecticism is due to the influences of variation in spatial data available (both detailed architectural information and artifact patterning) and the level and specificity at which activity inferences could be made using the MSM data. Yet even with preliminary occupational results, the door is opened onto a plethora of questions regarding the social use of space. As the following discussion illustrates, there remains much potential for examining the connections between activity, space, and sex composition of groups. Drawing "sexual maps" of domestic spaces and territories is a logical outgrowth of activity reconstructions.

Concern for reconstructing the spatial context of male and female activities requires differentiating tasks as much as possible. Furthermore, tacit assumptions about social groupings and mobility patterns need to be examined critically. Given the incipient stage of gender research in Near Eastern prehistoric settings (Crabtree 1991; Peterson 2000; Wright 1996), it is no surprise that there is still much work to be done.

Natufian

Three of the Natufian sites that produced skeletal data for the MSM study have architectural elements that have been interpreted as dwellings: Hayonim Cave, Nahal Oren, and Mallaha (for illustrations of dwellings, see Stekelis and Yizraely 1963; Valla 1991). Dwellings are circular, oval, or semicircular without internal partitions or subdivisions. Hearth areas are typically present. This generic description corresponds with architectural remnants from other Natufian sites (Edwards 1991). Lack of interior spatial divisions suggests that neither the people nor the activities within those spaces were conceptually separate at this stage, although more detailed studies of artifact distributions may eventually challenge that position.

Dwellings have been interpreted as both nuclear family (Henry 1989; Olszewski 1991) and individual residences (Valla 1991). Valla bases his interpretation on floor space estimates from 'Ain Mallaha. Given the small interior spaces enclosed, Valla's suggestion that these represent single-person dwellings remains a reasonable alternative hypothesis. This point is important because it frees us from some of the "mental baggage" associated with viewing the nuclear family as the only practical or viable organizational option in terms of either residential or productive groupings. Residential groups and productive activities need not have revolved exclusively around monogamous pairs. At this preliminary stage of social organization reconstruction, I would not rule out polygynous arrangements, particularly since 83 percent of societies permit it (Pasternak, Ember, and Ember 1997).

Unfortunately, artifacts within Natufian dwellings shed little additional light on the composition of residential units. Given the results of the MSM analysis, hunting tools might be the best candidates for defining engendered space. Yet the conundrum of multifunctionality plagues us. Microlithic tools were probably used as projectile elements (Byrd 1989b; Olszewski 1993). However, microliths have also been found hafted in sickle handles (Edwards 1991; Garrod and Bate 1937), and some have the typical gloss or luster associated with harvesting cereals (Anderson 1991). Other patterns of surface wear suggest use on softer, fleshy materials (Anderson 1991). So the presence of microlithic tools alone is not a sound inferential basis for defining activities related to hunting.

With these caveats in mind, spatial reconstructions focusing on larger, regional scales hold some promise (sensu Jackson 1991). Are there extractive camps that, by virtue of location, assemblages, features, and so on, suggest a narrow range of activities—either hunting or plant processing? Or are assemblages at limited activity sites more heterogeneous? By framing these questions, we begin to think about how male and female tasks and mobility patterns are interdigitated on the larger landscape. The distribution of bedrock-grinding installations and the composition of associated deposits may provide interesting results in this context (Peterson 1999).

Neolithic

Overall, there is a wealth of architectural data from the Neolithic periods. There is also substantial variation in domestic architecture over time and space in the southern Levant. Currently, I have difficulty envisioning males and females in these spaces. The coarse-grained results from the MSM analysis as well as the very real potential that male and female activity spheres overlapped considerably contribute to this lack of vision. However, important insights can still be gained by thinking about these spaces in light of the occupational patterning.

Pre-Pottery Neolithic A (PPNA) oval structures are related morphologically to their Natufian predecessors at Hatoula and Netiv Hagdud (Bar-Yosef, Gopher, et al. 1992; Lechevallier et al. 1990). Interior hearths are present. Ground stone artifacts, often slabs with cup holes, are typical finds within dwellings. At Netiv Hagdud, features identified as storage bins and silos are present in one dwelling (Bar-Yosef, Gopher, et al. 1992). Based on published estimates, the dwellings at Netiv Hagdud fall into two size groups, the smaller ranging from 8 to 12 square meters, the larger from 25 to 30 square meters. The smaller dwellings, like their Natufian counterparts, may have housed single individuals.

Several well-reported structures from Netiv Hagdud bear further description. Locus 55 is a small, circular dwelling, approximately 4 to 5 meters in diameter. Both in situ grinding equipment and a cache of hunting tools (shaft straighteners and whetstones) were found inside (Bar-Yosef, Gopher, et al. 1992). If we momentarily entertain the possibility that this small structure was the residence for one person, it is reasonable to suggest that its resident was involved in both processing and hunting activities. Recalling the convergence of MSM patterns between Neolithic males and females, one interpretation might be that the structure is a spatial and artifactual correlate of significant task overlap or task sharing.

Locus 8 at Netiv Hagdud is also worth discussing. It is a large (30 square meters), oval structure with an interior partition wall—a unique feature during the PPNA. In the smaller front room, closest to the entrance, is a slab with four cup-hole mortars. In the back room, there are two slabs with four or five cup-hole mortars. More than seventy pounding implements were also found in locus 8. The excavators recognized a higher degree of functional specificity here but do not speculate further. The three in situ slabs imply that three or more individuals could have been working simultaneously in or around the structure. Communal grinding areas in other parts of the world have been variously interpreted as evidence for extended family social structures (Jacobs 1979; Kramer 1979), matrilocal postmarital residence (James 1994), and increased formalization of food preparation as a ritual activity by groups crosscutting family lines (Mobley-Tanaka 1997). Whatever the case, the reconstructions imply a social structure removed from the self-sufficient, spatially discrete nuclear family. Based on MSM alone, I am not prepared to assign grinding to one sex or the other. So these may be single- or mixed-sex task groups. But given Molleson's conclusions, the suggestion of communal, female grinding spaces should be considered.

Among the Pre-Pottery Neolithic B (PPNB) sites sampled a number of significant spatial changes are evident. Rectangular residential architecture becomes the norm, and generally interior spaces increase in size. Careful stratigraphic excavations have revealed multiple remodeling episodes within structures at 'Ain Ghazal and Abou Gosh (Banning and Byrd 1987; Braun 1997; Lechevallier 1978). Remodeling consisted of subdividing interior spaces by additions of interior partition walls or piers, adding rooms, and demolishing rooms. While the partitions or piers offer some additional spatial differentiation, neither physical nor visual access was likely restricted (Banning and Byrd 1987).

Banning and Byrd (1987) argued convincingly that remodeling was a response to the changing needs of the household unit as members were added or dispersed. Even the largest remodeled structures, however, likely accommodated small families. There are no indications of large, agglutinated structures or compounds like those in the northern Levant (Akkermans, Fokken, and Waterbolk 1981; Watson 1979a). During the final PPNB phase at 'Ain Ghazal, in fact, dwellings decrease in average size (Rollefson, Simmons, and Kafafi 1992). It is reasonable to assume that PPNB households are now composed of small families, made up presumably of an adult male, an adult female, their unmarried children, and perhaps an elderly or unattached relative in some cases.

The search for domestic activity areas and the types of analyses that such areas require have not been high priorities. Excavations at Yiftahel suggest that houses were flanked by outdoor, unwalled courtyard areas (Garfinkel 1987b). A storage silo and an installation interpreted as a quern platform were excavated. Areas to process and cook animals, prepare plaster, and manufacture beads are also described (Garfinkel 1987a, 1987b). Single grinding tools and installations at other sites are often reported indoors or near dwelling entrances (Banning and

Byrd 1987; Lechevallier 1978; Moore 2000). Unlike Netiv Hagdud'o locus 8, no PPNB communal grinding areas have been described.

Extrapolating from the range of activities associated with a single house at Yiftahel and demographic estimates that suggest small co-residential groups, perhaps individual households are responsible for organizing and carrying out a number of productive tasks. The willingness to remodel existing space seems to reflect a new social cohesion in the household unit. This new sense of household identity may well arise jointly from a more fully sedentary settlement pattern and new subsistence pursuits that foster cooperation and dependence at the family level.

The MSM data suggest that both men and women are working harder to meet the demands of the new agricultural lifestyle. However, the musculature patterns do not indicate that clearly distinctive activities or more dichotomous patterns of sexual labor are a necessary corollary of this increase in household cohesion and identity. So while males and females are working harder, their MSM profiles are best summarized as converging. The source of this convergence is still unclear, plagued as we are by the possibility of equifinality. Similar MSM patterns between the sexes could result from activities that are sexually divided yet use the same suites of synergistic muscles. Alternatively, we can envision members of a tightly knit family sharing in a number of habitual tasks as a solution to the demands of a new, labor-intensive agricultural lifestyle. And despite evidence for cohesive family structures, particularly demanding tasks may have involved community-wide participation.

Early Bronze I

At Bab edh-Dhra and other EBI sites, there are several substantial problems in discussing domestic spatial patterning. This is extremely unfortunate given the interesting and profound reversals in sexual patterning derived from the MSM analysis.

Early Bronze I sites typically constitute the basal levels of large tell sites with extensive later occupations built over them. The combined limitations imposed by the logistics of stratigraphic excavation through these upper levels and destruction during rebuilding in antiquity often mean that complete EBI house plans are absent. At Ai, a site near Jericho, no complete EBI house plans were uncovered in eight years of excavation. From several wall fragments, excavators concluded that one house consisted of a single room with no internal divisions, covering about 13.5 square meters (Callaway 1993). The architectural descriptions of EBI houses from Bab edh-Dhra state that they consisted of single square or rectangular rooms made of mud brick. Some are plastered on the interior and exterior. Beam, thatch, and mud roofs are inferred. In general, the EBI houses sound very similar to their Neolithic predecessors. No interior features or in situ artifacts were described in the preliminary report (Schaub and Rast 1984).

There is, however, one recently excavated EBI site that has provided a wealth of information regarding domestic structures. Yiftahel, the same site that provided PPN skeletal material, also has EBI strata. Fortunately for the archaeologists, the site is relatively shallow with limited disruption or burial by later occupation. Interestingly, the houses vary considerably from the sketchy descriptions provided from Ai and Bab edh-Dhra. The primary difference is that they are not rectangular but curvilinear in outline. Braun describes the houses with their two long parallel walls and curved ends as "sausage shaped" (Braun 1997). The houses have stone foundations, hard-packed dirt floors, and superstructures presumably fashioned from mud brick.

There are pronounced size differences between structures. Some are small, almost circular, and lack internal partitions. Others are larger and divided into two or more rooms. Neither features nor artifacts suggested that functional differences explained the size differences (Braun 1997). Braun entertains a range of hypotheses to account for the size differences. Perhaps the larger houses were the homes of extended families. Perhaps they belonged to families of privileged status or wealth. Perhaps some were temporary housing for groups with some special status, for example, menstruating women or adolescents undergoing initiation. The author sees no empirical basis for choosing between these options at this time (Braun 1997).

At Yiftahel, carefully excavated and well-published inventories of house floors yield enticing data for reconstructing gendered spaces. Grinding installations suggest areas where grain was processed. A copper needle wedged between paving stones suggests an area where textiles or fibers were worked. Perhaps most interesting is the lack of hearths in and around houses. Cooking appears to have been an outdoor activity, possibly done in groups (Braun 1997). So even when small houses suggest that some families were living in nuclear groups, everyday tasks such as cooking supper may still have been carried out by larger groups. This serves as a caution against the danger of reconstructing labor organization on the basis of house dimensions alone. Small houses are often equated with nuclear families. Nuclear families are then equated with rigid sex-typed work patterns. Using Yiftahel as an example, this is clearly an oversimplification. This recurring problem has beset interpretations of prehistoric social organization for too long.

Models of Sexual Labor Changes with the Advent of Farming

Generalizations about the labor changes associated with the advent of farming appear in a number of places, most notably archaeological, feminist, and anthropological writings. These are not, of course, mutually exclusive sources. Before putting forward a preliminary model of sexual labor changes in the southern Levant, a critical review and analysis of these sources is a necessary step—not only to avoid previous mistakes but also to build on past insights.

Archaeology's Contributions

Several archaeologists have made general predictive statements about how sexual labor divisions were structured during the Natufian and how they were likely to be influenced by increased reliance on agricultural and domestic animal products (see Chapter 2). One potential value of the archaeological perspective is the time depth necessary to chart long-term changes and reliance on data typically ignored by other fields of inquiry. Unfortunately, much of the potential has yet to be actualized. Most typically, the social implications of the transition are ignored altogether (Blumler and Byrne 1990; Layton, Foley, and Williams 1991; McCorriston and Hole 1991; Redding 1989; Rindos 1980). Other researchers suggest that farming brought about increasing segregation in men's and women's labor, without considering the possible variations in farming labor patterns that are demonstrated in the ethnographic literature (Bar-Yosef 1995; Bar-Yosef and Belfer-Cohen 1992). Essentialist assumptions about appropriate, often biologically based activity spheres for males and females are still being perpetrated (Henry 1989).

Flannery (1972) published an influential study modeling prehistoric social organization using examples from the Near East and Mesoamerica. Sexual labor divisions were among the organizational variables he explored. Natufian sexual labor patterns were viewed as a continuum with preceding, more mobile hunter-gatherers, with adult male and female task groups sharply divided (Flannery 1972:25, 31). Groups of men hunted ungulates, and groups of women (and children) collected and processed plants and an increasingly "broad spectrum" of resources (Flannery 1969:79, 1972). The fundamental productive units were single-sex task groups organized to allow for communal use of resources among extended, loosely knit households. Task groups of either sex often operated at some distance from base camps (Flannery 1972).

Flannery describes massive social restructuring with the advent of farming and herding economies. The transition from circular to rectangular houses is the spatial manifestation of this reorganization. Flannery suggests that large nuclear or extended families living together perform daily tasks. He assumes that women's tasks include sewing, cooking, and food processing represented by awls, needles, grinding tools, and cooking pots (Flannery 1972:34, 39). Men make other stone tools and hunt using spear points, arrowheads, and microlithic projectiles (Flannery 1972:39). But who is doing all of the agricultural work? Who is clearing the land? Tilling the soil? Building the more substantial structures? Processing the tons of lime needed for floor and wall plaster? These questions are never directly addressed.

Overall, Flannery's point that social reorganization will accompany the development of agricultural economies is sound, and his point that architecture could reflect these changes is insightful. And the author should be credited for considering social variables and sexual labor when articulating his model some thirty years ago. His sexual labor reconstructions are, nonetheless, simplistic in terms of the ethnographic spectrum, and the omission of an engendered discussion of the organization of agricultural work makes it of limited utility to us.

Henry's synthesis of the terminal Pleistocene in the southern Levant attempts to define the social organization of the Natufians. Unfortunately, his gender reconstructions are severely limited by a lack of empirical verification, "naturalistic" and unsupported assumptions about the spheres of male and female activities, and a series of logical inconsistencies. Henry's discussion of sexual labor provides more fodder for critique than patterns useful in comparing with current data sets. He ultimately is conflicted between a biologically deterministic and narrow view of women's capacities and the necessities of the hunting and gathering lifestyle his own data suggest.

Henry begins by projecting the nuclear family structure even further back into the Epipaleolithic (Henry 1989:213). Henry infers this organization from the fact that both "men's" and "women's" artifacts are present in domestic dwellings. Artifacts are assigned to women if they represent items used at "base camps" and to men if they relate to activities carried out away from "base camps." The assumption is that women operate primarily within a domestic sphere and men in a public sphere. Henry is echoing early anthropological accounts that relate men:public sphere and women:domestic sphere (Evans-Pritchard 1961), but there is consensus that this polarization is analytically unproductive and empirically unjustified, particularly in nonstate contexts (Collier and Yanagisako 1987; Leacock 1978; Rapp 1975; Rosaldo 1980).

Women manufactured and used stone bowls, ostrich egg bottles, and hideworking tools (Henry 1989:202). Women used these while they stayed at the base camp overseeing the economic and social needs of the community (Henry 1989:209). Male objects are flint tools (Henry 1989:202). Men are viewed as more mobile, engaging in long-distance hunting, trading, and warfare that keep them away from camps for long periods. This stereotyped vision ignores an extensive corpus of data documenting female participation in hunting (Estioko-Griffin and Griffin 1981; Brumbach and Jarvenpa 1997), an array of child care options (Hewlett 1991), and the maintenance of mobility through periods of pregnancy and child rearing (Turnbull 1981). It implies a narrow, biologically deterministic view of women's capabilities.

A scenario that tethers women to base camps is inconsistent with Henry's own settlement and subsistence reconstructions. Base camps are seen as strategically located at the margins of lowland and upland zones. Lowland zones provided cereal grass and gazelle resources, uplands acorns and deer. Henry speaks about "the important role that women must have played in procuring . . . the plant resources on which the Natufian adaptive system depended" (Henry 1989:208). With men hunting and women collecting plant foods, does this not imply similar upland-to-lowland movements for both groups? Basalt, obsidian, greenstone, and marine shell are the usual exotic materials found at Natufian sites. However, these materials do not occur in very large quantities, nor are they typically obtained from great distances (Bar-Yosef 1983; Olszewski 1991). Down-the-line trade seems like a reasonable option to direct procurement and is one invoked for Chalcolithic and EBI nonlocal materials (Esse 1989). Whatever system one invokes, it requires neither long-distance time-consuming trade forays nor male exclusivity in maintaining them. And lastly, Henry ties high male mobility to warfare. Defensive structures are present in the Near Eastern archaeological record. But most so-called defensive structures substantially postdate the Natufian, for example, Early Bronze II (EBII) fortifications at Bab edh-Dhra (Rast and Schaub 1981) and enclosure walls at Tel es-Sawwan and Hacilar (Mellaart 1975). The wall and tower at Neolithic Jericho may be an early example of defensive architecture (Kenyon 1981), although their function is still debated (Bar-Yosef 1986) and they postdate the Natufian. Examinations of Natufian skeletal material betray an amazing lack of traumatic evidence. It is not clear what evidence Henry invokes to sustain the inference of male participation in warfare during the Natufian. An alternative scenario could just as easily be advanced, rooted more firmly in the data, that portrays men and women sharing important and complementary subsistence tasks with no great difference in mobility.

Crabtree (1991) synthesized many of these same concerns with Flannery's and Henry's models in her exploration of the role that women played in the transition from foraging to farming in the southern Levant. She makes the valid point that despite the profound lack of direct, empirical evidence on the sexual division of labor, past reconstructions of Natufian lifeways have not been gender neutral.

First, Crabtree attacks Flannery's notion that the emergence of a broad-spectrum diet during the Natufian served as a foundation for sexual labor patterns in the post-Pleistocene. She cites faunal literature that challenges the notion of increased resource base diversity during the Natufian (Edwards 1989; Henry 1989, in Crabtree 1991). She takes on Henry next, challenging his social organizational reconstructions on the basis of existing archaeological data. There is, for example, no clear link between occupation and tools or equipment found in burials (Crabtree 1991). She concludes that there is no real archaeological evidence to support a male hunting/female gathering scenario for the Natufian. She advances the alternative hypothesis, based on ethnographic parallels in the Great Basin, that communal mixed-sex collecting and hunting groups may have been the most effective social solution to take advantage of the short window of opportunity for collecting many important resources (Crabtree 1991).

I have argued that the task of killing gazelle may well have fallen primarily to males during the Natufian, although the data could support other habitual activities. So, males did play an active role in hunting. However, the corollary assumption that relegates females to domestic settings, exercising limited mobility and involved primarily in gathering and processing plants, does not follow logically given our current understanding of Natufian subsistence practices.

For example, recent faunal studies of the Hayonim Cave material suggests that small game made up a significant proportion of the Natufian meat diet. Hare and bird species in particular increase in frequency (Stiner, Munro, and Surovell 2000). The authors argue that these species, while more difficult to capture, were more highly resilient to increased predation by larger human groups (Stiner et al. 2000:56). Given the MSM patterns of male hunting using atlatl (presumably for gazelle), in conjunction with ethnographic examples of small-package protein acquisition by women and children, it no longer seems wise to attribute plant food collection and processing as the sole activity areas for Natufian females.

What about the Neolithic and EBI periods? Here the archaeological discussion of sexual labor divisions has been more limited. The archaeologists who have made statements pertaining to social organization among the first agricultural groups agree that significant restructuring of labor patterns occurred (Bar-Yosef 1995; Crabtree 1991; Flannery 1972). And there have been suggestions that women, with their assumed familiarity of the growth and propagation of wild plants, should be considered as likely innovators of agriculture (Ehrenberg 1989; Rohrlich-Leavitt 1975; Watson and Kennedy 1991).

As for the EBI, the period is still enigmatic in many regards. And in terms of household social organization, very little has been said. Increased utilization of domestic animal products implies fundamental lifestyle changes in terms of both mobility and activity. An increase in specialized craft production provides a glimpse into the urbanized EB II–III phenomenon in the southern Levant.

I think we can begin to speak broadly about the nature of this restructuring based on the Neolithic and EBI MSM data, but specific activity reconstructions still elude us. The potential for true sexual task differentiation awaits further empirical studies and methodological refinements.

Contributions from Feminist Scholarship

Conkey and Gero (1997) remind us that archaeological studies of gender need to be firmly anchored in feminist theory. The questions we ask and the behavioral models we build need to be conceived broadly with an understanding of gender's biological, social, political, and economic roots. But finding women and men archaeologically is a fundamentally different pursuit than finding them in history, literature, and art. There is a specific tension between the application of feminist theory with archaeological data that should not be ignored even in theoretical discussions. Much of the archaeological record does not contain text, and so we have to develop specific methodologies to "tease" sex and gender from these settings—methodologies without precedent elsewhere in feminist studies. We have to be prepared for more ambiguity, apply analyses that provide coarser-grained results, and accept that some realms may remain unknowable.

And while archaeologists have often failed to integrate feminist theories with much success, it is also imminently clear that feminist scholars have theorized about sexual labor divisions and the inception of gender-based inequalities largely without a critical use of the archaeological or ethnographic records (Gorman 1993). The presence of widespread, perhaps universal gender asymmetries in modern contexts has led some influential feminist scholars to posit a unilineal, developmental sequence based on original or pristine patterns in antiquity (Aaby 1977; Chevillard and LeConte 1986; Ehrenberg 1989; Lerner 1986; Meillassoux 1981). The archaeological record, or speculations about it, are used to locate the present in the past (Balme and Beck 1993). A major concern lies in identifying the origin of male-female social relationships, including sexual divisions of labor. This is where a discussion of prehistory is typically injected into historical discussions.

Several problems are inherent in these efforts. First, they imply an outdated, evolutionary view that assumes that an "original," or "pristine," state in fact existed. When cross-cultural cases are examined, no such monolithic or coherent phenomenon is found—not in modern, preindustrial contexts (Whyte 1978), let alone in the vast expanse of prehistory. And second, much of the feminist literature assumes that a division of labor by sex necessarily implies subordination, for example, that status inequality with respect to these tasks is inherent (Balme and Beck 1993). The quest for original causes has meant that feminists have been willing to accept universals about the sexual division of labor that betray an uncritical use of the ethnographic record—not at all unlike the criticism made against archaeologists (Balme and Beck 1993).

Over time, feminist research has become increasingly contextualized and nuanced, focusing instead on specific histories that critically reject causal evolutionary schemes (Silverblatt 1988). This has been less true, generally, in discussions of pre-historic labor scenarios where a paucity of textual data encourages more assumption-laden speculation.

Contributions from Ethnographic Studies of Sexual Labor Patterns

Lastly, cultural anthropologists have conducted cross-cultural research in attempts to identify variables that define and structure sexual labor patterns as groups become more dependent on domestic plant and animal products. Some efforts fall victim to the same naturalistic assumption about biology defining narrow sets of labor options. But detailed, cross-cultural studies have not borne these conclusions out. Current research trends deemphasize large-scale evolutionary schema that perpetuate the illusory portrait that labor pattern changes constitute a unitary subject with a unitary cause and unitary effects. Their lack of productive application and devolution into biologically deterministic arguments has led many to turn to more ethnographically circumscribed case studies. This research trajectory is documented in the following brief synopsis of a sample of studies examining sexual labor divisions.

As early as the late 1930s, anthropologists were investigating sexual labor patterns. The work of Murdock (1937) and Murdock and Provost (1973) consists of an extensive compilation of labor patterns in 185 societies drawn from the Human Relations Area Files. The sample covers a wide array of mobility, subsistence, and sociopolitical options. The regularities they identified cross-culturally provided the basis for a composite model of sexual labor divisions and their changes through time. The range of data collected and the variability in patterning is impressive. Their findings undercut their central argument that physiological differences between males and females are the basic imperative for sexual labor patterning (see a full discussion in Peterson 1994).

Child rearing and child care are seen as primary elements structuring female labor in a study by Brown (1970). Child rearing, she contends, is very widely construed as a female responsibility. Given the demands of child rearing, Brown identifies task characteristics that are compatible with looking after children. They include tasks that (1) can be performed close to home, (2) require little concentration (i.e., can be frequently interrupted), and (3) are not dangerous. Flexibility in sexual labor patterns is, then, linked to potential flexibility in the child-rearing options culturally available (Brown 1970). This scheme has received substantial feminist criticism, however.

Among preindustrial societies, an impressive array of child care options has been documented (DaVanza and Lee 1983; Hewlett 1991). Hewlett lists a number of child care alternatives to full-time care by biological mothers, including multiple caregivers, nonparental caregivers, wet nurses, stepparents, and foster parents. He concludes that "seldom does a child in pre-industrial society stay with his/her natural parents throughout the dependency period" (Hewlett 1991:19). This study is significant because it documents that the female reproductive role need not necessarily limit participation in activities to a narrowly domestic and maternal realm in preindustrial settings.

Leacock's prehistoric reconstruction meshes well with the flexible labor scenarios suggested by Hewlett. She suggests that the ethnographic present is a poor analog for sexual labor divisions in the past, arguing that prehistoric sexual labor was unlikely to have been as polarized, inflexible, or institutionalized as it is today (Leacock 1978, 1981). This is a point ignored by Murdock and Provost (1973). Modern hunter-gatherers and extensive farmers, for example, provide skewed labor configurations because they are not immune to the forces of commodity production, hierarchical social norms, wage labor, and pressures to decrease residential mobility imposed by the nation-states in which they are embedded.

In 1970, Esther Boserup published a book titled *Women's Role in Economic Development*, which formulated a general model for changing agricultural production. Her typology from extensive to increasingly intensive farming is evolutionary, with demographic change precipitating intensification and technological advance (Boserup 1970; Cloud 1985). At the technological level of hoe cultivation, Boserup claims that women do the bulk of agricultural work. Sparsely populated areas where shifting, extensive agriculture is practiced seem to follow this pattern. In more densely populated areas, where the agricultural system relies on plowing, men generally perform this task, often leaving hand operations of planting and weeding to women. In regions of extreme intensification (terraced rice fields and so on), men and women work the fields together.

Among feminist anthropologists, Boserup's formulation has been influential. It provided a basis for responding to those who supposed that modern divisions of labor and gender asymmetry are necessarily rooted in a set of biological limitations ultimately related to female reproductive capacities. Boserup's female farmer model seemed to demonstrate women's original, massive contribution to subsistence economy. In addition, many of the ethnographic examples cited document that child care need not restrict agricultural labor. Boserup's model supports the notion that women's relegation to the domestic, reproductive realm was a historically late phenomenon, one that meshes with Friedrich Engels's work making an explicit causal link between the rise of private property and the state to women's declining status (Guyer 1991; Silverblatt 1988).

But can Boserup's "female farmer" model, derived from twentieth-century ethnographic data, be taken as a fixed starting point for agricultural labor patterning? Can Boserup's first stage of extensive hoe agriculture be projected back into the prehistoric past to define women's activity patterns? From a number of perspectives, the response appears to be an emphatic "no."

Guyer (1991:259) skillfully argues that female farming among the Beti of Cameroon is the result of social and historic variables that have been developing over centuries. The ancient staple crops of millet and yams, for instance, have given way to maize and cassava production. While the production of these new crops has been grafted onto traditional agricultural systems, there are huge differences in the structure of the activities related to raising them.

Guyer cites ethnographic accounts of the yam and millet crop systems, which she characterizes as interdigitating male/female, individual/group tasks. In the case of millet, for example, men cut back tree branches, and women stack the branches. Men place the seeds in the ground, and women cover them with soil. Men fence the fields, and women tend the growing crop. Reaping was the sole domain of women. Each of these tasks took place in a ritualized, symbolic context, sometimes set to music and literally choreographed (Guyer 1991). With the introduction of maize and cassava and the colonial policies encouraging their production, much of this has changed. The new products were incorporated, but their cultivation became individuated, secularized, and field specific (Guyer 1991). These fundamentally altered systems are the basic units of Boserup's analysis.

This one African case study confirms the idea that the sexual division of labor is constantly being transformed and re-created as social and economic changes take place (Moore 1988). Despite the attraction Boserup's model holds for many, ignoring historical forces and the heterogeneity of gender constructs oversimplifies the dynamism and variability inherent in labor patterns. Wholesale adoption of Boserup's model for prehistoric systems seems especially tenuous, although we seem strangely attracted to evolutionary, systemwide schema that suggest sweeping causal circumstances.

The decline of women's contribution to agricultural production with intensification should clearly be defined as "relative" according to Ember (1983). Her research demonstrates that women typically continue to provide equivalent amounts of labor through time as agriculture intensifies. It is certainly not the case that women's agricultural contribution disappears when plowing or permanent fields are introduced (Ember 1983). Increasing demands on women's time are more responsible for widespread male plowing, not limitations of upper-body strength. Ethnographic examples of women participating in plowing (Stahl 1986) substantiate this point. With intensification, women typically spend more time processing crops, caring for more dependent children, and maintaining a more complex household. Men, conversely, have surplus time as hunting and other direct procurement tasks decrease (Ember 1983). Therefore, when more person-hours are needed to intensify production, the male labor pool has surplus time that can be drawn into service.

Burton and White (1984) broaden our conception of what intensification can imply. Plowing and irrigation are but two ways to increase productivity, but so are shortened fallow periods, terracing, and so on. The authors examined five variables to see how they correlated with variance in the sexual divisions of labor: (1) number of dry months, (2) importance of domesticated animals to subsistence, (3) use of the plow, (4) crop type, and (5) population density (Burton and White 1984). The first two variables are the best predictors of male agricultural participation. A long dry season precipitates seasonal time pressures, requiring males to increase their participation in agriculture. Marked dependence on domesticated animals draws women out of the agricultural labor pool, as they spend more of their time caring for animals and processing animal products. These factors are especially germane to the southern Levantine case.

Viewed through a multifaceted lens of integrated occupational data sets, spatial correlates of activity, and previous modeling efforts, a nascent model of sexual labor begins to emerge.

An Engendered Model

Integrating the material evidence from the archaeological record, the cross-cultural perspective of ethnographers, and the critical perspective of feminism has provided several important lessons that have shaped this modeling effort. The goal from the start was to formulate a local model appropriate to the southern Levant, perhaps yielding comparative insights for other areas but not intended as a generalizable scenario for changes in sexual labor division on a larger scale. Second, while recognizing that this still constitutes constructing the past, I wanted to do so with an empirical foundation rooted in archaeological data. Giving precedence to patterns in the data, with a clear-eyed view that we all construct the past, helps one avoid falling prey to essentialist assumptions that effectively remove sex and gender as analytic tools of interest for understanding social process. I strove to explore changing prehistoric sexual labor divisions, not to confirm some particular version of the past. And finally, I intentionally focus on sexual divisions of labor considered separately from questions of gender asymmetry and inequality. While there are undoubtedly important connections between the two realms of human experience, their relationship constitutes a sphere of inquiry outside the bounds of this particular study.

I am confident in concluding that substantial reorganization of activities and activity level is characteristic of the transition from hunter-gatherer to mixed farmer. Activity-specific reconstructions are the exception, as most frequently the data suggest relative activity levels with certain muscles and patterns of lateralization highlighted. In general, female activity levels (and perhaps activities) appear to be more stable through time. Males appear to experience more profound reorganization of activity moving from the Natufian to the Neolithic to the Early Bronze Age.

During the Natufian, the most specific sexually dimorphic MSM patterning occurs. Divergent patterns of symmetry and rank order differences suggest that overhand throwing motions, presumably associated with hunting using spear or atlatl, are a probable source of this variation. Female musculature is more tentatively linked with activities involving bilateral motions. Material culture and bioarchaeological evidence suggest cereal processing as one possible activity reconstruction. But it is premature to rule out other extractive and productive activities. Importantly, many strenuous activities and similar activity levels are shared by some members of both sex groups, as indicated in similarities in the rank order profiles of males and females as well as mixed-sex groupings in the cluster analysis.

Like Flannery (1972), we should probably entertain the possibility that Natufian gazelle kill sites may have been single-sex work areas. But more detailed engendered "readings" of those sites are needed since there are clearly ethnographic examples of men and women working together in hunting camps to butcher and process animal products (Brumbach and Jarvenpa 1997). Involvement of males with hunting gazelle does not exclude females and children from protein acquisition, particularly small game that did not employ projectile technology. It is also premature to exclude all males from participating in processing and gathering tasks, given the sex composition of certain cluster results (Figure 5.10).

Efforts to incorporate a growing corpus of survey data with large, site-based excavation results can be used productively to test some of the prevalent yet untested assumptions about differences in mobility patterns between males and females. And as a final cautionary note, I would only reiterate that the Natufian results should not serve as some kind of universal template for sexual divisions of labor within complex hunting and gathering societies. Instead, comparing these patterns with other groups will provide the basis for exploring a range of social relations of production on the eve of domestication as it occurred in the Levant.

A more physically demanding lifestyle is associated with the first appearance and use of domestic plants and animals and the suite of behaviors associated with Neolithic lifestyles. Males and females are both working harder at some tasks than their Natufian predecessors. Convergence in MSM mean scores and patterns of bilateralization between sexes during the Neolithic suggests that male activity patterns changed more profoundly. Perhaps as the need for hunting wild game decreased, males had more free time to devote to a number of laborious tasks associated with the new agricultural lifestyle.

During this transitional period, I would conjecture that many economic activities were widely shared, as experimentation with organizing the new productive tasks took place. The cumulative demands of procuring resources for and building substantial houses, tending domestic animals, cultivation, and processing were certainly not borne substantially by one sex over the other. I do not find that the MSM results support a "female farmer" model for early, extensive agriculture. Nor do I find evidence for a strong sex-based division of labor.

Architectural evidence mirrors the transitional nature of this period as we move from the PPNA to the PPNB. Ultimately, curvilinear domestic architecture structures give way to rectilinear houses (with and without piers). Good arguments have been advanced to link rectilinear structures, and their remodeling through time, with small nuclear family residential units. Large nuclear families and/or extended families are often assumed as the social organizational answer to the increased demands of agricultural work (see Flannery 1972). But house floor estimates for the southern Levantine PPN houses do not support this reconstruction. Architectural data do not indicate that nuclear families were increasing in size or that extended families lived under one roof.

Overall, the current evidence supports some portions of the brief statements by Bar-Yosef regarding sexed labor changes during the Neolithic and does not support others. For example, his suggestion that males are increasingly involved in domestic, household activities and that females participate in the agricultural sphere seems viable. However, Bar-Yosef's contention that females' child care requirements are increasing lacks support.

The Neolithic database offers the best supporting evidence from architecture, burial data, and village-level organization yet suffers from the least robust sample of human skeletal material. Small samples from a number of sites compress a large amount of variability across time and space. Clustering algorithms could not be used, meaning that I had to artificially impose sexual dichotomies into the analysis—forcing comparisons between male and female groups from the outset. With a large number of new and ongoing excavations at Neolithic sites around the southern Levant, there will be future opportunities to explore these issues further.

The EBI period can be characterized only as entailing major shifts in activity patterning. Pronounced reductions in muscle robusticity have to be interpreted as jointly reflecting the effects of activity change and declining nutritional and health status. Assuming that health problems were not affecting males differently than females, male activity levels decrease notably compared to females, as measured by a number of indices. Over time, the level and types of activities carried out by females appear to change less dramatically than do those of males. Now, for the first time, I see evidence for a well-established sex-based division of labor.

It is clear that both primary and secondary animal products had become increasingly important in EBI economies. The unprecedented shifts in sexual workloads are consistent with labor divisions among a number of ethnographically documented groups that retain a high degree of mobility in the practice of animal husbandry. The Sheikhanzi of Afghanistan provide a significant analog, made particularly relevant because of ethnographic research that has focused on time allocation by sex (Tavakalian 1984).

Women and adolescent girls in this group are responsible for all dairy operations and wool production. Along with the other daily tasks relating to maintaining their households, women and girls typically work seventeen or more hours a day. Because of their massive economic contribution, Tavakalian (1984) concludes that the number of productive women in the household ultimately determines manageable herd size. The group remains sedentary for a number of months at two seasonal pasturage sites. Short migrations are often necessary during these periods for grazing and watering. Men and adolescent boys are responsible for these herding tasks (Tavakalian 1984). The Sheikhanzi scenario parallels the results from the MSM analysis quite well and provides a useful interpretive analog.

Conclusion

The rationale of this study was to provide an empirically sound starting point from which to infer sexual task differentiation in a specific prehistoric context. Markers of occupational stress and habitual activity on the human skeleton identified a number of shifts in general workload trends and supported several specific activity reconstructions. The results may be unsatisfactory to those seeking definitive statements about particular activity realms, but to me they represent an archaeologically realistic starting point for necessary expansion and refinement. When the skeletal analyses are combined with archaeological and ethnographic data relevant to the human use of space and sexual labor patterns, they provide unique opportunities to integrate social variables more fully into our understanding of the original development of domestication economies. This is proof that incorporating sex and gender into our work generates models that are stronger and more intellectually satisfying.

References

Aaby, Peter. 1977. Engels and Women. *Critical Anthropology* 3(9–10):25–53.

Adovasio, J. M., and R. L. Andrews. 1981. Textile Remains and Basketry Impressions from Bab edh-Dhra and a Weaving Implement from Numeira. In *The Southeastern Dead Sea Plain Expedition,* edited by W. E. Rast and R. T. Schaub, pp. 181–185. Annual of the American Society of Oriental Research 46. American Schools of Oriental Research, Cambridge, MA.

Akkermans, P. A., H. Fokken, and H. T. Waterbolk. 1981. Stratigraphy, Architecture and Lay-Out of Bouqras. In *Préhistoire du Levant,* edited by J. Cauvin and P. Sanlaville, pp. 485–501. CNRS, Paris.

Alon, D. 1977. Two Cult Vessels from Gilat. *'Atiqot* 11:116–118.

Alon, D., and T. E. Levy. 1989. The Archaeology of Cult and the Chalcolithic Sanctuary at Gilat. *Journal of Mediterranean Archaeology* 2:163–221.

Amiran, R. 1970. *Ancient Pottery of the Holy Land.* Rutgers University Press, New Brunswick, NJ.

Anderson, Patricia C. 1991. Harvesting Wild Cereals during the Natufian as Seen from the Experimental Cultivation and Harvest of Wild Einkorn Wheat and Microwear Analysis of Stone Tools. In *The Natufian Culture in the Levant,* edited by O. Bar-Yosef and F. Valla, pp. 521–556. International Monographs in Prehistory, Ann Arbor, MI.

———. 1999. Experimental Cultivation, Harvest, and Threshing of Wild Cereals. In *Prehistory of Agriculture: New Experimental and Ethnographic Approaches,* edited by P. C. Anderson, pp. 118–144. Monograph 40, Institute of Archaeology, University of California, Los Angeles.

Anderson-Gerfaud, P. 1983. Consideration of the Uses of Certain Backed and "Lustred" Stone Tools from the Late Mesolithic and Natufian Levels of Abu Hureyra and Mureybat (Syria). In *Traces d'Utilisation sur les Outils Néolithiques du Proche Orient,* edited by M. C. Cauvin, pp. 77–105. Maison de l'Orient, Lyon, France.

Angel, J. L., J. O. Kelley, M. Parrington, and S. Pinter. 1987. Life Stresses of the Free Black Community as Represented by the First African Baptist Church, Philadelphia, 1823–1841. *American Journal of Physical Anthropology* 74:213–229.

Arensburg, B. 1985. The Natufian Skeleton H.01 of Hatula. In *Le Site Natoufien-Khiamien de Hatoula*, edited by M. Lechevallier and A. Ronen, pp. 103–104. Cahiers du Centre de Recherche Français de Jérusalem, Paris.

Arensburg, B., P. Smith, and R. Yakar. 1978. The Human Remains from Abou Gosh. In *Abou Gosh and Beisamoun*, edited by M. Lechevallier, pp. 95–105. Mémoires et Travaux du Centre de Recherches Préhistoriques de Jérusalem No. 2. Association Paleorient, Paris.

Balme, Jane, and Wendy Beck. 1993. Archaeology and Feminism—Views on the Origins of the Division of Labor. In *Women in Archaeology: A Feminist Critique*, edited by H. du Cros and L. Smith, pp. 61–74. Australian National University, Canberra.

Banning, E. B., and B. F. Byrd. 1987. Houses and the Changing Residential Unit: Domestic Architecture at PPNB 'Ain Ghazal, Jordan. *Proceedings of the Prehistoric Society* 53:309–325.

———. 1989. Alternative Approaches for Exploring Levantine Neolithic Architecture. *Paléorient* 15:154–160.

Banning, E. B., D. Rahimi, J. Siggers, and H. Ta'ani. 1996. The 1992 Season of Excavations in Wadi Ziqlab, Jordan. *Annual of the Department of Antiquities of Jordan* 40:29–49.

Barber, E. J. W. 1991. *Prehistoric Textiles*. Princeton University Press, Princeton, NJ.

Barrett, M. J. 1977. Masticatory and Non-Masticatory Uses of Teeth. In *Stone Tools as Markers*, edited by R. V. S. Wright, pp. 18–23. Australian Institute of Aboriginal Studies, Canberra.

Baruch, U., and S. Bottema. 1991. Palynological Evidence for Climatic Changes in the Levant ca. 17,000–9,000 B.P. In *The Natufian Culture in the Levant*, edited by O. Bar-Yosef and F. Valla, pp. 11–20. International Monographs in Prehistory, Ann Arbor, MI.

Bar-Yosef, Ofer. 1981. The "Pre-Pottery Neolithic" Periods in the Southern Levant. In *Préhistoire du Levant*, edited by J. Cauvin and P. Sanlaville, pp. 389–408. CNRS, Paris.

———. 1983. The Natufian of the Southern Levant. In *The Hilly Flanks and Beyond*, edited by T. C. Young, P. E. L. Smith, and P. Mortenson, pp. 16–38. Oriental Institute Studies in Ancient Oriental Civilization No. 36. University of Chicago Press, Chicago.

———. 1984. Seasonality among Neolithic Hunter-Gatherers in Southern Sinai. In *Animals and Archaeology: Vol. 3*, edited by J. Clutton-Brock and C. Grigson, pp. 145–160. British Archaeological Reports S202, Oxford.

———. 1986. The Walls of Jericho. *Current Anthropology* 27:157–162.

———. 1991. The Archaeology of the Natufian Layer at Hayonim Cave. In *The Natufian Culture in the Levant*, edited by O. Bar-Yosef and F. Valla, pp. 81–92. International Monographs in Prehistory, Ann Arbor, MI.

———. 1995. Earliest Food Producers—Pre-Pottery Neolithic (8,000–5,500). In *The Archaeology of Society in the Holy Land*, edited by T. E. Levy, pp. 190–201. Facts on File, New York.

Bar-Yosef, O., and A. Belfer-Cohen. 1989. The Origins of Sedentism and Farming Communities in the Southern Levant. *Journal of World Prehistory* 3:447–496.

———. 1991. From Sedentary Hunter-Gatherers to Territorial Farmers in the Levant. In *Between Bands and States*, edited by S. Gregg, pp. 181–202. Center for Archaeological Investigations Occasional Paper No. 9. Southern Illinois University, Carbondale.

————. 1992. From Foraging to Farming in the Mediterranean Levant. In *Transitions to Agriculture in Prehistory*, edited by A. B. Gebauer and T. D. Price, pp. 21–48. Prehistory Press, Madison, WI.

Bar-Yosef, O., and A. Gopher. 1997. *Netiv Hagdud. Part I: The Archaeology of Netiv Hagdud.* American School of Prehistoric Research Bulletin 43, Cambridge, MA.

Bar-Yosef, O., A. Gopher, E. Tchernov, and M. Kislev. 1992. Netiv Hagdud: An Early Neolithic Village Site in the Jordan Valley. *Journal of Field Archaeology* 18:405–424.

Bar-Yosef, O., and N. Goren. 1973. Natufian Remains in Hayonim Cave. *Paléorient* 1:49–68.

Bar-Yosef, O., and M. E. Kislev. 1989. Early Farming Communities in the Jordan Valley. In *Foraging and Farming*, edited by D. R. Harris and G. C. Hillman, pp. 632–642. Unwin Hyman, Boston.

Bar-Yosef, O., T. Schick, and D. Alon. 1993. Nahal Hemar Cave. In *The New Encyclopedia of Excavations in the Holy Land*, edited by E. Stern, pp. 1082–1084. Simon and Schuster, New York.

Bar-Yosef, O., and F. Valla. 1979. L'Evolutions du Natoufien, Nouvelles Suggestions. *Paléorient* 5:145–152.

Bar-Yosef, O., B. Vandermeersch, B. Arensburg, A. Belfer-Cohen, P. Goldberg, H. Laville, L. Meignen, Y. Rak, J. D. Speth, and S. Weiner. 1992. The Excavations in Kebara Cave, Mt. Carmel. *Current Anthropology* 33:497–550.

Bass, William M. 1971. *Human Osteology.* Missouri Archaeological Society, Columbia.

Beck, L. 1978. Women among Qashaq'i Nomadic Pastoralists in Iran. In *Women in the Muslim World*, edited by L. Beck and N. Keddie, pp. 351–373. Harvard University Press, Cambridge, MA.

Becker, Marshall Joseph. 2000. Reconstructing the Lives of South Etruscan Women. In *Reading the Body*, edited by A. Rautman, pp. 55–67. University of Pennsylvania Press, Philadelphia.

Belfer-Cohen, Anna. 1988. The Natufian Graveyard in Hayonim Cave. *Paléorient* 14:297–308.

————. 1991. The Natufian in the Levant. *Annual Review of Anthropology* 20:167–186.

————. 1995. Rethinking Social Stratification in the Natufian Culture: The Evidence from Burials. In *The Archaeology of Death in the Near East*, edited by Stuart Campbell and Anthony Green, pp. 9–16. Oxbow Books, Oxford.

Belfer-Cohen, A., B. Arensberg, O. Bar-Yosef, and A. Gopher. 1990. Human Remains from Netiv Hagdud—A PPNA Site in the Jordan Valley. *Mitekufat Haeven* 23:79–85.

Belfer-Cohen, A., L. A. Schepartz, and B. Arensburg. 1991. New Biological Data for the Natufian Populations in Israel. In *The Natufian Culture in the Levant*, edited by O. Bar-Yosef and F. Valla, pp. 411–424. International Monographs in Prehistory, Ann Arbor, MI.

Bender, A. E. 1996. Nutritional Effects of Food Processing. *Journal of Food Technology* 1:262–289.

Bender, B. 1978. Gatherer-Hunter to Farmer: A Social Perspective. *World Archaeology* 10:204–222.

————. 1985. *Farming in Prehistory: From Hunter-Gatherer to Food Producer.* St. Martin's Press, New York.

Ben-Tor, Ammon. 1992. The Early Bronze Age. In *The Archaeology of Ancient Israel,* edited by A. Ben-Tor, pp. 81–125. Yale University Press, New Haven, CT.

Berget, K. A., and Steven E. Churchill. 1994. Subsistence Activity and Humeral Hypertrophy among Western Aleutian Islanders (abstract). *American Journal of Physical Anthropology* 18(Suppl.):55.

Betts, A. V. G. 1988. The Black Desert Survey: Prehistoric Sites and Subsistence Strategies in Eastern Jordan. In *The Prehistory of Jordan,* edited by A. Garrard and H. G. Gebel, pp. 369–391. BAR International Series No. 396. BAR International, Oxford.

Blakey, R. L., and Lane A. Beck. 1984. Tooth-Tool Use versus Dental Modification: A Case Study from the Prehistoric Southeast. *Midcontinental Journal of Archeology* 9:269–276.

Blumler, M. A. 1996. Ecology, Evolutionary Theory and Agricultural Origins. In *The Origins and Spread of Agriculture and Pastoralism in Eurasia,* edited by D. R. Harris, pp. 25–50. Smithsonian Institution Press, Washington, DC.

Blumler, M. A., and R. Byrne. 1990. The Ecological Genetics of Domestication and the Origins of Agriculture. *Current Anthropology* 32:23–54.

Boserup, E. 1970. *Women's Role in Economic Development.* St. Martin's Press, New York.

Bourke, Stephen J. 1997. The "Pre-Ghassulian" Sequence at Teleilat Ghassul: Sydney University Excavations 1975–1995. In *Prehistory of Jordan II,* edited by H. Gebel, Z. Kafafi, and G. Rollefson, pp. 395–417. Ex oriente, Berlin.

Bourke, Stephen J., Peta L. Seaton, Rachael T. Sparks, Jaimie L. Lovell, and Lachlan D. Mairs. 1995. The First Season of Renewed Excavation by the University of Sydney at Tulaylat al-Ghassul. *Annual of the Department of Antiquities of Jordan* 39:31–63.

Braun, Eliot. 1997. *Yiftah'el: Salvage and Rescue Operations at a Prehistoric Village in Lower Galilee, Israel.* IAA Reports No. 2. Israel Antiquities Authority, Jerusalem.

Bridges, Patricia S. 1985. *Changes in Long-Bone Structure with the Transition to Agriculture: Implications for Prehistoric Activities.* Ph.D. dissertation, University of Michigan, Ann Arbor.

————. 1989. Changes in Activities with the Shift to Agriculture in the Southeastern United States. *Current Anthropology* 30:385–394.

————. 1991a. Degenerative Joint Disease in Hunter-Gatherer and Agriculturalists from the Southeastern United States. *American Journal of Physical Anthropology* 85:379.

————. 1991b. Skeletal Evidence of Changes in Subsistence Activities between Archaic and Mississippian Time Periods in Northwestern Alabama. In *What Mean These Bones,* edited by M. L. Powell, P. S. Bridges, and A. W. Mires, pp. 102–113. University of Alabama Press, Tuscaloosa.

————. 1992. Prehistoric Arthritis in the Americas. *Annual Review of Anthropology* 21:67-91.

————. 1995. Skeletal Biology and Behavior in Ancient Humans. *Evolutionary Anthropology* 4:112–120.

————. 1997. The Relationship among Humeral Muscle Markings and Bone Strength in Prehistoric Remains from West-Central Illinois. Paper presented at the annual meeting of the American Association of Physical Anthropologists, St. Louis, MO.

Bronowski, J. 1973. *Harvest of the Seasons* (videotape). Time-Life Multimedia, New York.

Brown, J. K. 1970. A Note on the Division of Labor by Sex. *American Anthropologist* 72:1073–1078.

Brumbach, Hetty Jo, and Robert Jarvenpa. 1997. Ethnoarchaeology of Subsistence Space and Gender: A Subarctic Dene Case. *American Antiquity* 62:414–436.

Brumfiel, E. M. 1991. Weaving and Cooking: Women's Production in Aztec Mexico. In *Engendering Archaeology: Women and Prehistory,* edited by J. M. Gero and M. W. Conkey, pp. 241–255, Basil Blackwell, Oxford.

———. 1992. Distinguished Lecture in Archaeology: Breaking and Entering the Eco-System—Gender, Class, and Faction Steal the Show. *American Anthropologist* 94:551–567.

Bumsted, M. P., J. E. Booker, R. M. Barnes, T. W. Boutton, G. J. Armelagos, J. C. Lerman, and K. Brendel. 1990. Recognizing Women in the Archaeological Record. In *Powers of Observation: Alternative Views in Archeology,* edited by S. M. Nelson and A. B. Kehoe, pp. 89–101. Archaeological Papers of the American Anthropological Association No. 2. American Anthropological Association, Washington, DC.

Burrell L., M. Maas, and D. Van Gerven. 1986. Patterns of Long-Bone Fracture in Two Nubian Cemeteries. *Human Evolution* 1:495–506.

Burton, M. L., and D. R. White. 1984. Sexual Divisions of Labor in Agriculture. *American Anthropologist* 86:568–583.

Butler, C. 1989. The Plastered Skull of 'Ain Ghazal: Preliminary Findings. In *People and Culture in Change,* edited by I. Hershkovitz, pp. 141–145. BAR International Series No. 508, Bar International, Oxford.

Byrd, Brian F. 1989a. *The Natufian Encampment at Beidha: Late Pleistocene Adaptation in the Southern Levant.* Jutland Archaeological Society, Hojbjerg, Denmark.

———. 1989b. The Natufian: Settlement Variability and Economic Adaptations in the Levant at the End of the Pleistocene. *Journal of World Prehistory* 3:159–197.

———. 2000. Households in Transition: Neolithic Social Organization within Southwest Asia. In *Life in Neolithic Farming Communities,* edited by I. Kuijt, pp. 63–98. Kluwer Academic/Plenum Publishers, New York.

Byrd, B. F., and E. B. Banning. 1988. Southern Levantine Pier Houses: Intersite Architectural Patterning during the Pre-Pottery Neolithic B. *Paléorient* 14:65–72.

Byrd, B. F., and S. M. Colledge. 1991. Early Natufian Occupation along the Edge of the Southern Jordanian Steppe. In *The Natufian Culture in the Levant,* edited by O. Bar-Yosef and F. Valla, pp. 265–276. International Monographs in Prehistory, Ann Arbor, MI.

Callaway, J. A. 1993. 'Ai. In *The New Encyclopedia of Excavations in the Holy Land,* edited by E. Stern, pp. 39–45. Simon and Schuster, New York.

Campana, D. V. 1989. *Natufian and Protoneolithic Bone Tools: The Manufacture and Use of Bone Implements in the Zagros and the Levant.* BAR International Series No. 494. BAR International, Oxford.

———. 1991. Bone Implements from Hayonim Cave: Some Relevant Issues. In *The Natufian Culture in the Levant,* edited by O. Bar-Yosef and F. Valla, pp. 459–466. International Monographs in Prehistory, Ann Arbor, MI.

Cauvin, J. 1972. *Religions Néolithique de Syro-Palestine.* Adrien Maisonneuve, Paris.

Cauvin, M. C. 1991. Du Natoufien au Levant Nord? Jayroud and Mureybet (Syrie). In *The Natufian Culture in the Levant,* edited by O. Bar-Yosef and F. Valla, pp. 295–314. International Monographs in Prehistory, Ann Arbor, MI.

Charles, Douglas K., and Jane E. Buikstra. 1983. Archaic Mortuary Sites in the Central Mississippi Drainages: Distribution, Structure and Implications. In *Archaic Hunters and Gatherers in the Midwest,* edited by J. Phillips and J. Brown, pp. 117–145. Academic Press, New York.

Charles, M. 1984. Present Day Field Practices in Near Eastern Agriculture: Possible Parallels for Ancient Sumer. *Bulletin for Sumerian Agriculture* I.

Chevillard, N., and S. LeConte. 1986. The Dawn of Lineage Societies. In *Women's Work, Men's Property,* edited by S. Coontz and P. Henderson, pp. 76–107. Verso, London.

Churchill, Steven E. 1994. *Human Upper Body Evolution in the Eurasian Later Pleistocene.* Ph.D. dissertation, University of New Mexico, Albuquerque.

Churchill, Steven E., and Alan G. Morris. 1998. Muscle Marking Morphology and Labour Intensity in Prehistoric Khoisan Foragers. *International Journal of Osteoarchaeology* 8:390–411.

Claassen, Cheryl. 1996. Mother's Work Loads and Children's Labor in the Midwest-Midsouth Region. Paper presented at the Fourth Gender and Archaeology Conference, East Lansing, MI.

Cloud, K. 1985. Women's Productivity in Agricultural Systems: Considerations for Project Design. In *Gender Roles in Development Projects,* edited by C. Overholt, M. B. Anderson, K. Cloud, and J. R. Austin, pp. 17–56. Kumarian Press, West Hartford, CT.

Clutton-Brock, J. 1979. Mammalian Remains from the Jericho Tell. *Proceedings of the Prehistoric Society* 45:135–157.

Cohen, Mark Nathan, and Sharon Bennett. 1993. Skeletal Evidence for Sex Roles and Gender Hierarchies in Prehistory. In *Sex and Gender Hierarchies,* edited by B. Miller, pp. 273–296. Cambridge University Press, New York.

Collier, J. F., and S. J. Yanagisako. 1987. *Gender and Kinship: Essays toward a Unified Analysis.* Stanford University Press, Stanford, CA.

Commenge-Pellerin, C. 1987. *La Poterie d'Abou Matar et de l'Ouadi Zoumeila (Beersheva) au IVe Millénaire Avant l'Ere Chrétienne.* Association Paléorient, Paris.

Conkey, Margaret W., and Joan M. Gero. 1997. Programme to Practice: Gender and Feminism in Archaeology. *Annual Reviews of Anthropology* 26:411–437.

Conkey, M., and J. Spector. 1984. Archaeology and the Study of Gender. In *Advances in Archaeological Method and Theory,* edited by M. J. Schiffer, pp. 1–38. Academic Press, New York.

Conkey, M. W., and S. H. Williams. 1991. Original Narratives: The Political Economy of Gender in Archaeology. In *Gender at the Crossroads of Knowledge,* edited by M. DiLeonardo, pp. 102–139. University of California Press, Berkeley.

Cook, D. C., J. E. Buikstra, C. J. DeRousseau, and D. C. Johanson. 1983. Vertebral Pathology in the Afar Australopithecines. *American Journal of Physical Anthropology* 60:83–101.

Copeland, L. 1991. Natufian Sites in Lebanon. In *The Natufian Culture in the Levant,* edited by O. Bar-Yosef and F. Valla, pp. 27–42. International Monographs in Prehistory, Ann Arbor, MI.

Cosar, F. M. 1978. Women in Turkish Society. In *Women in the Muslim World*, edited by L. Beck and N. Keddie, pp. 124–140. Harvard University Press, Cambridge, MA.

Cowgill, G. L. 1975. On the Causes and Consequences of Ancient and Modern Population Changes. *American Anthropologist* 77:505–525.

Crabtree, P. J. 1991. Gender Hierarchies and the Sexual Division of Labor in the Natufian Culture of the Southern Levant. In *The Archaeology of Gender*, edited by D. Walde and N. D. Willows, pp. 384–391. University of Calgary Archaeological Association, Calgary.

Crabtree, P. J., D. V. Campana, and A. Belfer-Cohen. 1989. Salibiya I: First Results. Paper presented at the Conference on Le Natoufien ou les Premices du Néolithique au Levant, Valbone, France.

Cribb, R. 1991. *Nomads in Archaeology*. Cambridge University Press, New York.

Crognier, E., and M. Dupouy-Madre. 1974. Les Natufiens de Nahal Oren (Ouadi Fallah): Etude Anthropologique. *Paléorient* 2:103–121.

Crowfoot Payne, J. 1983. The Flint Industries of Jericho. In *Excavation at Jericho, Vol. V*, edited by K. Kenyon and T. A. Holland, pp. 622–759. British School of Archaeology in Jerusalem, London.

DaVanza, J., and D. L. P. Lee. 1983. The Compatibility of Child Care with Market and Nonmarket Activities: Preliminary Evidence from Malaysia. In *Women and Poverty in the Third World*, edited by M. Buvinic, M. A. Lycette, and W. P. McGreevey, pp. 62–91. Johns Hopkins University Press, Baltimore.

Davis, S. J. M. 1983. The Age Profiles of Gazelles Predated by Ancient Man in Israel: Possible Evidence for a Shift from Seasonality to Sedentism in the Natufian. *Paléorient* 8:5–16.

Divale, William, and Marvin Harris. 1976. Population, Warfare, and the Male Supremacist Complex. *American Anthropologist* 78:521–538.

Dobres, Marcia-Anne. 1995. Gender and Prehistoric Technology: On the Social Agency of Technical Strategies. *World Archaeology* 27(1):25–49.

Dollfus, G., and Z. Kafafi. 1986. Preliminary Results of the First Season of the Joint Jordano-French Project at Abu Hamid. *Annual of the Department of Antiquities of Jordan* 30:353–379.

Draper, P. 1975. !Kung Women: Contrasts in Sexual Egalitarianism in Foraging and Sedentary Contexts. In *Towards an Anthropology of Women*, edited by R. Reiter, pp. 77–109. Monthly Review Press, New York.

Ducos, P. 1978. La Faune d'Abou Gosh: Proto-Élevage de la Chèvre au Néolithique Pré-Céramique. In *Abou Gosh and Beisamoun*, edited by M. Lechevallier, pp. 107–123. Association Paléorient, Paris.

Dunand, M. 1973. *Fouilles de Byblos*. Adrien Maisonneuve, Paris.

Dutour, O. 1986. Enthesopathies (Lesions of Muscular Insertions) as Indicators of the Activities of Neolithic Saharan Populations. *American Journal of Physical Anthropology* 71:221–224.

Edwards, P. C. 1989. Revising the Broad Spectrum Revolution. *Antiquity* 63:225–246.

———. 1991. Wadi Hammeh 27: An Early Natufian Site at Pella, Jordan. In *The Natufian Culture in the Levant*, edited by O. Bar-Yosef and F. Valla, pp. 123–148. International Monographs in Prehistory, Ann Arbor, MI.

Ehrenberg, M. 1989. *Women in Prehistory.* British Museum Publications, London.

El-Najjar, M., A. Al-Shiyab, and I. Al-Sarie. 1997. Cases of Tuberculosis at 'Ain Ghazal, Jordan. *Paléorient* 22/2:123–128.

Ember, C. R. 1983. The Relative Decline in Women's Contribution to Agriculture with Intensification. *American Anthropologist* 85:285–304.

Epstein, C. 1977. The Chalcolithic Culture of the Golan. *Biblical Archaeologist* 40:57–62.

———. 1985. Laden Animal Figurines from the Chalcolithic Period in Palestine. *Bulletin of the American Schools of Oriental Research* 258:53–62.

Esse, D. L. 1989. Secondary State Formation and Collapse in Early Bronze Age Palestine. In *L'Urbanization de la Palestine à l'Age du Bronze Ancien,* edited by P. de Miroschedji, pp. 81–96. BAR International Series No. 527(i). BAR International, Oxford.

Estioko-Griffin, A., and P. Bion Griffin. 1981. Woman the Hunter: The Agta. In *Woman the Gatherer,* edited by F. Dahlberg, pp. 121–152. Yale University Press, New Haven, CT.

Evans-Pritchard, E. E. 1961. *The Position of Women in Primitive Society and Other Essays.* The Free Press, New York.

Farquharson-Roberts, M. A., and P. C. Fulford. 1980. Stress Fracture of the Radius. *Journal of Bone Joint Surgery* 62:194–195.

Fausto-Sterling, Anne. 2000. The Five Sexes Revisited. *The Sciences,* July/August, 19–23.

Ferembach, D. 1976. Influence Nutritionelle et Différences Morphologiques chez des Populations Préhistoriques (Natoufiens-Israël). *Eretz Israel* 13:240–251.

Fiedel, S. J. 1979. *Intra- and Inter-Cultural Variability in Mesolithic and Neolithic Mortuary Practices.* Ph.D. dissertation, University of Pennsylvania, Philadelphia.

Finnegan, M. 1981. Faunal Remains from Bab edh-Dhra and Numeira. In *The Southeastern Dead Sea Plain Expedition,* edited by W. E. Rast and R. T. Schaub, pp. 177–180. Annual of the American Schools of Oriental Research 46, American Schools of Oriental Research, Cambridge, MA.

Flannery, K. V. 1969. Origins and Ecological Effects of Early Domestication in Iran and the Near East. In *The Domestication and Exploitation of Plants and Animals,* edited by P. J. Ucko and G. W. Dimbleby, pp. 73–100. Duckworth, London.

———. 1972. The Origins of the Village as a Settlement Type in Mesoamerica and the Near East: A Comparative Study. In *Man, Settlement and Urbanism,* edited by P. J. Ucko, R. Tringham, and G. W. Dimbleby, pp. 23–53. Duckworth, London.

———. 1973. Origins of Agriculture. *Annual Review of Anthropology* 2:271–301.

———. 1983. Early Pig Domestication in the Fertile Crescent: A Retrospective Look. In *The Hilly Flanks and Beyond,* edited by T. C. Young, P. E. L. Smith, and P. Mortensen, pp. 163–188. University of Chicago Press, Chicago.

Frayer, David W. 1988. Auditory Exostoses and Evidence for Fishing at Flasac. *Current Anthropology* 29:346–349.

Frayer, D. W., and M. H. Wolpoff. 1985. Sexual Dimorphism. In *Annual Review of Anthropology,* edited by B. J. Siegel, pp. 429–473. Annual Reviews, Inc., Palo Alto, CA.

Fresia, Anne E., Christopher B. Ruff, and Clark Spencer Larsen. 1990. Chapter 8: Temporal Decline in Bilateral Asymmetry of the Upper Limb on the Georgia Coast. In *The Archaeology of Mission Santa Cataline de Guale: 2. Biocultural Interpretations of a Population in Transition,* edited by Clark Spencer Larsen, pp. 121–132. Anthropological Papers of the American Museum of Natural History No. 68. American Museum of Natural History, New York.

Frolich, B., and D. J. Ortner. 1982. Excavations of the Early Bronze Age Cemetery at Bab edh-Dhra, Jordan 1981, a Preliminary Report. *Annual of the Department of Antiquities of Jordan* 26:247–269.

Garfinkel, Y. 1987a. Bead Manufacture on the Pre-Pottery Neolithic B Site of Yiftahel. *Mitekufat Haeven* 20:79–89.

———. 1987b. Yiftahel: A Neolithic Village from the Seventh Millennium B.C. in Lower Galilee, Israel. *Journal of Field Archaeology* 14:199–212.

Garrard, A. N., A. Betts, B. Byrd, S. Colledge, and C. Hunt. 1989. Summary of the Palaeoenvironmental and Prehistoric Investigations in the Azraq Basin. In *The Prehistory of Jordan*, edited by A. N. Garrard and H. G. Gebel, pp. 311–337. BAR International Series No. 396. BAR International, Oxford.

Garrod, D. A. E. 1932. A New Mesolithic Industry: The Natufian of Palestine. *Journal of the Royal Anthropological Institute* 62(2):257–269.

Garrod, D. A. E., and D. M. A. Bate. 1937. *The Stone Age of Mount Carmel: Excavations at the Wady el-Mughara, Vol. I.* Clarendon Press, Oxford.

Gebel, Hans Georg K., and Hans-Dieter Bienert. 1997. Ba'ja Hidden in the Petra Mountains: Preliminary Report on the 1997 Excavations. In *Prehistory of Jordan II*, edited by H. G. K. Gebel, Z. Kafafi, and G. O. Rollefson, pp. 221–262. Ex oriente, Berlin.

Gebel, Hans Georg K., Bo Dahl Hermansen, and Carsten Niebuhr. 1999. Ba'ja Neolithic Project 1999: Short Report on Architectural Findings. *Neo-Lithics* 3/99:18–21.

Gero, Joan M. 1991. Genderlithics: Women's Roles in Stone Tool Production. In *Engendering Archaeology: Women and Prehistory*, edited by J. M. Gero and M. W. Conkey, pp. 163–193. Basil Blackwell, Oxford.

Gilead, I. 1988. The Chalcolithic Period in the Levant. *Journal of World Prehistory* 2:397–443.

———. 1990. The Neolithic-Chalcolithic Transition and the Qatifian of the Northern Negev and Sinai. *Levant* 22:47–63.

Gopher, A. 1995. Early Pottery-Bearing Groups in Israel—The Pottery Neolithic Period. In *The Archaeology of Society in the Holy Land*, edited by T. E. Levy, pp. 205–221. Facts on File, New York.

Gopher, Avi, and Estelle Orrelle. 1995. New Data on Burials from the Pottery Neolithic Period (Sixth–Fifth Millennium BC) in Israel. In *The Archaeology of Death in the Ancient Near East*, edited by Stuart Campbell and Anthony Green, pp. 24–28. Oxbow Books, Oxford.

Gopher, Avi, and Tsvika Tsuk. 1996. *The Nahal Qanah Cave: Monograph 12.* Institute of Archaeology, Tel Aviv University, Tel Aviv.

Gophna, Ram. 1995. Early Bronze Age Canaan: Some Spatial and Demographic Observations. In *The Archaeology of Society in the Holy Land*, edited by T. E. Levy, pp. 269–276. Facts on File, New York.

Goodman, A. H., J. Lallo, George Armelagos, and J. Rose. 1984. Health Changes at Dickson Mounds, Illinois (A.D. 950–1300). In *Paleopathology at the Origins of Agriculture*, edited by Mark N. Cohen and George J. Armelagos, pp. 271–305. Academic Press, Orlando.

Goring-Morris, A. N. 1987. *At the Edge: Terminal Pleistocene Hunter-Gatherers in the Negev and Sinai.* BAR International Series No. 361. BAR International, Oxford.

Goring-Morris, A. N., and A. Gopher. 1983. Nahal Issaron: A Neolithic Settlement in the Southern Negev. *Israel Exploration Journal* 33:149–162.

Gorman, Alice C. 1993. Theories of Prehistoric Inequality: Hobbes, Freud and Engels. In *Women in Archaeology: A Feminist Critique,* edited by H. du Cros and L. Smith, pp. 46–50. Australian National University, Canberra.

Gray, H. 1974. *Gray's Anatomy.* Running Press, Philadelphia.

Gray, Kimberle. 1995. Digging the Bronze Age Woman. Paper presented at the Fourth Gender and Archaeology Conference, East Lansing, MI.

Grigson, C. 1987. Shiqmim: Pastoralism and Other Aspects of Animal Management in the Chalcolithic of the Northern Negev. In *Shiqmim I: Studies Concerning Chalcolithic Societies in the Northern Negev Desert, Israel (1982–1984),* edited by T. E. Levy, pp. 219–241. BAR International Series No. 356(i). BAR International, Oxford.

Guyer, J. 1995. Plough and Pasture in the Early Economy of the Southern Levant. In *The Archaeology of Society in the Holy Land,* edited by T. E. Levy, pp. 245–268. Facts on File, New York.

Grindell, Beth. 1997. *Unmasked Equalities: An Example of Mortuary Practices and Social Complexity in the Levantine Natufian and Pre-Pottery Neolithic.* Ph.D. dissertation, University of Arizona, Tucson.

Guyer, J. 1991. Female Farming in Anthropology and African History. In *Gender at the Crossroads of Knowledge,* edited by M. diLeonardo, pp. 257–277. University of California Press, Berkeley.

Hanbury-Tenison, J. W. 1986. *The Late Chalcolithic to Early Bronze I in Palestine and Transjordan.* BAR International Series No. 311. BAR International, Oxford.

Harris, D. R. 1986. Plant and Animal Domestication and the Origins of Agriculture: The Contribution of Radiocarbon Accelerator Dating. In *Archaeological Results from Accelerator Dating,* edited by J. A. J. Gowlett and R. E. M. Hedges, pp. 5–12. Oxford Committee for Archaeology Monograph No. 11, Oxford.

———. 1996. Introduction: Themes and Concepts in the Study of Early Agriculture. In *The Origins and Spread of Agriculture and Pastoralism in Eurasia,* edited by D. R. Harris, pp. 1–9. Smithsonian Institution Press, Washington, DC.

Hastorf, C. A. 1991. Gender, Space, and Food in Prehistory. In *Engendering Archaeology: Women and Prehistory,* edited by J. M. Gero and M. W. Conkey, pp. 132–159. Basil Blackwell, Oxford.

Hauptmann, A., and G. Weisgerber. 1986. Archaeometallurgical and Mining—Archaeological Investigations in the Area of Feinan, Wadi 'Arabah (Jordan). *Annual of the Department of Antiquities of Jordan* 31:419–437.

Hawkey, Diane E. 1988. *Use of Upper Arm Extremity Enthesopathies to Indicate Habitual Activity Patterns.* M.A. thesis, Arizona State University, Tempe.

———. 1998. Disability, Compassion and the Skeletal Record: Using Musculoskeletal Stress Markers (MSM) to Construct an Osteobiography from Early New Mexico. *International Journal of Osteoarchaeology* 8:326–340.

Hawkey, Diane E., and Charles F. Merbs. 1995. Activity-Induced Musculoskeletal Stress Markers (MSM) and Subsistence Strategy among Ancient Hudson Bay Eskimos. *International Journal of Osteoarchaeology* 5:324–338.

Hawkey, Diane, and Steven R. Street. 1992. Activity-Induced Stress Markers in Prehistoric Human Remains from the Eastern Aleutian Islands (abstract). *American Journal of Physical Anthropology* 14(Suppl.):89.

Hayden, Brian. 1990. Nimrods, Piscators, Pluckers, and Planters: The Emergence of Food Production. *Journal of Anthropological Archaeology* 9:31–69.

Heilman, Jill L., Charlotte Roberts, and Christopher J. Knuesel. 1997. Skeletal Response to Differential Labor in an Early Twentieth Century Population from Urban St. Louis, Missouri. Paper presented at the annual meeting of the American Association of Physical Anthropologists, St. Louis.

Hennessy, J. B. 1982. Teleilat Ghassul: Its Place in the Archaeology of Jordan. In *Studies in the History and Archaeology of Jordan*, edited by A. Hadidi, pp. 55–58. Department of Antiquities, Amman.

Henry, D. O. 1976. Rosh Zin: A Natufian Settlement near Ein Ardat. In *Prehistory and Paleoenvironments in the Central Negev, Israel, Vol. I*, edited by A. E. Marks, pp. 317–348. Southern Methodist University Press, Dallas.

———. 1985. Preagricultural Sedentism: The Natufian Example. In *Prehistoric Hunter-Gatherers: The Emergence of Cultural Complexity*, edited by T. D. Price and J. A. Brown, pp. 365–384. Academic Press, New York.

———. 1986. The Prehistory and Paleoenvironments of Jordan: An Overview. *Paléorient* 2:5–26.

———. 1989. *From Foraging to Agriculture: The Levant at the End of the Ice Age.* University of Pennsylvania Press, Philadelphia.

Henry, D. O., and A. Leroi-Gourhan. 1976. The Excavation of Hayonim Terrace: An Interim Report. *Journal of Field Archaeology* 3:391–405.

Hershkovitz, I., and E. Galili. 1990. 8000-Year-Old Human Remains on the Sea Floor Near Atlit, Israel. *Human Evolution* 5:319–358.

Hershkovitz, I., E. Galili, and B. Ring. 1991. Des squelettes humains 8000 ans sous la mer: Indications sur la vie sociale et économique des habitants de la côte sud du Levant à la periode néolithique précéramique. *L'Anthropologie* 95:639–650.

Hershkovitz, I., Y. Garfinkel, and B. Arensburg. 1986. Neolithic Skeletal Remains at Yiftahel, Area C (Israel). *Paléorient* 12:73–81.

Hershkovitz, Israel, and Avi Gopher. 1988. Human Remains from Horvat Galil: A Pre-Pottery Neolithic Site in the Upper Galilee, Israel. *Paleorient* 14:119–125.

———. 1990. Paleodemography, Burial Customs, and Food-Producing Economy at the Beginning of the Holocene: A Perspective from the Southern Levant. *Mitekufat Haeven* 23:9–47.

Hewlett, B. S. 1991. Demography and Childcare in Preindustrial Societies. *Journal of Anthropological Research* 47:1–37.

Hillman, G. C. 1984. Traditional Husbandry and Processing of Archaic Cereals in Recent Times: The Operations, Products, and Tools Which Might Feature in Sumerian Tests. *Bulletin for Sumerial Agriculture* 1:114–152.

———. 1985. Traditional Husbandry and Processing of Archaic Cereals in Recent Times: The Operations, Products and Equipment Which Might Feature in Sumerian Texts. Part II. Free Threshing Cereals. *Bulletin on Sumerian Agriculture* 2:1–31.

———. 1996. Late Pleistocene Changes in Wild Plant-Foods Available to Hunter-Gatherers of the Northern Fertile Crescent: Possible Preludes to Cereal Cultivation. In *The Origins and Spread of Agriculture and Pastoralism in Eurasia,* edited by D. R. Harris, pp. 159–203. Smithsonian Institution Press, Washington, DC.

Hillman, G. C., S. M. Colledge, and D. R. Harris. 1989. Plant-Food Economy during the Epipaleolithic Period at Tell Abu Hureyra, Syria: Dietary Diversity, Seasonality, and Modes of Exploitation. In *Foraging and Farming,* edited by D. Harris and G. Hillman, pp. 240–268, Unwin Hyman, London.

Hole, Frank. 2000. Is Size Important? Function and Hierarchy in Neolithic Settlements. In *Life in Neolithic Farming Communities,* edited by I. Kuijt, pp. 191–209. Kluwer Academic/Plenum Publishers, New York.

Holliman, Sandra E. 1991. Health Consequences of Divisions of Labor among the Chumash Indians of Southern California. In *The Archaeology of Gender,* edited by D. Walde and N. Willows, pp. 462–469. Archaeology Association of the University of Calgary, Calgary.

———. 2000. Sex, Health, and Gender Roles among the Arikara of the Northern Plains. In *Reading the Body,* edited by A. Rautman, pp. 25–37. University of Pennsylvania Press, Philadelphia.

Hooton, E. A. 1930. *The Indians of Pecos Pueblo: A Study of Their Skeletal Remains.* Papers of the Southwestern Expedition No. 4. Yale University Press, New Haven, CT.

Hopf, M. 1969. Plant Remains and Early Farming in Jericho. In *The Domestication and Exploitation of Plants and Animals,* edited by P. J. Ucko and G. W. Dimbleby, pp. 355–359. Duckworth, London.

Horne, L. 1994. *Village Spaces: Settlement and Society in Northeastern Iran.* Smithsonian Institution Press, Washington, DC.

Horwitz, L. K., and E. Tchernov. 1989. Animal Exploitation in the Early Bronze Age of the Southern Levant: An Overview. In *L'Urbanization de la Palestine à l'Age du Bronze Ancien,* edited by P. de Miroschedji, pp. 279–296. BAR International Series No. 527(ii). BAR International, Oxford.

Hovers, E. 1993. Judea. In *The New Encyclopedia of Excavations in the Holy Land,* edited by E. Stern, p. 814. Simon and Schuster, New York.

Iscan, Mehmet Yasar, and Kenneth A. R. Kennedy (editors). 1989. *Reconstructions of Life from the Skeleton.* Alan R. Liss, New York.

Jackson, T. L. 1991. Pounding Acorns: Women's Production as Social and Economic Focus. In *Engendering Archaeology,* edited by J. M. Gero and M. W. Conkey, pp. 301–325. Basil Blackwell, Cambridge.

Jacobs, K. 1993. Human Postcranial Variation in the Ukrainian Mesolithic-Neolithic. *Current Anthropology* 34:311–324.

Jacobs, L. 1979. Tell-i-Nun: Archaeological Implications of a Village in Transition. In *Ethnoarchaeology: Implications of Ethnography for Archaeology,* edited by C. Kramer, pp. 175–191. Columbia University Press, New York.

James, S. R. 1994. *Variation in Pueblo Household Use of Space: A Processual Approach to Prehistoric Social Organization.* Ph.D. dissertation, Arizona State University, Tempe.

Johnson, A. W., and T. Earle. 1987. *The Evolution of Human Societies.* Stanford University Press, Stanford, CA.

Jurmain, Robert D. 1980. The Pattern of Involvement of Appendicular Degenerative Joint Disease. *American Journal of Physical Anthropology* 53:143–150.

———. 1990. Paleoepidemiology of a Central California Prehistoric Population from Ca-Ala-329. II. Degenerative Disease. *American Journal of Physical Anthropology* 83:83–94.

———. 1991. Degenerative Changes in Peripheral Joints as Indicators of Mechanical Stress: Opportunities and Limitations. *International Journal of Osteoarchaeology* 1:247–252.

———. 1999. *Stories from the Skeleton.* Gordon and Breach Publishers, Amsterdam.

Kafafi, Zeidan. 1988a. Jebel Abu Thawwab: A Pottery Neolithic Village in North Jordan. In *Prehistory of Jordan,* edited by A. N. Garrard and H. G. Gebel, pp. 451–471. BAR International Series No. 396. BAR International, Oxford.

———. 1988b. The Pottery Neolithic in Jordan in Connection with Other Near Eastern Regions. In *Studies in the History and Antiquity of Jordan, Volume III,* pp. 33–39. Department of Antiquities, Amman.

———. 1998. The Late Neolithic in Jordan. In *The Prehistoric Archaeology of Jordan,* edited by D. O. Henry, pp. 127–138. BAR International Series No. 705. BAR International Series, Oxford.

Kafafi, Zeidan, Isabella Caneva, and Gaetano Palumbo. 1999. The Neolithic Site of es-Sayyah: Preliminary Report on the 1999 Season. *Neo-Lithics* 3/99:10–12.

Kafafi, Zeidan, and Gary Rollefson. 1995. The 1994 Excavation Season at 'Ayn Ghazal: Preliminary Report. *Annual of the Department of Antiquities of Jordan* 39:13–29.

Kamp, Kathryn A. 1987. Affluence and Image: Ethnoarchaeology in a Syrian Village. *Journal of Field Archaeology* 14:283–296.

———. 1993. Towards an Archaeology of Architecture: Clues from a Modern Syrian Village. *Journal of Anthropological Research* 49(4):293–317.

Kaplan, J. 1954. Two Chalcolithic Vessels from Palestine. *Palestine Exploration Quarterly* 86:97–101.

———. 1969. 'Ein el-Jarba: Chalcolithic Remains in the Plain of Esdraelon. *Bulletin of the American School of Oriental Research* 194:2–38.

———. 1976. Giv'atayim. In *Encyclopedia of Excavations in the Holy Land,* edited by M. Avi-Yonah, pp. 451–452. Massada, Jerusalem.

Keeley, Lawrence H. 1991. The Introduction of Agriculture to the Western North European Plain. In *Transitions to Agriculture in Prehistory,* edited by A. B. Gebauer and T. D. Price, pp. 81–96. Prehistory Press, Madison, WI.

Kehoe, Alice B. 1990. Points and Lines. In *Powers of Observation: Alternative Views in Archaeology,* edited by S. M. Nelson and A. B. Kehoe, pp. 23–38. Archaeological Papers of the American Anthropological Association No. 2. American Anthropological Association, Washington, DC.

———. 1991. No Possible, Probable Shadow of Doubt. *Antiquity* 65:129–131.

Keith, A. 1931. *The Antiquity of Man.* Williams and Norgate, London.

Kelley, J. O., and J. L. Angel. 1987. Life Stresses of Slavery. *American Journal of Physical Anthropology* 74:199–211.

Kennedy, K. A. R. 1983. Morphological Variations in Ulnar Supinator Crests and Fossae as Identification Markers of Occupational Stress. *Journal of Forensic Science* 28:871–876.

———. 1989. Skeletal Markers of Occupational Stress. In *Reconstruction of Life from the Skeleton*, edited by M. Y. Iscan and K. A. R. Kennedy, pp. 129–160. Alan R. Liss, New York.

Kennedy, K. A. R., T. Plummer, and J. Chiment. 1986. Identification of the Eminent Dead: Penpi, a Scribe in Ancient Egypt. In *Forensic Osteology: Advances in the Identification of Human Remains*, edited by K. J. Reich, pp. 290–301. Charles C. Thomas, Springfield, IL.

Kenyon, K. M. 1957. *Digging Up Jericho*. Frederick A. Praeger, New York.

———. 1981. *Excavations at Jericho, Vol. II: The Architecture and Stratigraphy of the Tell*. British School of Archaeology in Jerusalem, London.

Kerner, Susanne. 1997. Specialization in the Chalcolithic in the Southern Levant. In *The Prehistory of Jordan II*, edited by H. G. Gebel, Z. Kafafi, and G. Rollefson, pp. 419–427. Ex oriente, Berlin.

Kirkbride, D. V. W. 1966. Five Seasons at the Pre-Pottery Neolithic Village of Beidha in Jordan. *Palestine Exploration Quarterly* 98:8–72.

Kohler-Rollefson, I. 1989. Changes in Goat Exploitation at Neolithic 'Ain Ghazal: A Metrical Analysis. *Paléorient* 14:87–93.

Kramer, C. 1979. An Archaeological View of a Contemporary Kurdish Village: Domestic Architecture, Household Size, and Wealth. In *Ethnoarchaeology: Implications of Ethnography for Archaeology*, edited by C. Kramer, pp. 139–163. Columbia University Press, New York.

———. 1982a. Ethnographic Households and Archaeological Interpretation: A Case from Iranian Kurdistan. *American Behavioral Scientist* 25:663–675.

———. 1982b. *Village Ethnoarchaeology: Rural Iran in Archaeological Perspective*. Academic Press, New York.

Krogman, W. M. 1989. Representative Early Bronze Crania from Bab edh-Dhra. In *Bab edh-Dhra: Excavations in the Cemetery Directed by Paul Lapp (1965–1967)*, edited by R. T. Schaub and W. E. Rast, pp. 507–520. Eisenbrauns, Winona Lake, IN.

Kuijt, Ian. 1996. Negotiating Equality through Ritual: A Consideration of Late Natufian and PPNA Period Mortuary Practices. *Journal of Anthropological Archaeology* 15:313–336.

———. 2000. Keeping the Peace: Ritual, Skull Caching, and Community Integration in the Levantine Neolithic. In *Life in Neolithic Farming Communities*, edited by I. Kuijt, pp. 137–164. Kluwer Academic/Plenum Publishers, New York.

Kuijt, I., J. Mabry, and G. Palumbo. 1991. Early Neolithic Use of Upland Areas of Wadi el-Yabis: Preliminary Evidence from the Excavations of 'Iraq ed-Dubb, Jordan. *Paléorient* 17:99–108.

Kurth, Gottfriend, and Olav Rohrer-Ertl. 1981. On the Anthropology of the Mesolithic to Chalcolithic Human Remains from the Tell es-Sultan in Jericho, Jordan. In *Excavations at Jericho, Vol. III*, edited by K. M. Kenyon, pp. 407–499. British School of Archaeology, Jerusalem.

Lai, Ping, and Nancy C. Lovell. 1992. Skeletal Markers of Occupational Stress in the Fur Trade: A Case Study from the Hudson's Bay Company Fur Trade Post. *International Journal of Osteoarchaeology* 2:221–234.

Larsen, Clark Spencer. 1982. The Anthropology of St. Catherine's Island 3. Prehistoric Human Biological Adaptation. *American Museum of Natural History Anthropological Papers* 57:119–122.

———. 1984. Health and Disease in Prehistoric Georgia: The Transition to Agriculture. In *Paleopathology at the Origins of Agriculture,* edited by M. N. Cohen and G. J. Armelagos, pp. 367–392. Academic Press, New York.

———. 1985. Dental Modifications and Tool Use in the Western Great Basin. *American Journal of Physical Anthropology* 67:367–402.

———. 1987. Bioarchaeological Interpretations of Subsistence Economy and Behavior from Human Skeletal Remains. In *Advances in Archaeological Method and Theory, Vol. 10,* edited by Michael B. Schiffer, pp. 339–445. Academic Press, New York.

———. 1997. *Bioarchaeology.* Cambridge University Press, New York.

———. 2000. *Skeletons in Our Closet.* Princeton University Press, Princeton, NJ.

Larsen, Clark Spencer, and Marc A. Kelley. 1991. Introduction. In *Advances in Dental Anthropology,* edited by Marc A. Kelley and Clark Spencer Larsen, pp. 1–5. Wiley-Liss, New York.

Layton, R., R. Foley, and E. Williams. 1991. The Transition between Hunting-Gathering and the Specialized Husbandry of Resources. *Current Anthropology* 32:255–274.

Leacock, E. 1978. Women's Status in Egalitarian Society: Implications for Social Evolution. *Current Anthropology* 19:247–275.

———. 1981. History, Development, and the Division of Labor by Sex. *Signs* 7:474–491.

LeBlanc, S. A. 1971. An Addition to Naroll's Suggested Floor Area and Settlement Population Relationship. *American Antiquity* 36:210–211.

Lechevallier, M. (editor). 1978. *Abou Gosh et Beisamoun.* Mémoires et Travaux du Centre de Recherches Préhistoriques Français de Jérusalem No. 2. Association Paléorient, Paris.

Lechevallier, M., D. Philibert, A. Ronen, and A. Samzun. 1990. Une Occupation Khiamienne et Sultanienne à Hatoula (Israel)? In *Préhistoire du Levant,* edited by O. Aurenche, M.-C. Cauvin, and P. Sanlaville, pp. 323–332. CNRS, Paris.

Leibowitz, Lila. 1986. In the Beginning . . . : The Origins of the Sexual Division of Labour and the Development of the First Human Societies. In *Women's Work, Men's Property,* edited by S. Coontz and P. Henderson, pp. 43–75. Verso, London.

LeMort, F. 1989. PPNA Burials from Hatoula (Israel). In *People and Culture in Change,* edited by I. Hershkovitz, pp. 133–140. BAR International Series No. 508. BAR International, Oxford.

Lerner, Gerda. 1986. *The Creation of Patriarchy.* Oxford University Press, New York.

Levy, L. F. 1968. Porter's Neck. *British Medical Journal* 2:16–19.

Levy, Thomas E. 1986. The Chalcolithic Period. *Biblical Archaeologist* 49:82–108.

———. 1993. Tuleilat el-Ghassul. In *The New Encyclopedia of Excavations in the Holy Land,* edited by E. Stern, pp. 506–511. Simon and Schuster, New York.

———. 1995. Cult, Metallurgy and Rank Societies—Chalcolithic Period (ca. 4500–3500 BCE). In *The Archaeology of Society in the Holy Land,* edited by T. E. Levy, pp. 226–243. Facts on File, New York.

Levy, T. E. (editor). 1987. *Shiqmim I: Studies concerning Chalcolithic Societies in the Northern Negev Desert, Israel (1982–1984).* BAR International Series No. 356. BAR International, Oxford.

Liphschitz, N. 1989. Plant Economy and Diet in the Early Bronze Age in Israel: A Summary of Present Research. In *L'Urbanization de la Palestine à l'Age du Bronze Ancien,* edited by P. de Miroschedji, pp. 296–277. BAR International Series No. 527(ii). BAR International, Oxford.

Lipschultz, Joshua G. 1996. *Who Were the Natufians? A Dental Assessment of Their Population Affinities.* M.A. thesis, Arizona State University, Tempe.

Little, K. 1973. *Bone Behavior.* Academic Press, New York.

Lovejoy, C., and K. Heiple. 1981. The Analysis of Fractures in Skeletal Populations with an Example from the Libben Site, Ottawa County, Ohio. *American Journal of Physical Anthropology* 55:529–541.

Lovejoy, C. O., and Eric Trinkaus. 1980. Strength and Robusticity of the Neandertal tibia. *American Journal of Physical Anthropology* 53:465–470.

MacDonald, B. (editor). 1988. *The Wadi el Hasa Archaeological Survey 1979–1983, West-Central Jordan.* Wilfrid Laurier University Press, Waterloo, Ontario.

———. 1992. *The Southern Ghor and Northeast 'Arabah Archaeological Survey.* Sheffield Archaeological Monographs 5. Sheffield University, Sheffield.

MacNeish, R. S. 1992. *The Origins of Agriculture and Settled Life.* University of Oklahoma Press, Norman.

Mahasneh, Hamzeh M. 1997. The 1995 Season at the Neolithic Site of Es-Sifiya, Wadi Mujib, Jordan. In *The Prehistory of Jordan II,* edited by H. G. K. Gebel, Z. Kafafi, and G. O. Rollefson, pp. 203–214. Ex oriente, Berlin.

Marder, O., H. Khalaily, E. Barzilay, and M. Patrson-Solemani. 1996. Recent Excavations at Abu Ghosh. *Neo-Lithics* 1/96:3–4.

Marks, A. E., and P. A. Larson, Jr. 1977. Test Excavations at the Natufian Site of Rosh Horesha. In *Prehistory and Paleoenvironments in the Central Negev, Israel, Vol. II,* edited by A. E. Marks, pp. 191–232. Southern Methodist University Press, Dallas.

McCorriston, J. 1992. *The Early Development of Aggriculture in the Ancient Near East: An Ecological and Evolutionary Study.* Ph.D. dissertation, Yale University, New Haven CT.

McCorriston, J., and F. Hole. 1991. The Ecology of Seasonal Stress and the Origins of Agriculture in the Near East. *American Anthropologist* 93:46–69.

McCown, T. D., and A. Keith. 1939. *The Stone Age of Mount Carmel, Vol II.* Clarendon Press, Oxford.

McCreery, D. W. 1981. Flotation of the Bab edh-Dhra and Numeira Plant Remains. In *The Southeastern Dead Sea Plain Expedition,* edited by W. E. Rast and R. T. Schaub, pp. 165–169. Annual of the American Schools of Oriental Research 46. American Schools of Oriental Research, Cambridge, MA.

Meillassoux, Claude. 1981. *Maidens, Meal and Money.* Cambridge University Press, New York.

Mellaart, J. 1975. *The Neolithic of the Near East.* Thames and Hudson, London.

Merbs, Charles F. 1983. *Patterns of Activity-Induced Pathology in a Canadian Inuit Population.* Archaeological Survey of Canada Paper No. 119. National Museum of Canada, Ottawa.

————. 1989. Trauma. In *Reconstruction of Life from the Skeleton*, edited by K. Kennedy and M. Iscan, pp. 161–190. Alan R. Liss, New York.

Milner, George R., and Clark Spencer Larsen. 1991. Teeth as Artifacts of Human Behavior: Intentional Mutilation and Accidental Modification. In *Advances in Dental Anthropology*, edited by Marc A. Kelley and Clark Spencer Larsen, pp. 357–378. Wiley-Liss, New York.

Milner, George R., Virginia C. Smith, and Eve Anderson. 1991. Conflict, Mortality, and Community Health in an Illinois Oneota Population. In *Between Bands and States*, edited by Susan A. Gregg, pp. 245–264. Center for Archaeological Investigations Occasional Paper No. 9. Southern Illinois University, Carbondale.

Mobley-Tanaka, Jeannette L. 1997. Gender and Ritual Space during the Pithouse to Pueblo Transition: Subterranean Mealing Rooms in the North American Southwest. *American Antiquity* 62:437–448.

Molleson, T. I. 1989. Seed Preparation in the Mesolithic: The Osteological Evidence. *Antiquity* 63:356–362.

————. 1994. Eloquent Bones of Abu Hureyra. *Scientific American*, August, 70–75.

————. 2000. People of Abu Hureyra. In *Village on the Euphrates: From Foraging to Farming at Abu Hureya*, by A. M. T. Moore, G. C. Hillman, and A. J. Legge, pp. 301–324. Oxford University Press, Oxford.

Moore, A. M. T. 1985. The Development of Neolithic Societies in the Near East. In *Advances in World Archaeology 4*, edited by F. Wendorf and A. E. Close, pp. 1–69. Academic Press, New York.

————. 1991. Abu Hureyra I and the Antecedents of Agriculture on the Middle Euphrates. In *The Natufian Culture in the Levant*, edited by O. Bar-Yosef and F. Valla, pp. 277–294. International Monographs in Prehistory, Ann Arbor, MI.

————. 2000. The Excavation of Abu Hureyra 2. In *Village on the Euphrates*, edited by A. M. T. Moore, G. C. Hillman, and A. J. Legge, pp. 189–260. Oxford University Press, Oxford.

Moore, A. M. T., G. C. Hillman, and A. J. Legge. 2000. *Village on the Euphrates: From Foraging to Farming at Abu Hureya.* Oxford University Press, Oxford.

Moore, H. L. 1988. *Feminism and Anthropology.* University of Minnesota Press, Minneapolis.

Moss, Madonna L. 1993. Shellfish, Gender, and Status on the Northwest Coast: Reconciling Archaeological, Ethnographic, and Ethnohistorical Records of the Tlingit. *American Anthropologist* 95:631–652.

Muheisen, M., H. G. Gebel, C. Hannss, and R. Neef. 1988. Excavations at 'Ain Rahub, a Final Natufian and Yarmoukian Site near Irbid (1985). In *Prehistory of Jordan*, edited by A. N. Garrard and H. G. Gebel, pp. 473–495. BAR International Series No. 396. BAR International, Oxford.

Murdock, G. P. 1937. Comparative Data on Division of Labor by Sex. *Social Forces* 15:551–553.

————. 1949. *Social Structure.* Macmillan, New York.

Murdock, G. P., and C. Provost. 1973. Factors in the Division of Labor by Sex: A Cross-Cultural Analysis. *Ethnology* 12:203–225.

Nagy, Bethel L. B. 1997. Musculoskeletal Stress Markers, Osteoarthritis, and Habitual Activity in the Prehistoric American Southwest. Paper presented at the annual meeting of the American Association of Physical Anthropologists, St. Louis, MO.

Nagy, Bethel L., and Diane E. Hawkey. 1993. Correspondence of Osteoarthritis and Muscle Use in Reconstructing Prehistoric Activity Patterns. Paper presented at the annual meeting of the Paleopathology Association, Toronto.

Naroll, R. S. 1962. Floor Area and Settlement Population. *Antiquity* 27:587–589.

Neff, R. 1988. Note on the Yarmoukian Plant Remains. In *The Prehistory of Jordan: The State of Research in 1986*, edited by A. Garrard and H. G. Gebel, pp. 472–502. BAR International Series No. 396(ii), British Archaeological Reports. Oxford.

Nelson, Sarah M. 1997. *Gender and Archaeology: Analyzing Power and Prestige.* AltaMira Press, Walnut Creek, CA.

Neuville, R. 1951. *Le Paléolithique et le Mésolithique du Désert de Judée.* Archives de l'Institut de Paléontologie Humaine Memoire 24. Masson et Cie, Paris.

Norusis, M. J. 1990. *SPSS User's Guide.* SPSS Inc., Chicago.

Noy, T. 1977. Nahal Oren. Distribution of Carbonized Seeds According to Layer. In *Encyclopedia of Archaeological Excavations in the Holy Land*, edited by M. Avi-Stern and E. Stern, p. 903, Massada Press, Jerusalem.

Noy, T., A. J. Legge, and E. S. Higgs. 1973. Recent Excavations at Nahal Oren, Israel. *Proceedings of the Prehistoric Society* 39:75–99.

Noy, T., J. Schuldenrein, and E. Tchernov. 1980. Gilgal, a Pre-Pottery Neolithic A Site in the Lower Jordan Valley. *Israel Exploration Journal* 30:63–82.

O'Kelley, C. G., and L. S. Carney. 1986. *Women and Men in Society: Cross-Cultural Perspectives on Gender Stratification.* Wadsworth, Belmont, CA.

Olin, M. S., H. A. Young, D. Seligson, and H. H. Schmidek. 1982. An Unusual Cervical Injury Occurring during Cow Milking. *Spine* 7:514–515.

Olszewski, D. I. 1991. Social Complexity in the Natufian? Assessing the Relationship of Ideas and Data. In *Perspective on the Past*, edited by G. A. Clark, pp. 322–340. University of Pennsylvania Press, Philadelphia.

———. 1993. Zarzian Microlithis from Warwasi Rockshelter, Iran: Scalene Triangles as Arrow Components. In *Hunting and Animal Exploitation in the Later Palaeolithic and Mesolithic of Eurasia*, edited by G. L. Peterkin, H. M. Bricker, and P. Mellars, pp. 199–205. American Anthropological Association, Washington, DC.

Ortner, D. J. 1979. Disease and Mortality in the Early Bronze Age People of Bab edh-Dhra, Jordan. *American Journal of Physical Anthropology* 51:589–598.

———. 1981. A Preliminary Report on the Human Remains from the Bab edh-Dhra Cemetery. In *The Southeastern Dead Sea Plain Expedition*, edited by W. E. Rast and R. T. Schaub, pp. 119–132. Annual of the American Schools of Oriental Research No. 46. American Schools of Oriental Research, Cambridge, MA.

———. 1982. The Skeletal Biology of an Early Bronze IB Charnel House at Bab edh-Dhra, Jordan. *Studies in the History and Archaeology of Jordan*, edited by A. Hadidi, pp. 93–95. Department of Antiquities, Amman.

Ortner, D. J., and W. G. J. Putschar. 1985. *Identification of Pathological Conditions in Human Skeletal Remains.* Smithsonian Contributions to Anthropology No. 28. Smithsonian Institution Press, Washington, DC.

Ortner, S. B. 1974. Is Female to Male as Nature Is to Culture? In *Culture and Society,* edited by M. Z. Rosaldo and L. Lamphere, pp. 67–88. Stanford University Press, Stanford, CA.

Pasternak, B., C. E. Ember, and M. Ember. 1997. *Sex, Gender, and Kinship: A Cross-Cultural Perspective.* Prentice Hall, Upper Saddle River, NJ.

Perrot, J. 1966. Le Gisement Natoufien de Mallaha (Eynan), Israël. *L'Anthropologie* 7:437–484.

———. 1984. Structures d'Habitat, Mode de Vie, et Environment: Les Villages Souterrains des Pasteurs de Beershéba dan le Sud d'Israel au IV Millénium Avant l'Ère Chris. *Paléorient* 10:75–96.

———. 1993a. 'Enan. In *The New Encyclopedia of Excavations in the Holy Land,* edited by E. Stern, pp. 389–393. Simon and Schuster, New York.

———. 1993b. Horvat Minha. In *The New Encyclopedia of Excavations in the Holy Land,* edited by E. Stern, pp. 1046–1050. Simon and Schuster, New York.

Perrot, J., and D. Ladiray. 1988. Les Sepultures. In *Les Hommes de Mallaha,* pp. 1–106. Mémoires et Travaux du Centre Recherche Français de Jérusalem No. 7. Association Paléorient, Paris.

Peters, E. L. 1978. The Status of Women in Four Middle East Communities. In *Women in the Muslim World,* edited by L. Beck and N. Keddie, pp. 311–350. Harvard University Press, Cambridge, MA.

Peterson, Jane D. 1994. *Changes in the Sexual Division of Labor in the Prehistory of the Southern Levant.* Ph.D. dissertation, Arizona State University, Tempe.

———. 1997. Tracking Activity Patterns through Skeletal Remains: A Case Study from Jordan and Palestine. In *Prehistory of Jordan II,* edited by H. G. Gebel, Z. Kafafi, and G. O. Rollefson, pp. 475–492. Ex oriente, Berlin.

———. 1998. The Natufian Hunting Conundrum: Spears, Atlatls, or Bows? Musculoskeletal and Armature Evidence. *International Journal of Osteoarchaeology* 8:378–389.

———. 1999. Early Epipaleolithic Settlement Patterns: Insights from the Study of Ground Stone Tools from the Southern Levant. *Levant* 31:1–17.

———. 2000a. Labor Patterns in the Southern Levant in the Early Bronze Age. In *Reading the Body,* edited by A. E. Rautman, pp. 38–54. University of Pennsylvania Press, Philadelphia.

———. 2000b. Test Excavations at PPNB/PPNC Khirbet Hammam, Wadi el-Hasa, Jordan. *Neo-Lithics* 1/2000:4–5.

———. 2000c. Where the Water Flows: Neolithic Settlement at Khirbet Hammam, Jordan. Paper presented at the 65th annual meeting of the Society for American Archaeology, Philadelphia.

Peterson, J., and D. Hawkey. 1998. Preface. *International Journal of Osteoarchaeology* 8:303–304.

Pickering, R. B. 1984. *Patterns of Degenerative Joint Disease in Middle Woodland, Late Woodland, and Mississippian Skeletal Series from the Lower Illinois Valley.* Ph.D. dissertation, Northwestern University, Evanston, IL.

Postgate, J. N. 1986. The Equids of Sumer, Again. In *Equids in the Ancient World*, edited by R. H. Meadow and H. P. Uerpmann, pp. 194–206. Reichert, Wiesbaden, Germany.

Potts, T. F., S. M. Colledge, and P. C. Edwards. 1985. Preliminary Report on a Sixth Season of Excavation at Pella in Jordan (1983/1984). *Annual of the Department of Antiquities of Jordan* 29:181–206.

Powell, Mary Lucas. 1992. In the Best of Health? Disease and Trauma among the Mississippian Elite. In *Lords of the Southeast*, edited by Alex W. Barker and Timothy R. Pauketat, pp. 81–97. Archaeological Papers of the American Anthropological Association No. 3. American Anthropological Association, Washington, DC.

Quintero, L. A., and P. J. Wilke. 1995. Evolution and Economic Significance of Naviform Core-and-Blade Technology in the Southern Levant. *Paléorient* 21(1):17–33.

Rapp, R. 1975. *Toward an Anthropology of Women*. Monthly Review Press, New York.

Rast, W. E. 1981. Patterns of Settlement at Bab edh-Dhra. In *The Southeastern Dead Sea Plain Expedition*, edited by W. E. Rast and R. T. Schaub, pp. 7–34. Annual of the American Schools of Oriental Research No. 46. American Schools of Oriental Research, Cambridge, MA.

———. 1999. Society and Mortuary Customs at Bab edh-Dhra'. In *Archaeology, History and Culture in Palestine and the Near East*, edited by T. Kapitan, pp. 164–182. ASOR Books Volume 3. Scholars Press, Atlanta.

Rast, W. E., and R. T. Schaub (editors). 1981. *The Southeastern Dead Sea Plain Expedition*. Annual of the American Schools of Oriental Research No. 46. American Schools of Oriental Research, Cambridge, MA.

Rathbun, T. A. 1984. Skeletal Pathology from the Paleolithic through the Metal Ages in Iran and Iraq. In *Pathology at the Origins of Agriculture*, edited by R. Cohen and G. Armelagos, pp. 137–167. Academic Press, New York.

Redding, R. 1989. A General Explanation of Subsistence Change: From Hunting and Gathering to Food Production. *Journal of Anthropological Archaeology* 7:56–97.

Redman, C. L. 1978. *The Rise of Civilization: Early Farmers to Urban Society in the Ancient Near East*. Freeman, San Francisco.

Richard, S. 1987. Early Bronze Age. *Biblical Archaeologist* 50:22–43.

Rindos, D. 1980. Symbiosis, Instability, and the Origins and Spread of Agriculture: A New Model. *Current Anthropology* 21:751–772.

Robb, John. 1994. Skeletal Signs of Activity in the Italian Metal Ages: Methodological and Interpretive Notes. *Human Evolution* 9:215–229.

———. 1998. The Interpretation of Skeletal Muscle Sites: A Statistical Approach. *International Journal of Osteoarchaeology* 8:363–377.

Roehrer-Ertl, O., K. W. Frey, and H. Newesely. 1998. Preliminary Note on Early Neolithic Human Remains from Basta and Sabra. In *The Prehistory of Jordan*, edited by A. Garrard and H. G. Gebel, pp. 135–136. BAR International Series No. 396. BAR International, Oxford.

Rohrlich-Leavitt, R. 1975. *Women Cross-Culturally: Continuity and Change*. Mouton, The Hague.

Rollefson, Gary O. 1990. Neolithic Chipped Stone Technology at 'Ain Ghazal: The Status of the PPNC. *Paléorient* 16:119–124.

———. 1996. The Neolithic Devolution: Ecological Impact and Cultural Compensation at 'Ain Ghazal, Jordan. In *Retrieving the Past*, edited by J. D. Seger, pp. 219–229. Eisenbrauns, Winona Lake, IN.

———. 1998. The Aceramic Neolithic of Jordan. In *The Prehistoric Archaeology of Jordan*, edited by D. O. Henry, pp. 102–126. BAR International Series No. 705, BAR International, Oxford.

———. 1999. El-Hemmeh: A Late PPNB-PPNC Village in the Wade el-Hasa, Southern Jordan. *Neo-Lithics* 2/99:6–8.

Rollefson, Gary, and Zeidan Kafafi. 1994. The 1993 Season at 'Ain Ghazal: Preliminary Report. *Annual of the Department of Antiquities of Jordan* 38:11–32.

———. 1996. The 1995 Season at 'Ayn Ghazal: Preliminary Report. *Annual of the Department of Antiquities of Jordan* 40:11–28.

Rollefson, G. O., E. Banning, B. Byrd, Z. Kafafi, I. Kohler, D. Petocz, S. Rolston, and L. Villiers. 1984. The Pre-Pottery Neolithic B Village of 'Ain Ghazal (Jordan): Preliminary Report of the 1982 Excavation Season. *Mitteilungen der Deutschen Orient Gesellschaft* 116:139–184.

Rollefson, G. O., and I. Kohler-Rollefson. 1989. The Collapse of Early Neolithic Settlements in the Southern Levant. In *People and Cultures in Change*, edited by I. Hershkovitz, pp. 73–89. BAR International Series No. 508(i). BAR International, Oxford.

Rollefson, G. O., A. H. Simmons, and Z. Kafafi. 1992. Neolithic Cultures at 'Ain Ghazal, Jordan. *Journal of Field Archaeology* 19:443–470.

Ronen, A., and M. Lechevallier. 1991. The Natufian of Hatoula. In *The Natufian Culture in the Levant*, edited by O. Bar-Yosef and F. Valla, pp. 149–160. International Monographs in Prehistory, Ann Arbor, MI.

Rosaldo, M. Z. 1980. The Use and Abuse of Anthropology: Reflections on Feminism and Cross-Cultural Understanding. *Signs* 5:389–417.

Rosaldo, M. Z., and L. Lamphere. 1974. *Culture and Society.* Stanford University Press, Stanford, CA.

Roscoe, Will. 1991. *The Zuni Man-Woman.* University of New Mexico Press, Albuquerque.

Rosen, S. A. 1983. The Canaanean Blade and the Early Bronze Age. *Israel Exploration Journal* 33:15–29.

———. 1986. The Analysis of Trade and Craft Specialization in the Chalcolithic Period: Comparisons from Different Realms of Material Culture. *Michmanim* 3:2–32.

———. 1997. *Lithics after the Stone Age: A Handbook of Stone Tools from the Levant.* AltaMira Press, Walnut Creek, CA.

Rothenberg, B. 1972. *Timna: Valley of the Biblical Copper Mines.* Thames and Hudson, London.

Ruff, Christopher B., and Clark Spencer Larsen. 1990. Chapter 7: Postcranial Biomechanical Adaptations to Subsistence Strategy Change on the Georgia Coast. In *The Archaeology of Mission Santa Cataline de Guale: 2. Biocultural Interpretations of a Population in Transition*, edited by Clark Spencer Larsen, pp. 94–120. Anthropological Papers of the

American Museum of Natural History No. 68. American Museum of Natural History, New York.

Ruff, Christopher B., Eric Trinkaus, Alan Walker, and Clark Spencer Larsen. 1993. Postcranial Robusticity in HOMO. I: Temporal Trends and Mechanical Interpretation. *American Journal of Physical Anthropology* 91:21–53.

Schaub, R. T. 1981. Patterns of Burial at Bab edh-Dhra. In *The Southeastern Dead Sea Plain Expedition*, edited by W. E. Rast and R. T. Schaub, pp. 45–68. Annual of the American Schools of Oriental Research No. 46. American Schools of Oriental Research, Cambridge, MA.

Schaub, R. Thomas, and Walter E. Rast. 1984. Preliminary Report of the 1981 Expedition to the Dead Sea Plain, Jordan. *Bulletin of the American Schools of Oriental Research* 254:35–60.

Schultz, Michael. 1987. Report on the First Two Field Seasons at Basta (1986–7): Human Skeletal Remains. *Annual of the Department of Antiquities of Jordan* 31:96–97.

Schultz, Michael, and Andreas Scherer. 1991. Report on the Excavation of Basta: Human Skeletal Remains. *Annual of the Department of Antiquities of Jordan* 35:18–19.

Schulz, P. D. 1977. Task Activity and Anterior Tooth Grooving in Prehistoric California Indians. *American Journal of Physical Anthropology* 46:87–91.

Sellars, Jonathan R. 1998. The Natufian of Jordan. In *The Prehistoric Archaeology of Jordan*, edited by D. O. Henry, pp. 83–101. BAR International Series No. 705, BAR International, Oxford.

Shaibani, A., R. Workman, and B. M. Rothschild. 1993. The Significance of Enthesopathy as a Skeletal Phenomenon. *Clinical and Experimental Rheumatology* 11:399–403.

Shalev, S., and P. J. Northover. 1987. Chalcolithic Metal and Metalworking from Shiqmim. In *Shiqmim I: Studies concerning Chalcolithic Societies in the Northern Negev Desert, Israel (1982–1984)*, edited by T. E. Levy, pp. 357–371. BAR International Series No. 356(i). BAR International, Oxford.

Sherratt, H. 1981. Plough and Pastoralism. In *Patterns of the Past*, edited by I. Hodder, G. Isaac, and N. Hammond, pp. 261–306. Cambridge University Press, Cambridge.

———. 1983. The Secondary Products Revolution of Animals in the Old World. *World Archaeology* 15:90–104.

Sillen, A. 1984. Dietary Change in the Epi-Paleolithic and Neolithic of the Levant: The Sr/Ca Evidence. *Paléorient* 10:149–155.

Sillen, A., and J. A. Lee-Thorp. 1991. Dietary Change in the Late Natufian. In *The Natufian Culture in the Levant*, edited by O. Bar-Yosef and F. Valla, pp. 399–410. International Monographs in Prehistory, Ann Arbor, MI.

Silverblatt, Irene. 1988. Women in States. *Annual Review of Anthropology* 17:427–460.

Simmons, Alan H., and Mohammad al-Najjar. 1999. Preliminary Field Report of the 1998–1999 Excavations at Ghwair I, a Pre-Pottery Neolithic B Community in the Wadi Feinan Region of Southern Jordan. *Neo-Lithics* 1/99:4–6.

Simmons, Alan H., Gary O. Rollefson, Zeidan Kafafi, Rolfe D. Mandel, Maysoon al-Nahan, Jason Cooper, Ilse Kohler-Rollefson, and Kathy Roler Durand. 2000. Wadi Shu'eib, a Large Neolithic Community in Central Jordan: Final Report of Test Excavations. *Bulletin of the American Schools of Oriental Research* 321:1–39.

Smith, Patricia. 1972. Diet and Attrition in the Natufians. *American Journal of Physical Anthropology* 37:233–238.

———. 1989a. Paleonutrition and Subsistence Patterns in the Natufians. In *People and Cultures in Change*, edited by I. Hershkovitz, pp. 375–384. BAR International Series No. 508(ii). BAR International, Oxford.

———. 1989b. The Skeletal Biology and Paleopathology of Early Bronze Age Populations in the Levant. In *L'Urbanization de la Palestine à l'Age du Bronze Ancien*, edited by P. de Miroschedji, pp. 297–313. BAR International Series No. 527(ii). BAR International, Oxford.

———. 1991. The Dental Evidence for Nutritional Status in the Natufians. In *The Natufian Culture in the Levant*, edited by O. Bar-Yosef and F. Valla, pp. 425–432. International Monographs in Prehistory, Ann Arbor, MI.

———. 1995. People of the Holy Land from Prehistory to the Recent Past. In *The Archaeology of Society in the Holy Land*, edited by T. E. Levy, pp. 58–74. Facts of File, New York.

Smith, P. E. L. 1976. *Food Production and Its Consequences*. Cummings Publishing Company, Menlo Park, CA.

Smith, P., O. Bar-Yosef, and A. Sillen. 1984. Archaeological and Skeletal Evidence for Dietary Changes during the Late Pleistocene/Early Holocene in the Levant. In *Paleopathology at the Origins of Agriculture*, edited by R. Cohen and G. Armelagos, pp. 101–136. Academic Press, New York.

Smith, P., R. A. Bloom, and J. Berkowitz. 1984. Diachronic Trends in Humeral Cortical Thickness of Near East Populations. *Journal of Human Evolution* 13:603–611.

Smith, P., and L. K. Horwitz. 1984. Radiographic Evidence for Changing Patterns of Animal Exploitation in the Southern Levant. *Journal of Archaeological Science* 11:467–475.

Soliveres-Massei, O. 1978. Etude Anthropologique: Les Restes Post-Cephaliques. In *Abou Gosh and Beisamoun*, edited by M. Lechevallier, pp. 181–191. Mémoires et Travaux du Centre de Recherches Préhistoriques Français de Jérusalem No. 2. Association Paléorient, Paris.

———. 1988. Etude Anthropologique. In *Les Hommes de Mallaha*, pp. 110–208. Memoires et Travaux du Centre de Recherche Français de Jérusalem No. 7. Association Paléorient, Paris.

Spector, J. D. 1982. Male/Female Task Differentiation among the Hidatsa: Toward the Development of an Archaeological Approach to the Study of Gender. In *The Hidden Half*, edited by B. Medicine and P. Albers, pp. 77–99. University Press of America, Washington, DC.

Stager, L. E. 1992. The Periodization of Palestine from Neolithic through Early Bronze Times. In *Chronologies in Old World Archaeology*, edited by R. W. Ehrich, pp. 22–41. University of Chicago Press, Chicago.

Stahl, A. B. 1989. Plant-Food Processing: Implications for Dietary Quality. In *Foraging and Farming: The Evolution of Plant Exploitation*, edited by D. R. Harris and G. C. Hillman, pp. 171–194. Unwin Hyman, Boston.

Stahl, P. M. 1986. *Household, Village and Village Confederation in Southeastern Europe*. East European Monographs No. CC. Columbia University Press, New York.

Stark, B. L. 1986. Origins of Food Production in the New World. In *American Archaeology Past and Future*, edited by D. J. Meltzer, D. D. Fowler, and J. A. Sabloff, pp. 277–321. Smithsonian Institution Press, Washington, DC.

Steen, Susan L., and Robert W. Lane. 1998. Evaluation of Habitual Activities among Two Alaskan Eskimo Populations Based on Musculoskeletal Stress Markers. *International Journal of Osteoarchaeology* 8:341–353.

Steinbock, R. T. 1976. *Paleopathological Diagnosis and Interpretation.* C. C. Thomas, Springfield, IL.

Stekelis, M. 1972. *The Yarmoukian Culture.* Magness Press, Jerusalem.

Stekelis, M., and T. Yizraely. 1963. Excavations at Nahal Oren: Preliminary Report. *Israel Exploration Journal* 13:1–12.

Stiner, Mary C., Natalie D. Munro, and Todd A. Surovell. 2000. The Tortoise and the Hare: Small-Game Use, the Broad-Spectrum Revolution, and Paleolithic Demography. *Current Anthropology* 41:39–73.

Stirland, Ann. 1991. Diagnosis of Occupationally Related Paleopathology: Can It Be Done? In *Human Paleopathology: Current Synthesis and Future Options*, edited by Donald J. Ortner and Arthur C. Aufderheide, pp. 40–47. Smithsonian Institution Press, Washington, DC.

———. 1998. Musculoskeletal Evidence for Activity: Problems of Evaluation. *International Journal of Osteoarchaeology* 8:354–362.

Stuart-Macadam, Patty, and Bonnie Glencross. 1997. Interpreting Activity Patterns: A Synthetic Approach. Paper presented at the annual meeting of the American Association of Physical Anthropologists, St. Louis, MO.

Sullivan, Norman C. 1977. *The Physical Anthropology of Chiggerville: Demography and Pathology.* M.A. thesis, Western Michigan University, Kalamazoo.

Sumner, D. R., B. Mockbee, K. Morse, T. Cram, and M. Pitt. 1985. Computed Tomography and Automated Image Analysis of Prehistoric Femora. *American Journal of Physical Anthropology* 68:225–232.

Tainter, J. 1980. Behavior and Status in a Middle Woodland Mortuary Population from the Illinois Valley. *American Antiquity* 45:308–313.

Tapper, N. 1978. The Women's Subsociety among the Shahseven Nomads of Iran. In *Women in the Muslim World*, edited by L. Beck and N. Keddie, pp. 374–398. Harvard University Press, Cambridge, MA.

Tavakalian, B. 1984. Women and Socio-Economic Change among Sheikhanzai Nomads of Western Afghanistan. *Middle East Journal* 38:433–453.

Tchernov, E. 1984. Commensal Animals and Human Sedentism. In *Animals and Archaeology, Vol. 3: Early Herders and Their Flocks*, edited by J. Clutton-Brock and C. Grigson, pp. 91–116. BAR International Series No. 202. BAR International, Oxford.

———. 1994. Netiv Hagdud. Part II: The Fauna of Netiv Hagdud. American School of Prehistoric Research Bulletin 44, Cambridge, MA.

Trinkaus, Eric. 1975. Squatting among the Neanderthals: A Problem in the Behavioral Interpretation of Skeletal Morphology. *Journal of Archaeological Science* 2:327–351.

Trinkaus, Eric, Steven E. Churchill, and Christopher B. Ruff. 1994. Postcranial Robusticity in HOMO. II: Humeral Bilateral Asymmetry and Bone Plasticity. *American Journal of Physical Anthropology* 93:1–34.

Tubb, Kathryn Walker, and Carol A. Grissom. 1995. 'Ayn Ghazal: A Comparative Study of the 1983 and 1985 Statuary Caches. In *Studies in the History and Archaeology of Jordan V*, pp. 435–447. Department of Antiquities, Amman.

Turnbull, C. M. 1981. Mbuti Womanhood. In *Woman the Gatherer*, edited by F. Dahlberg, pp. 205–220. Yale University Press, New Haven, CT.

Turner, C. J., and J. D. Cadien. 1969. Dental Chipping in Aleuts, Eskimos, and Indians. *American Journal of Physical Anthropology* 31:303–310.

Turville-Petre, F. 1932. Excavations in the Mugharet el-Kebarah. *Journal of the Royal Anthropological Institute* 62(2):271–276.

Ubelaker, D. H. 1979. Skeletal Evidence for Kneeling in Prehistoric Ecuador. *American Journal of Physical Anthropology* 51:679–686.

Unger-Hamilton, R. 1991. Natufian Plant Husbandry in the Southern Levant and Comparison with That of the Neolithic Periods: The Lithic Perspective. In *The Natufian Culture in the Levant*, edited by O. Bar-Yosef and F. Valla, pp. 483–520. International Monographs in Prehistory, Ann Arbor, MI.

Ussishkin, D. 1980. The Ghassulian Shrine at Ein Gedi. *Tel Aviv* 7:1–44.

Valla, F. A. 1987a. Chronologie relative et Chronologie absolute dans le Natoufien. In *Chronologies in the Near East*, edited by O. Aurenche, J. Evin, and F. Hours, pp. 267–294. BAR International Series No. 379. BAR International, Oxford.

———. 1987b. Les Natoufiens Connaisient-ils l'Arc? In *La Main et l'Outil, Manches et Emanchements Préhistoriques: Travaux de la Maison de l'Orient No. 15*, edited by D. Stordeur, pp. 165–174. Diffusion de Boccard, Paris.

———. 1991. Les Natoufiens de Mallaha et l'Espace. In *The Natufian Culture in the Levant*, edited by O. Bar-Yosef and F. Valla, pp. 111–122. International Monographs in Prehistory, Ann Arbor, MI.

———. 1995. The First Settled Societies—Natufian (12,500–10,200 BP). In *The Archaeology of Society in the Holy Land*, edited by T. E. Levy, pp. 169–185. Facts on File, New York.

Vallois, H. 1937. Les ossements Natoufiens d'Erq el Ahmar (Palestine). *L'Anthropologie* 46:529–539.

Voigt, Mary M. 1990. Reconstructing Neolithic Societies and Economies in the Middle East: An Essay. *Archeomaterials* 4:1–14.

Waheeb, Mohammed, and Nazeh Fino. 1997. 'Ayn el-Jammam: A Neolithic Site near Ras en-Naqb, Southern Jordan. In *Prehistory of Jordan II*, edited by H. G. K. Gebel, Z. Kafafi, and G. O. Rollefson, pp. 215–219. Ex oriente, Berlin.

Walker, Phillip L. 1981. Cranial Injuries as Evidence for the Evolution of Prehistoric Warfare in Southern California. *American Journal of Physical Anthropology* 54:287.

Wallace, J. A. 1974. Approximal Grooving of Teeth. *American Journal of Physical Anthropology* 40:385–390.

Watson, P. J. 1978. Architectural Differentiation in Some Near Eastern Communities, Prehistoric and Contemporary. In *Social Archaeology: Beyond Subsistence and Dating*, edited by C. L. Redman, pp. 131–158. Academic Press, New York.

———. 1979a. *Archaeological Ethnography in Western Iran*. Viking Fund Publications in Anthropology No. 57. Wenner-Gren Foundation, New York.

———. 1979b. The Idea of Ethnoarchaeology: Notes and Comments. In *Ethnoarchaeology*, edited by C. Kramer, pp. 277–287. Columbia University Press, New York.

Watson, P. J., and M. C. Kennedy. 1991. The Development of Horticulture in the Eastern Woodlands: Women's Role. In *Engendering Archaeology*, edited by J. M. Gero and M. W. Conkey, pp. 255–275. Basil Blackwell, Oxford.

Weineck, J. 1986. *Functional Anatomy in Sports.* Year Book Medical Publishers, Chicago.

Weisberg, H.F. 1992. *Central Tendency and Variability.* Sage Publications, Newbury Park, CA.

Whyte, M. K. 1978. *The Status of Women in Preindustrial Societies.* Princeton University Press, Princeton, NJ.

Wilczak, Cynthia A. 1998. Consideration of Sexual Dimorphism, Age, and Asymmetry in Quantitative Measurements of Muscle Insertion Sites. *International Journal of Osteoarchaeology* 8:311–325.

Williamson, Matthew A. 2000. A Comparison of Degenerative Joint Disease between Upland and Coastal Prehistoric Agriculturalists from Georgia. In *Bioarchaeological Studies of Life in the Age of Agriculture*, edited by P. M. Lambert, pp. 134–147. University of Alabama Press, Tuscaloosa.

Wilson, Diane E. 1994. Division of Labor and Stress Loads at the Sanders Site (41Lr2), Lamar County, Texas. *Bulletin of the Texas Archaeological Society* 65:129–160.

———. 1997. Gender, Diet, Health and Social Status in the Mississippian Powers Phase Turner Cemetery Population. In *Women in Prehistory*, edited by Cheryl Claassen and Rosemary A. Joyce, pp. 119–135. University of Pennsylvania Press, Philadelphia.

Wirhed, R. 1984. *Athletic Ability and the Anatomy of Motion.* Wolfe Medical Publishers, London.

Wolff, J. 1892. *The Law of Bone Remodelling.* Translated by P. Maquet and R. Furlong. Springer-Verlag, Berlin.

Wreschner. E. E. 1983. The Submerged Neolithic Village "Newe Yam" on the Israeli Mediterranean Coast. In *Quaternary Coastlines and Marine Archaeology*, edited by P. M. Masters and N. C. Fleming, pp. 325–333. Academic Press, London.

Wright, G. A. 1978. Social Differentiation in the Early Natufian. In *Social Archaeology*, edited by C. L. Redman, M. J. Berman, E. V. Curtain, W. T. Langhorne, Jr., N. H. Versaggi, and J. C. Wanser, pp. 201–224. Academic Press, New York.

Wright, K. I. 1992. *Ground Stone Assemblage Variations and Subsistence Strategies in the Levant, 22,000–5,500 B.P.* Ph.D. dissertation, Yale University, New Haven, CT.

———. 1993. Early Holocene Ground Stone Assemblages in the Levant. *Levant* 25:93–111.

Wright, Rita P. 1996. Technology, Gender, and Class: Worlds of Difference in Ur III Mesopotamia. In *Gender and Archaeology*, edited by R. P. Wright, pp. 79–110. University of Pennsylvania Press, Philadelphia.

Wylie, A. 1991a. Feminist Critiques and Archaeological Challenges. In *The Archaeology of Gender*, edited by D. Walde and N. D. Willows, pp. 17–23. The Archaeological Association of the University of Calgary, Calgary.

———. 1991b. Gender Theory and the Archaeological Record: Why Is There No Archaeology of Gender? In *Engendering Archaeology*, edited by J. M. Gero and M. W. Conkey, pp. 31–56. Basil Blackwell, Oxford.

Index

Page numbers in italic refer to illustrations.

About the Author

Jane Peterson is an assistant professor of anthropology at Marquette University in the Department of Social and Cultural Sciences. Among the courses she teaches are Bioarchaeology, Origins of Agriculture, and Gender in Cross-Cultural Perspective. Her research interests focus on questions of social organization among early farming groups, particularly those who lived in arid climates. Her published work ranges topically from an examination of regional obsidian exchange among the Hohokam of Arizona to an analysis of household labor patterns during the Pre-Pottery Neolithic in the Levant. Her fieldwork has taken her to Ireland, Italy, Turkey, and various locations in the United States. Ongoing fieldwork in Jordan will include the analysis of ancient DNA in order to examine the structure of prehistoric kin networks. She holds a B.A. in philosophy from the University of Virginia and M.A. and Ph.D. degrees in anthropology from Arizona State University.

4890